Advanced Aquarist's Online Magazine

Volume VII, Book I
2008 Edition

Pomacanthus Publications, Inc.

ADVANCED AQUARIST'S ONLINE MAGAZINE
VOLUME VII, BOOK I
2008 EDITION

ISBN 10: 1440422354
EAN 13: 9781440422355

Chief Editor: Terry Siegel
Layout & Design: Shane Graber
Cover Photo: *Pseudanthias bimaculatus*, Leonard Ho
Publisher: Pomacanthus Publications, Inc.
Printing: Self-Published at CreateSpace.com

http://www.advancedaquarist.com/

This book is dedicated to all of Advanced Aquarist's readers that have helped advance this hobby one step at a time.

ACKNOWLEDGMENTS

Advanced Aquarist would like to thank all of our authors, sponsors, and readers who have made this publication possible over these last seven years. Without everyone's support, this publication would not be the high quality publication that it is today.

We'd especially like to thank all of our contributing authors for the first six months of 2008: Jake Adams, Suzy Q Applegarthm Adam Blundell, Charles J. DeVito, Mark E. Evans, Ken S. Feldman, Todd Gardner, Shane Graber, Jay Hemdal, Elizabeth A. Huber, Sanjay Joshi, Kelly M. Maers, Jim McDavid, Karl T. Mueller, Christopher Paparo, Dana Riddle, Pavaphon Supanantananont, Matthew R. Test, Greg Timms, and Lauren F. Vernese for all of their excellent articles.

We'd also like to thank our sponsors: AquaCave, Inc., HelloLights, Marine Depot, Premium Aquatics, and Two Part Solution along with Deltec USA, Global Aquarium Supply, J & L Aquatics, Marine Garden, Reef Nutrition / Reed Mariculture, and Sunlight Supply – all of whom provided significant financial support for the online magazine. We'd also like to thank Alti's Reef, AquaFX, AquariumPart.com, Champion Lighting & Supply, EcoSystem Aquarium, ESV, Jelliquarium, Marineland, Midnight Sun Aquaculture, Phishybusiness, Red Sea, Salty Critter, and Two Little Fishies for their financial support. Without all of these businesses financial support, this magazine would not be able to be provided for free online and we wouldn't be able to provide you with the print edition that you are now reading.

We'd also like to thank you, the reader, for your readership and for the continued suggestions. You've helped shape this publication into what it is currently.

Terry Siegel, this publication's Chief Editor, would like to thank Doug Robbins (deceased), Greg Schiemer (deceased), Julian Sprung, J. Charles Delbeek, Peter Wilkens, Martin Moe, and Craig Bingman.

Shane Graber, this publication's Design and Layout Editor, would like to thank his wife, Jama, for her love and support. Things get pretty hectic around the 15th of the month and he greatly appreciates her patience with him as he scrambles to put the finishing touches on each issue.

CHIEF EDITOR

Terry Siegel:
terry@advancedaquarist.com

WEBSITE AND PRINT DESIGNERS

Shane Graber: liquid@reefs.org

Leonard Ho: len@reefs.org

FEATURED AQUARIUMS

D. Wade Lehmann: wade@reefs.org

INFORMATION

Publisher:
Pomacanthus Publications, Inc.

Website:
http://www.advancedaquarist.com/

Advertising:
advertising@advancedaquarist.com

Feedback:
feedback@advancedaquarist.com

COVER PHOTO

Pseudanthias bimaculatus, a deepwater species that typically inhabits coastal drop-offs in excess of 100 feet. Also known as the Twin or Two-Spot Anthias.

Photograph by Leonard Ho

PUBLICATION INFORMATION

Advanced Aquarist's Online Magazine (ISSN 1931-6895) is published monthly online by Pomacanthus Publications, Inc. A central goal of this publication is to promote exchange between the scientific community and amateur aquarists, for the benefit of both disciplines and the environment. To achieve our combined goals of greater understanding of the natural world and honing our husbandry skills we will rely heavily on science and scientists. Advanced Aquarist's Online Magazine will always emphasize protection and understanding of the natural environment.

a reefs.org publication

ADVANCED AQUARIST'S ONLINE MAGAZINE

TABLE OF CONTENTS

Volume VII, Book I   2008 Edition

JANUARY

FEBRUARY

MARCH

APRIL

MAY

June

FEATURE ARTICLE

GRANULAR ACTIVATED CARBON, PART 1: MODELING OF OPERATIONAL PARAMETERS FOR DISSOLVED ORGANIC CARBON REMOVAL FROM MARINE AQUARIA

By Ken S. Feldman, Lauren F. Vernese, Karl T. Mueller, Kelly Maers

Chemistry Department, The Pennsylvania State University. In this first part of a two part series, the authors will introduce granular activated carbon and explain the experimental goals and mathematical models used in their research.

Published January 2008, Advanced Aquarist's Online Magazine

© Pomacanthus Publications, LLC

Keywords: Feature Article, Filtration, GAC, Granular Activated Carbon, Karl T. Mueller, Kelly Maers, Ken S. Feldman, Lauren F. Vernese, Water Quality, Water Testing
Link to original article: http://www.advancedaquarist.com/2008/1/aafeature1

INTRODUCTION

GAC AND THE AQUARIUM

The use of granular activated carbon (GAC) for decolorizing marine aquarium water has had a long and successful history. In fact, prior to the introduction of this filtering agent into the saltwater aquarium hobby, the central role of this technology in water remediation efforts ensured that a large body of data existed which spoke to the basics of contaminant removal from drinking water and wastewater by carbon-based media (Bansal, 2005; Cheremisinoff, 1993; Kvech, 1997). Through extensive experimental and theoretical (i.e., model building) studies, many of the parameters that define success have been identified. Optimization of GAC source, water flow rate through fixed-bed reactors, media presentation, and time-in-use, among other features, has led to successful protocols for the removal of many small-molecule organic contaminants, such as benzene, phenol, chlorinated hydrocarbons, pesticides, etc. from potable water sources (Bansal, 2005; Khan, 1997; Singh, 2006). It is not surprising that many of the lessons learned from these studies accompanied the technology as it was adapted to marine aquarium use. Some empirical and largely divergent "rules for use", which have emerged from these initial inputs combined with the numerous observations of aquarists, have been proposed by many authors (http://www.carbochem.com/activatedcarbon101.html; http://www.articlefishtalk.com/Article/

Activated-Carbon-in-the-Aquarium/78; Hovanec, 1993; Harker, 1998; Schiemer, 1997). Although there is by no means a uniform consensus, recommendations 1 and 2 below seem to have stood the test of time. On the other hand, opinions conflict on the questions of how much (#3), how fast (#4), and how often (#5).

1. Use GAC formulated from either bituminous coal (Hovanec, 1993) or lignite coal (Harker, 1998), but not coconut shell.

2. Use active flow through the media and not passive diffusion (Hovanec, 1993; Harker, 1998).

3. Use about 0.3 gm of GAC per gallon of tank water ("3 tablespoons per 50 gallons") (Harker, 1998) to 19 gm/gal (Lliopoulos, 2002) (no consensus here).

4. Use water flow rates of about 4 gph (Harker, 1998) to several hundred gph [many canister filter manufacturers] (again, no consensus).

5. Replace with new GAC every week (Harker, 1998) to once every 4-6 weeks (Schiemer, 1997) (once again, no consensus).

6. Run continuously (Schiemer, 1997) or sporadically (Harker, 1998) (no consensus!).

DISSOLVED ORGANIC CARBON

The precise chemical species that GAC removes have not been determined. Rather, the catchall phrases "DOC" (dissolved organic carbon) and/or "marine humic/fulvic acids" are frequently employed to categorize the uncharacterizable (Holmes-Farley, 2004; Bingman, 1996; Rashid, 1985; Romankevich, 1984). In fact, both descriptors have little intrinsic meaning and give no insight into the actual chemicals involved. Romankevich has estimated that there is approximately 2×10^{12} tons of DOC in the world's oceans (for comparison, Romankevich reports that there are approximately 2.5×10^{12} tons of organic carbon in oil deposits in the world), and about 94% of that material is phytoplantonic in origin (Romankevich, 1984). Most (all?) of these dissolved organic materials are subjected to both biological (bacterial) and non-biological degradative processes until eventually refractory (= inert) compounds, which survive exposure to the marine environment's inhabitants and conditions, result. Occasionally, marine scientists have attempted to provide some structural details for these substances on the basis of the spectroscopic signatures of specific chemical functionalities observed. In particular, solid-state carbon nuclear magnetic resonance spectroscopy has provided an unrivaled window into this complex problem (Gillam, 1986; Sardessal, 1998). Representative polycyclic species derived from oxidation and then cyclization of unsaturated lipids have been proposed (Harvey, 1983), whereas other authors have suggested that some humic acid components originate from oligosaccharide-protein condensations to form polycyclic materials that have a high nitrogen content (Francois, 1990). The former process has a direct analogy to the curing of oil-based varnishes for wood treatment, whereas the latter process is related to the chemistry of food browning upon cooking, a sequence of transformations called the Maillard reaction. In both cases, colored, soluble material can be formed. Both of these chemical transformations require condensation of different chemical reaction partners that each exist in concentrations of approximately 1 ppm, and so any hypothesis for DOC formation that cites these reactions must address this low-concentration-of-reactants issue.

OUR EXPERIMENTAL GOALS

With this information as background, we set out to experimentally probe some of the unresolved issues surrounding the use of GAC in the marine aquarium:

1. How much GAC should be used to deplete the DOC by 90% (arbitrarily chosen) for a given water volume?

2. When should the GAC charge be changed?

3. Does GAC differentially remove different types of arguably reef-relevant organic molecules with different facility? That is, are all yellow, or more generally, colored, compounds removed with equal facility, and are there non-yellow-colored but possibly undesirable organic compounds that GAC removes as well?

4. How does the rate of impurity removal relate to water flow rate?

5. Do organics leach back out of GAC upon saturation?

Some tentative answers (not THE answers) to these questions are presented below.

Prior to framing these questions in experimentally addressable terms, some basics must be considered: For example, what experimental quantity should be measured - the amount of the impurity that a given amount of GAC removes, or the rate by which the GAC removes the impurity? Actually, both quantities will be required to address these questions. Historically, measurements of the ability of GAC to remove an impurity from water have looked at both issues. Some background:

1. Thermodynamics. Thermodynamic measurements attempt to describe the quantity of impurity that can be removed by a given quantity of GAC (Suzuki, 2004; Walker, 2000). These types of measurements are run to "infinite" time; that is, the system (= GAC + impurity in water) is allowed to settle until the measured concentration of impurity in the water is constant; or, in chemical terms, the system has reached *equilibrium*. From these measurements of GAC's adsorbing capacity (different for each chemically unique impurity) and application of mathematical treatments relying on either the Freundlich or Langmuir isotherms [Potgieter, 1991], many useful system parameters can be calculated. This type of analysis provides data pertaining to which type of GAC can adsorb the most impurity-per unit-weight. Many authors have applied this technique in analyzing the use of GAC with marine aquaria, and some of their conclusions (cf. # 1 and # 5 in the Introductory section) have been presented. These data do not address how fast impurities are removed.

2. Kinetics. Kinetic measurements attempt to describe how fast GAC removes an impurity (Ganguly, 1996; Baup, 2000). These data do not reveal the ultimate adsorption capacity of the GAC. The kinetic approach to developing figures of merit for GAC has been explored by some aquarist authors (Cerreta, 2006; Walker, 1999; Harker, 1998), and conclusions about active vs. passive flow (# 2 above), preferred type of GAC precursor (#1 above), and amount of GAC to use (# 3 above) have been derived from these data.

It should be emphasized that the kinetic approach and the thermodynamic approach actually measure different things, and data garnered from these two different experimental protocols will not necessarily lead to the same conclusions about which is the "best" GAC, depending upon the criteria used to define "best". It is possible, for example, for a particular sample of GAC to remove an impurity very rapidly but actually have a rather low capacity. Conversely, another sample of GAC may exhibit the exact opposite behavior; there is no reason why the kinetics of impurity removal and the capacity of the GAC sample should correlate or even run in parallel.

These assertions can be better understood when viewing GAC on the molecular level. As many authors have detailed in earlier accounts (Hovanec, 1993; Kvech, 1997), GAC is essentially a refractory solid honeycombed with passages and chambers that are chemically active enough to bind some types of organic molecules. The sizes of the interior spaces are exceedingly heterogeneously distributed, and vary as per the technique(s) used to activate the carbon. Likewise, the chemical nature of the active binding surfaces is heterogeneous and the details of the surface molecular constituents depend upon the activation procedure. This heterogeneity all works towards the good, as GAC in the aggregate then offers many differently sized and functionally distinct binding sites to act as complementary partners for the myriad of structurally different organic impurities that might be found in a marine aquarium, lumped under the aegis of DOC. The thermodynamics (= capacity at equilibrium) of impurity removal typically scales with the number, or amount, of available binding sites for impurities. If a GAC sample has a greater porosity due to its activation procedure, it will have the capacity to trap and hold more impurity. The kinetics (= rate of impurity capture) of DOC removal is dependent on several factors: (a) the rate of diffusion of the impurity to the surface of the GAC particle, (b) the rate of diffusion of the impurity inside the potentially restricting space of the pores, (c) the rate of surface diffusion once the impurity is bound, and (d) the strength of the specific molecular-level interactions between the GAC surface and the impurity in question. All of these rate components are sensitive to the specific shape, charge, size and chemical functionality of the impurity. Therefore, there is no real correlation, or expectation of a correlation, between the amount of surface area for binding within the pores and channels in GAC (proportional to thermodynamic capacity) and the diffusion rates and surface chemistry within these pores and channels (influences the kinetic rate of removal).

Both kinetic and thermodynamic data are necessary for probing the central questions outlined above. Quantifying the rates of impurity removal (kinetics) as a function of different chemical impurity structures will allow question (3) to be tested, whereas the kinetic approach will directly address the questions posed in (1) and (4). Measurement of impurity leaching rates of impurity-saturated GAC (question (5)) will address concerns that used GAC itself might be a source of DOCs if not removed when saturated. Finally, the GAC's thermodynamic adsorption capacity should provide direction with question (2).

THE MATHEMATICAL MODELS

There are two distinct tank scenarios that require different mathematical models to obtain useful information.

1. There is a fixed amount of impurity (DOC), and no more is being added, at least at a rate competitive with the rate of impurity removal by the GAC. This case most likely might be encountered if GAC has not been used for a while, and so the DOC level has built up, or if the tank has been medicated, and it is important to remove excess medication quickly. The key question here is, "How much GAC should I use to remove this large amount of impurity?"

2. GAC is in continuous use, and the steady-state DOC level reflects the trade-off between the rate of DOC introduction by biological processes, and the rate of DOC removal by the GAC. This situation would pertain if GAC is used continuously. The key question here is, "When should I change my GAC?"

We will first examine scenario (1), and then use the results obtained to arrive at an approach to address scenario (2).

The fundamental Case 1 chemical equation that describes the removal of an organic dye molecule (as a model for DOC) from solution by GAC is

$$(1) \quad dye \quad + \quad GAC_{bs} \quad \rightleftharpoons \quad dye \cdot GAC_{bs}$$

Note that this equation does not have any provision for adding dye to the water, and so it describes Case (1) and not Case (2). The symbol "GAC_{bs}" in this chemical equation is defined for our purposes as one binding site in the GAC matrix. In words, this equation indicates that one molecule of dye (or one mole, which equals 6.02×10^{23} molecules - it is often convenient to discuss chemical process in terms of moles, or fractions of a mole - millimol, micromol, etc.) binds to one binding site in the GAC (or one mole of binding sites) and therefore is removed from solution. An assumption of this model is that the dye can leach from the GAC and reenter the solution, leading to a situation called "equilibrium binding". That is, the GAC will become saturated with dye at some point, and that saturation point is a complex function of how much dye is present, how much GAC is present, and the molecular-level affinity of the GAC for the dye. A test of this assumption will be described later in the article. This one-to-one interaction between the dye molecule and a GAC binding site (GAC_{bs}) lends itself to a mathematical analysis characterized by the relationship in Eq. (2). In words, this expressions indicates that the rate of removal of dye from solution (symbolized by the differential $-d[dye]/dt$, t = time in minutes) is proportional to the product of the concentration of dye (in moles per liter, often abbreviated as mol/L, or M, and indicated by the symbol $[dye]$), and the concentration of GAC binding sites available ($[GAC_{bs}]$, in moles per liter of total solution). Of course, the GAC binding sites are not spread throughout the whole solution, but rather they are confined to the GAC particles in a Phosban (or equivalent) reactor. However, the experimental design is such that this distinction is not significant. This proportionality expression can be converted to an equality by including a constant of proportionality denoted as k (Eq. (3)).

$$(2) \qquad -\frac{d[dye]}{dt} \propto [dye][GAC_{bs}]$$

$$(3) \qquad \frac{d[dye]}{dt} = -k[dye][GAC_{bs}]$$

Although it may seem that the introduction of this "fudge factor" k is somewhat arbitrary and perhaps not even germane to the problem, it turns out that it is possible to use this single figure-of-merit to describe the key rate characteristics of the system - k is often called a *rate constant*. The larger k is, the faster that the GAC removes the dye from solution. Note that k is independent of the amount of GAC used - in principle, the same k should be obtained for any amount of GAC from the same source. In practice, we shall see that the reality is somewhat different, perhaps reflecting the crudeness of some of the assumptions of our model, and the inconsistencies that attend any repetitive experimental measurement procedure. Whereas the rate constant k should be invariant with respect to GAC amount, the actual *rate* of dye removal ($d[dye]/dt$) is a function of the amount of GAC present, since the amount of GAC binding sites ($[GAC_{bs}]$) will scale with the amount of GAC used. In typical aquarium use, the amount of DOC will be relatively small and constant, and the amount of GAC used is the real variable available to the aquarist in terms of accelerating the removal of unwanted DOC's.

It will be our goal to calculate this value k under different conditions. The rate constant k is a function of all of the intrinsic features of the system, such as the flow rate through a Phosban Reactor, the physical configuration of the plumbing and Reactor, the dimensions and aspect ratio of the GAC bed, the GAC particle size and porosity, the diffusion rate to the GAC surface and along the GAC surface/pores as discussed earlier, etc. It is not possible at this level of analysis to deconvolute the calculated k value in terms of these specific parameters, but it is possible to use this rate constant value for a given set of experimental parameters to calculate useful attributes of the system, such as (1) how long will it take to cut the amount of dye (or DOC) by 90% for a given tank size

and GAC amount, and (2) how long will it take to saturate 90% the GAC binding sites with dye (or DOC's in a real aquarium) for a given tank size and GAC amount. These practical issues will aid in making informed decisions on the related questions of "How much GAC should I use?" and "When do I need to change my GAC?"

It is possible to derive a mathematical expression from Eq. (3) that relates the desired rate constant k to experimentally measurable (or derivable) quantities. This derivation can be found in any standard Chemical Kinetics treatment/textbook, and the expression is

$$(4) \qquad \frac{1}{[GAC_{bs}]_o - [dye]_o} \cdot Ln\left[\frac{[GAC_{bs}]_t / [GAC_{bs}]_o}{[dye]_t / [dye]_o}\right] = kt$$

where

t = time, in minutes

$[dye]_t$ = the concentration of dye, in moles/liter (M), at time t

$[dye]_o$ = the concentration of dye (M) at t = 0 (i.e., the beginning of the experiment)

$[GAC_{bs}]_t$ = the concentration of binding sites in the GAC, in moles/liter (M) at time = t

$[GAC_{bs}]_o$ = the concentration of binding sites in the GAC (M) at t = 0

k = rate constant from Eq. (3), in $M^{-1}min^{-1}$

We can measure $[dye]_o$, the amount of dye that we put into the system in the beginning, and we can measure $[dye]_t$, the concentration of dye at some time t after the experiment begins. Obtaining the other necessary quantities, $[GAC_{bs}]_o$ and $[GAC_{bs}]_t$, requires some mathematical manipulation and some assumptions.

The total binding capacity of the GAC, which is equal to $[GAC_{bs}]_o$, can be indirectly measured by placing a known quantity of GAC in solution with a known and excess quantity of dye. The GAC will absorb the dye until it becomes saturated and can no longer bind any more dye. As a consequence, the concentration of the dye in solution will decrease as some of the dye is bound to the GAC. Eventually, the concentration of dye in solution will remain constant, as the now saturated GAC can no longer accept any more dye. We can monitor the decrease in dye concentration over time, and when the concentration levels out and no longer changes, we assume that we have reached the GAC saturation point. The difference in dye concentration between the initial value and this terminal value can be used to determine the amount of dye absorbed by the GAC, and we can use a mathematical treatment called a Langmuir isotherm to calculate the total binding capacity of the GAC for the dye. The mathematical form of the Langmuir isotherm is given in Eq. (5) [Potgieter, 1991]:

$$(5) \qquad \frac{1}{x} = \frac{1}{x_m \cdot K} \cdot \frac{1}{C} + \frac{1}{x_m}$$

where

x = milligrams (mg) of dye absorbed per mg of GAC, at equilibrium

C = the concentration of dye (mg/L), at equilibrium

K = a constant of no interest in this analysis

x_m = the total amount of dye (mg) that can be absorbed by 1 mg of GAC, at equilibrium

The total binding capacity of the dye is x_m, the quantity that we seek. Simply running several parallel trials to equilibrium, all differing in the amount of GAC used (leading to differing x values), and measuring the dye concentration, C, will provide the necessary data. Then, plotting $1/C$ vs. $1/x$ should provide a straight line whose Y-intercept is $1/x_m$. The desired quantity for this experiment, x_m, is then in hand.

In order to use this experimentally derived quantity of binding capacity, x_m, to calculate $[GAC_{bs}]_o$, we must define a new quantity, m, as the # of moles of dye that bind to one gram (abbreviated 1g) of GAC at equilibrium. Note that x_m originally is determined in units of mg of dye/mg of GAC, but that ratio is equivalent to gms of dye/gms of GAC. Thus, simply dividing x_m by the dye's molecular weight (MW, in g/mol) provides m:

$$(6) \qquad m = \frac{x_m}{MW}$$

In addition, $[GAC_{bs}]_o$ requires knowledge of the system water volume (V) and the amount (mass) of GAC used (G):

V = the volume of the water in the system, in liters (experimentally measured)

G = the grams of GAC used (experimentally measured)

So, $m \cdot G$ = the total # of moles of binding sites for a given mass of GAC, and therefore

$$(7) \qquad [GAC_{bs}]_o = m \cdot G / V$$

In words, this expression indicates that the concentration of the total amount of GAC binding sites is equal to the total #

of moles of binding sites divided by the system volume. As indicated earlier, the GAC binding sites are not evenly dispersed throughout the solution, but are confined to the GAC bed. This distinction is of no consequence, however, since our experimental protocol is equivalent to just adding a portion of GAC to the tank volume itself. The fact that dye can only be removed when the solution passes through the GAC bed is taken into account by the rate constant k.

In addition, it is convenient to formulate another definition:

$c = [dye]_t/[dye]_o$, which again is an experimentally measured quantity.

Substituting these two expressions into Eq. (4) leads to

$$(8) \qquad \frac{1}{m \cdot G/V - [dye]_o} \cdot Ln \left[\frac{[GAC_{bs}]_t / [GAC_{bs}]_o}{c} \right] = kt$$

Arriving at a experimentally accessible expression for $[GAC_{bs}]_t$ is a bit trickier. We can start by noting that there is a fundamental mass balance expression that defines the removal of dye by GAC:

$$(9) \qquad [dye]_o - [dye]_t = [GAC_{bs}]_o - [GAC_{bs}]_t$$

In words, this expression indicates that the amount of dye removed from solution up to a time t (= $[dye]_o - [dye]_t$) must be equal to the amount of dye absorbed onto the GAC during that same time, which, in turn, must equal the decrease in the amount of GAC binding sites (= $[GAC_{bs}]_o - [GAC_{bs}]_t$). Rearranging and substituting for $[dye]_t$ gives

$$(10) \qquad [GAC_{bs}]_t = [GAC_{bs}]_o - [dye]_o \cdot (1 - c)$$

Substituting back into Eq. (8) then gives

$$(11) \qquad \frac{1}{m \cdot G/V - [dye]_o} \cdot Ln \frac{[GAC_{bs}]_o - [dye]_o \cdot (1-c)}{c \cdot [GAC_{bs}]_o} = kt$$

Substituting $[GAC_{bs}]_o = m \cdot G/V$ and rearranging furnishes

$$(12) \qquad \frac{1}{m \cdot G/V - [dye]_o} \cdot Ln \left[\frac{1}{c} - \frac{V \cdot [dye]_o \cdot (1-c)}{c \cdot m \cdot G} \right] = kt$$

which simplifies to

$$(13) \quad \frac{1}{m \cdot G/V - [dye]_o} \cdot Ln \left[\frac{1}{c} - \frac{V \cdot [dye]_o}{m \cdot G} \left(\frac{1}{c} - 1 \right) \right] = kt$$

The quantities m (derived from the Langmuir isotherm experimental data) and $[dye]_o$ are measured initially, and remain constant throughout all of the experiments. The amount of GAC, G, is measured at the beginning of each experimental run, and $[dye]_t$ (from which c is derived) is measured at different times t. The quantity on the left-hand side of Eq. (13) is graphed against time t, and the slope of that line is k, the desired quantity.

It will be valuable to define a new quantity, t_{90}, as the length of time required to reduce a given starting dye concentration by 90%. The t_{90} value can be extracted from Eq, (13) by setting c = 0.1 (= 90% depletion of the dye concentration), and solving for t:

$$(14) \quad t_{90} = \frac{1}{k(m \cdot G/V - [dye]_o)} \cdot Ln \left[10 - \frac{9V \cdot [dye]_o}{m \cdot G} \right]$$

This Case (1) mathematical modeling ultimately can be applied to answering the question, "How much GAC should I use?" (see Section 3.1). That is, this model will have the most utility is a situation where GAC has not been used before, and the DOC level in the water has built up, or a situation where the tank has been medicated, and so there is a specific level of impurity (excess medication) that must be removed quickly.

To address the Case (2) scenario, where GAC is used continuously and DOC (modeled by dye) is continuously being added to the water, we must explicitly incorporate a DOC source into the simple expression Eq. (1). Specifically, we can allocate that role to PoOP (Precursors of Organic Particulates), and then assign a generic rate constant k_1 to describe the overall rate of conversion of PoOP into DOC's (modeled by dye in Eq. (15)). This simplistic model allows for a continuous and gradual introduction of DOC's (dyes) into the water column of an aquarium as a consequence of a wide range of biological processes that degrade the PoOP into soluble organic material. Thus, Eq. (15) illustrates how dye (as a model for DOC) is both formed from PoOP with a rate constant k_1, and removed by the GAC with a rate constant k, as previously discussed.

$$(15) \quad PoOP \xrightarrow{k_1} dye + GAC_{bs} \underset{}{\overset{k}{\rightleftharpoons}} dye \cdot GAC_{bs}$$

Surprisingly, the expansion of Eq. (1) into Eq. (15), which includes the dye generation term, renders the kinetics mathematically unsolvable, at least in terms of arriving at an analytical solution like that expressed in Eq. (13). This problem has long been recognized, and Chien has developed a workaround using mathematical approximations (Bessel functions) that are applicable if certain criteria are met (Chien, 1948). However, there are two factors that mitigate against using the Chien formalism to solve this problem:

1. It is not clear whether the criterion for its use, which involves the relative magnitudes of k and k_1, is met.

2. We can only guess at the concentration of PoOP and the value of the rate constant k_1 (necessary inputs for Chien's mathematical model).

This second point is really a critical one, as it will cloud any attempt to arrive at a solution based on Eq. (15). However, all is not lost, as there is another approach to solving kinetic (rate) expressions that is applicable in this case; kinetics simulations. It is possible to use one of the commercially available kinetics modeling programs to make guesses for [PoOP] and k_1, and then calculate desirable quantities like $[GAC_{bs}]_t$ or $[dye]_t$ based on experimentally determined k values (from the Case (1) math and experimental measurements). Even with this approach, we must have some basis for making guesses about [PoOP] and k_1, and fortunately, we do. As discussed later in more detail, we have measured the concentration of oxidizable organics in the water of several reef tanks, and so we have an idea of the steady-state concentration, [DOC], in an actual GAC-treated tank. With that constraint, we can then adjust the product $[PoOP] \cdot k_1$ in the kinetics simulation program to hold [DOC] within a realistic range. That is, the rate of DOC removal will be measured experimentally, and then we just have to balance that rate of removal with a rate of DOC introduction via a $[PoOP] \cdot k_1$ quantity that keeps the overall DOC level around the steady-state values measured in actual marine tanks. For these studies, we use the shareware program KinTekSim (http://www.kintek-corp.com/members/).

THE EXPERIMENTAL VARIABLES

The experimental variables examined in this study are:

1. The type of GAC: Two Little Fishes Hydrocarbon and Marineland's Black Diamond.

2. The flow rate: 49 gph (= 0.81 gpm) and 72 gph (= 1.2 gpm).

3. The amount of GAC: 6.25 g/gal up to 50 g/gal.

4. The dye molecule probes. This latter experimental variable is quite important to the success of these experiments, and so some more elaboration and a few digressions are in order. First, a digression about the pros and cons of model use in science:

Some scientific disciplines have a "look but don't touch character" to their experimentation. For example, cosmology and paleontology ask questions about events so distant in time (the birth of the Universe or the behavior of dinosaurs) that it is impossible to construct real-time experiments to gain hard data. Thus, model building and model testing are the primary experimental tools of these types of disciplines. Other fields of science are readily probed by direct experiment, like chemistry and biology. However, even within these hands-on sciences, the type of experiments, and the quality of data retrievable, varies significantly. For example, directly probing a biological or chemical system of interest is possible, but sometimes the system is so complicated that the data obtained is uninterpretable or compromised. For example, such a situation might pertain to the question of what, exactly, is GAC removing. Sure, it can be labeled as "DOC", or "marine humic substances", but those categories reveal nothing about its chemical structure and hence its reactivity with GAC or any other component of an aquarium. In reality, the DOC is so complex and so heterogeneous that it would be a Herculean analytical task to try to determine its constituents and their relative amounts. So, how can experiments whose goal involves DOC chemistry be performed? In principle, it might be possible to isolate and concentrate DOC, and use that preparation as an experimental starting point without ever knowing its composition. That type of procedure would hew closest to the goal of performing experiments on a "real" system, but the downsides of this approach are many: there is currently no effective way to isolate all of the DOC's, although some subset of DOC components can be isolated; there is no effective way to ensure that whatever might be isolable actually corresponds to the DOC of an aquarium; there is no way of testing whether the DOC isolated from one aquarium is similar to, or different from, the DOC isolated from another aquarium. In light of these types of technical (but not conceptual!) problems in working with complex "real" systems, scientists often turn to simplified model systems that presume to capture the essential elements of the real system but reduce the experimental variables to a manageable number. In this approach, experiments can be designed and executed, but the real challenge lies in choosing appropriate model systems that can give insight into the real system. In the case of GAC and DOC removal studies, several authors used a blue dye, the Salifert test kit reagent methylene blue (1), as a model for organic impurities that might be found in a reef tank (Cerreta, 2006; Schiemer, 1997). Harker, on the other hand, used the yellow exudates from stewed seaweed as a model for DOC, reasoning that (a) it was yellow in color like DOC, and (b) it was derived from a marine source (Harker, 1998). In actuality, both approaches share both the strength of the reductionist approach by defining a system upon which useful experiments can be performed, and its weaknesses by assuming that some model compound(s), known in the case of the Salifert test kit, and unknown in the case of the Harker experiment, accurately mimic the constituents of DOC with respect to their interactions with GAC.

With these thoughts as background, we chose our models for DOC by asking the following question: what are the likely types of components, at least as broad classes, in DOC, and what commercially available dye molecules might have similar chemical and/or structural characteristics to these components? The premise underlying this approach to model system selection is that if the chosen dyes share chemical/structural characteristics with some of the presumed DOC components, then perhaps their diffusion properties and chemical interactions with the chemically active sites in GAC might be similar to those of the actual DOC components. As a starting point for this analysis, it is worth noting that the chemical composition of both bacterial and mammalian cells can be averaged to give the following values (Alberts, 2002):

- Proteins: 50 - 60%

- Lipids: 7 - 17%

- Nucleic acids: 5 - 23%

- Oligosaccharides: 7%

- Small metabolites: 10%

Some illustrative examples from each class of biomolecule are given in Figure 1. Proteins, nucleic acids and oligosaccharides are polymers (= large molecules composed of many linked small molecule repeat units; beads on a string is an apt analogy) whose sizes range from millions of repeat units (nucleic acids) to hundreds of repeat units (proteins) to tens of repeat units (oligosaccharides). Lipids and metabolites, on the other hand, are discrete small molecules that are not built up from joining repeat units. The category "metabolites" actually is an all-encompassing class that includes many organic molecules (vitamins, hormones, enzyme co-factors, etc.) that are diverse in structure and chemistry. The chlorophyll molecule (Figure 1) was chosen as an example because of its obvious color, and because it is representative of a class of small metabolites called porphyrins that are both highly colored and ubiquitous in living organisms (hemoglobin, myoglobin, many enzyme co-factors). As cells are ruptured and the contents are released, these "molecules of life" become food for bacteria, whose metabolic processes function to both chop up polymers to their individual repeat units and also to modify the basic chemical structures of the components, typically by oxidation. In this way, these species serve as carbon-based fuels whose ultimate fate, in many cases, is conversion to CO_2. However, not all molecules are susceptible to complete oxidation to form CO_2, and some of the organic residues are chemically inert to further oxidative or degradative action by bacterial enzymes. In this case, the waste material cannot be further modified, at least at an appreciable rate, and so it accumulates. This leftover organic trash is part of what we call dissolved organic carbon, DOC.

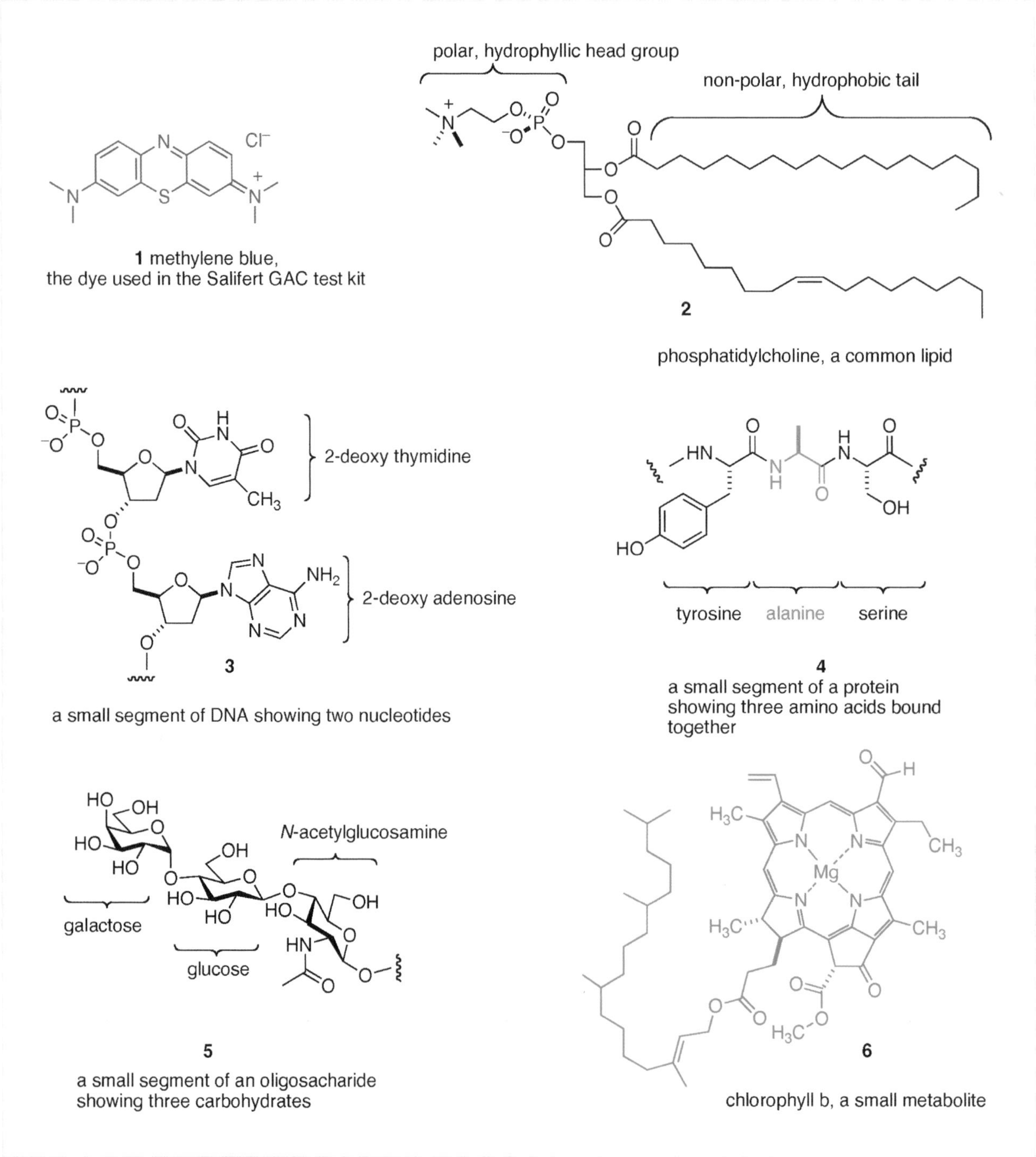
polar, hydrophyllic head group
non-polar, hydrophobic tail
1 methylene blue,
the dye used in the Salifert GAC test kit
2
phosphatidylcholine, a common lipid
2-deoxy thymidine
2-deoxy adenosine
3
a small segment of DNA showing two nucleotides
tyrosine
alanine
serine
4
a small segment of a protein showing three amino acids bound together
N-acetylglucosamine
galactose
glucose
5
a small segment of an oligosacharide showing three carbohydrates
6
chlorophyll b, a small metabolite

Figure 1. Examples of the molecules of life, and methylene blue, the Salifert GAC test kit reagent.

With this information as background, we can now ask, "What type of dye molecules might resemble, in structure and/or chemical functionality, elements of DOC?" This question, of course, is impossible to answer with precision for the reasons discussed above, but we can make some educated guesses as to what type of chemical units might survive intact, or be formed from, the input species of Figure 1. The fact that DOC is soluble (= dissolved) requires that it contains functional

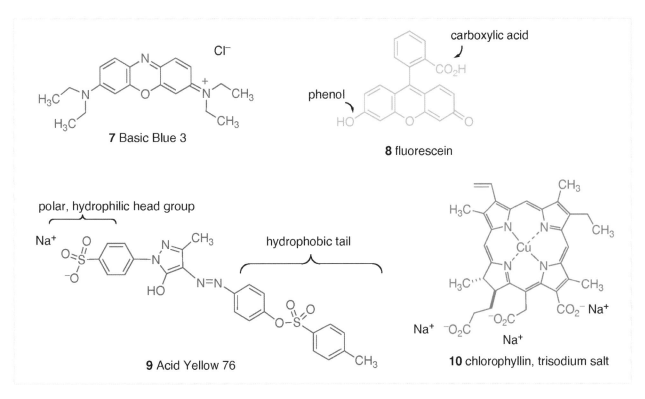

Figure 2. The dyes used in the GAC-based adsorption assays.

groups which are hydrophilic (= water loving). In addition, the nucleic acids and some of the proteins' individual amino acid components (e.g., histidine) contain flat 5- and 6-membered nitrogen-containing ring units that are generally resistant to chemical transformation. Therefore, choosing a dye that contains both flat nitrogen-containing rings and water solubilizing charges seems appropriate. This line of reasoning led to the inclusion of Basic Blue 3 (7) in our study, Figure 2. This dye is structurally similar to methylene blue (1) from the Salifert test kit.

The inevitable oxidation and chemical condensations that define much of the pathway from cell metabolite to DOC typically results in the formation of compounds featuring condensed ring systems, and also to the generation of oxidized chemical functionality like carboxylic acids and phenols. One dye that embodies both of these likely DOC characteristics is fluorescein (8), Figure 2. This orange dye might be a simple model for the "humic substances" that contain acids and phenols on rings similar to the presentation depicted in the structure 8.

Many organic molecules of the type produced by biological metabolism have a dual character with respect to water. These molecules have both a hydrophilic portion and a hydrophobic (= water hating) portion, and they are termed amphoteric. Lipids are good examples of amphoteric molecules, as illustrated in Figure 1. In particular, amphoteric molecules might be good candidates for removal by GAC, as the hydrophilic portion will keep them in solution, whereas the hydrophobic portion is similar in character to the binding surface of GAC and therefore is susceptible to strong association. The dye molecule Acid Yellow 76 (9) has just such amphoteric character, as it has both a hydrophilic, charged sulfonate group and a carbon-rich and uncharged tail (Figure 2). In addition, the 6-membered ring residues in 9 are characteristic of many biological metabolites, and this very stable and unreactive ring often survives bacterial action either intact or only slightly modified. Thus, it may serve as a useful model for amphoteric molecules in DOC.

Finally, the common occurrence of porphyrin-based metabolites in cells, and the relative resistance of the porphyrin superstructure to complete degradation (porphyrins are used as biomarkers in geological samples millions of years old (Callot, 2000)), suggests that a dye mimicking this color source might be a useful contributor to modeling DOC in GAC-based removal studies. Towards this end, the porphyrin derivative chlorophyllin (10) was selected as the final probe dye for use in the GAC studies.

These model compounds were chosen for their resemblance to presumed DOC components, although this point cannot be experimentally verified. Argument-by-analogy will be our strongest ally upon employing this modeling approach to investigating GAC's properties. Thus, using these model compounds will allow us to acquire meaningful data and provide a framework for interpretation of the results, which in turn will, hopefully, provide some guidance for the aquarist contemplating the details of GAC use in his/her aquarium. In Part 2 next month, we will continue with the Results and Discussion of the data.

FEATURE ARTICLE

CORAL COLORATION, PART 9: TRIDACNA AND OTHER PHOTOSYNTHETIC CLAM COLORATION, WITH OBSERVATIONS ON POSSIBLE FUNCTIONS

By Dana Riddle

This month, we will continue our observations of marine invertebrate coloration with a slightly different subject - that of the impressive appearance of photosynthetic clams.

Published January 2008, Advanced Aquarist's Online Magazine

© Pomacanthus Publications, LLC

Keywords: Clams, Coloration, Coral, Dana Riddle, Feature Article
Link to original article: http://www.advancedaquarist.com/2008/1/aafeature3

With full realization that I'll get email stating that 'clams are not corals', I can not be content to leave it at that. So, I will make an even bolder statement - *Tridacna* clams' tissues (along with certain other genera) are colorless and contain *no* spectacular pigments. You are paying good money for an optical illusion. But what an illusion!

This month, we will continue our observations of marine invertebrate coloration with a slightly different subject - that of the impressive appearance of photosynthetic clams (mostly *Tridacna* and *Hippopus* species, but also including *Fragum*, and *Corculum* specimens). Strangely enough, and contrary to information in many hobbyist references, these clams do *not* contain colorful pigments. The 'metallic' iridescent colors we often see are caused by light reflected from tiny internal structures. Also involved are refraction, light interference and possibly diffraction. To understand why these colors are apparent necessitates a review of a few optical physics terms.

DEFINITIONS AND EXAMPLES

Coral coloration (due to reflection and fluorescence) is relatively simple when compared to the science involved with clam coloration. Take a deep breath, and we'll get started.

Diffraction: Bending of light waves around an object. The colorful surfaces of CDs and DVDs are good examples of diffraction.

Hue: One of three attributes of color (along with chroma and lightness). This attribute is described with names such as 'red', 'yellow', etc.

Interference: A characteristic of light waves under certain circumstances to reinforce or cancel hue. Reinforcement is called 'constructive' interference while cancellation is called 'destructive' interference. Interference is caused by light waves traveling at different speeds and staying in or out of

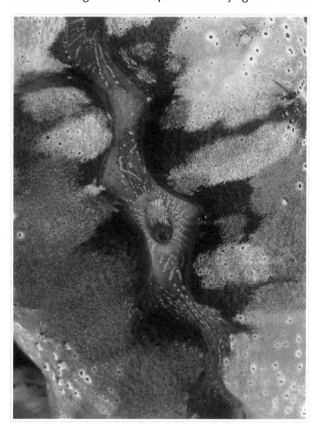

phase. If the light beams are of the same orientation after reflection/refraction, no color will be apparent. However, certain colors will be amplified if beams are out of phase (within a very small range).

An example of interference can be seen when two pebbles are dropped into a tub of water. Some waves will combine and become larger while others' energies meet and 'cancel out.' Basically, the same thing can happen with light waves during constructive or destructive interference.

The colors of soap bubbles or oil on water (and *Tridacna* iridescence) are due to constructive and destructive interference (See Figure 1).

For a tutorial on interference, see:

http://www.glenbrook.k12.il.us/gbssci/phys/class/waves/u10l3c.html

Iridophore: For our purposes, iridophores are the iridescent patches of color scattered across the mantle of *Tridacna* clams. An iridophore consists of numerous smaller bodies or cells called *iridocytes*. In turn, iridocytes contain uniform, regularly spaced stacks ('laminate' *iridosomes*) of sulfur-rich protein called *iridosomal platelets*. See Figure 2.

Iridophores and their various substructures have been described in *T. maxima* (Fankboner, 1971; Farmer et al., 2001; Kawaguti, 1966); *T. gigas* (Griffiths et al., 1992); *T. crocea* (Griffiths et al., 1992); *T. squamosa* (Fankboner, 1971); *Hippopus hippopus* (Griffiths et al., 1992); and *T. tevoroa* (Klumpp and Lucas, 1994). It is believed other photosynthetic clams contain them as well.

Note that clam iridophores are made of different proteins than many other animals' iridophores. For instance,

cephalopod (squid, octopus, etc.) iridophores are based on a different material (guanine, which is why their iridophores are sometimes called guanophores. If that sounds a little odd - it is. Guanine was originally isolated from guano, or bird poop. This little known fact can make you the life of the next black tie cocktail party you attend... and make you wonder about the motivation of some scientists!).

Iridescence: An optical phenomenon in which hue ('color') changes with the viewing angle.

Reflection: The 'return' or 'bouncing back' of light waves, sometimes (but not always) without alteration of the light and incident angle.

Refraction: Deviation or 'bending' of light waves as they pass from one medium to another of different optical density. The amount of 'bending' caused by a material is called its refractive index.

Mirages are due to refraction caused by layers of cool and warm air.

Schemochromes or **'Structural Colors'**: Those colors caused by presence of tiny light-reflecting structures and optical physics such as refraction, interference and others. *Schemochromes* are the opposite of *biochromes* (which contain true colored pigments). Therefore, schemochromes are not

Figure 2. Tridacna reflective (and refractive/diffractive) proteins are arranged in neat rows. After a photomicrograph by Griffiths et al., 1992.

Figure 1. A common example of interference. These bubbles do not, nor do Tridacna clams, contain pigments that make them iridescent. Light reflected from the inside and outside surfaces of the bubble recombine and, if out of phase, cause constructive interference and different hues. If in phase, no color is apparent due to destructive interference.

actually pigments but only an optical illusion caused by structural properties (and widely seen in many bird feathers, reptile and fish scales and tissues, insects and marine invertebrates).

To stitch this information together - the 'metallic', iridescent colors displayed by *Tridacna* and other taxa are not true pigments (biochromes) - they are schemochromes. Schemochromes are due to physical structures within tissues. In the case of colorful clams, these structures are called iridophores. Iridophores contain uniform, protein-rich cells called iridosomal platelets. When light strikes the iridosomal platelets, it is reflected but not without modification. The color reflected is dependent upon the refractive index of the protein, its orientation, number of platelets in the stack, angle of illumination and other factors. Thus, light falling upon the platelets is refracted (due to different optical densities). Construction and destructive interference now come into play. Again, depending upon the refractive index and possibly the orientation of the proteins, interference can reinforce certain colors, or cancel them. These refracted/reflected light waves can be very dramatic in appearance if the background is dark.

If the exact refractive index is known (and, to my knowledge, it is not for *Tridacna* and others), then the apparent color can be predicted. Constructive interference (assuming a refractive index of 1.42) would occur at wavelengths in the range of ultraviolet (355nm) through blue (468nm; Griffiths et al., 1992)*. In other words, the structural colors reflect ultraviolet light (which we cannot see) and those visible wavelengths of violet and blue (which is the color of many clams' mantles). Different refractive indices could lend any number of visible colors.

* Note: These researchers believed preparation of mantle samples may have caused some shrinkage, thus throwing a small monkey wrench into the works. When the calculation is 'corrected' for this potential error, the constructive interference range is extended into the green portion of the spectrum (and, as we know, violet, blue and greens are quite visible in mantles' reflected light).

DISCUSSION

If we have in mind a concept of what causes clam iridescence, then the next logical question is 'why?'

The most popular theory seems to be one of photoprotection, where potentially harmful ultraviolet (UV) radiation and Photosynthetically Active Radiation (PAR, especially in the violet/blue/green portions of the spectrum) are simply reflected away from the animal and its symbiotic algae.

A simple test, though certainly not conclusive, would be to compare clam coloration to depth. Theoretically, clams reflecting blue and green light would be found in shallow depths. See Table 1.

Table 1. Common clam coloration and depths. Casual observation suggests blue and green colors are common in clams from shallow water, while yellows and browns are often seen in specimens from deeper water. Is it really so?

Species	Common Depth	Common Colors
Tridacna crocea	to ~6m	Blue, Green
Tridacna maxima	Common to 7m, but to ~20m	Blue, Green, Violet
Tridacna squamosa	To 15-20m	Golden Brown
Tridacna trevoroa	20-33m	Brownish-Gray
Tridacna gigas	20m	Green-Brown
Tridacna derasa	4-10m, but to 25m	Golden Brown
Hippopus hippopus	to ~6m	Dull Greenish Brown

Before continuing, it should be noted that any attempt to associate fashion (coloration, in this case) with function is notoriously difficult. However, with that said, generally we see blue and green coloration associated with clams often found in shallow depths, with yellow-browns at deeper depths. However, there are major exceptions to this apparent trend where clams of a single species at the same depth display radically different coloration (see Fatherree, 2006 for some striking examples). *Hippopus* specimens also buck the trend.

So, other factors should be considered, such as genetic variability among specimens and possible effects of environmental factors. 'Types' (clades) of zooxanthellae found in photosynthetic clams should be studied when examining maximal depth ranges of clams.

GENETIC DIFFERENCES BETWEEN DIFFERENTLY COLORED TRIDACNA GIGAS AND EFFECTS OF LIGHT INTENSITY AND QUALITY ON T. MAXIMA

Burton (1997) used a laboratory procedure called electrophoresis in an attempt to link mantle 'coloration' and genetic variations. No clear relationship was established (although some interesting anomalies were observed in some of his colorful *T. gigas* specimens). This researcher believed unspecified environmental conditions (perhaps in conjunction with genetic predisposition) could cause 'expression of color'.

The most common environmental factor mentioned in hobby literature is that of light intensity or spectral quality. Alo (2005), in tests involving almost 400 *T. maxima* specimens distributed in 12 greenhouse systems and using different lighting setups in each system ('full greenhouse' light - peak

PAR of 1,300-1,400mmol×m²×sec; 'shaded greenhouse' light - peak PAR of 700-1,000 mmol×m²×sec; and 10,000K metal halide light - maximum PAR of 1,450 mmol×m×sec, decreasing to 280 mmol×m²×sec (!) after 13 weeks, found *only* **one** *T. maxima* to shift coloration (from green to yellow) during the experiment's progress (this specimen was held in a 'shaded greenhouse' tank). However, during the clams' light acclimation period (an initial 5-hour photoperiod increased by 30 minutes daily until a 12-hour photoperiod was obtained) *fourteen* clams changed from green to gold, and two switched from blue to gold.

Of interest to many hobbyists is one of Alo's observations - those clams maintained under the 10,000K metal halide lamps never expanded their mantles as fully as those exposed to natural sunlight of any intensity. His work suggests spectral quality was in play, and he attributes statistically significant high clam mortality to the UV-A spike at 365nm in the metal halide's spectrum (which is an interesting observation, since other researchers have suggested refractive/reflective qualities produced by iridophores protect mantle tissues/ zooxanthellae from UV-A radiation. Since the metal halide lamps were suspended 20 cm (8 inches) above the water surface, is it possible that infrared radiation - heat - generated by the lamps was transferred to the clams resulting in stress?). For those wondering, Alo keep careful records of nutrients within his systems.

This researcher also includes some interesting work determining reflectance of clams' mantles using an Ocean Optics spectrometer and its software (See Figures 3, 4 and 5).

AND... A FINAL CLUE

If *Tridacna* clams' coloration plays a part in preventing zooxanthellae from getting too much light, we would see this as

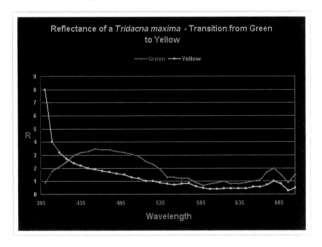

Figure 3. Reflectance of a single T. maxima specimen before and after its transition from 'green' to 'yellow'. (The 'R' legend on the y-axis stands for 'reflectance'.)

lack of photoinhibition in photosynthesis (or specifically, a linear increase of electron flow as light intensity increases - this determined by a PAM fluorometer).

And this is exactly what we see (as shown in Figure 6). However, this is not proof that the mantle coloration is responsible - it could be due to self-shading of zooxanthellae within the relatively thick mantle, or some other factor.

This experiment was conducted while using an Iwasaki 400-watt 'daylight' metal halide as the illumination source. No photosaturation (much less dynamic photoinhibition) was noted at PAR values approaching 600 µmol·m²·sec, or ~30,000 lux. This does not mean the clam requires this amount of light; merely that it can tolerate it. *T. maxima* specimens can do just fine when maintained under much less

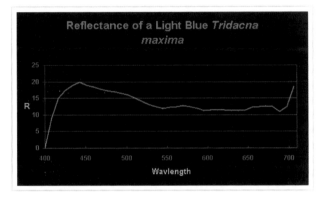

Figure 4. Reflectance of a 'light blue' T. maxima. Note the unusual and very strong reflectance at ~440nm - ~20% of the light falling upon the mantle is reflected. There is a muted spectral signature of zooxanthellae seen at 575nm and 650nm.

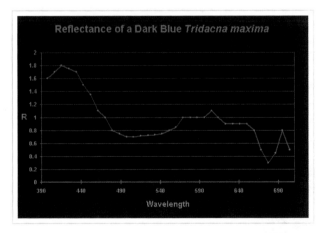

Figure 5. Reflectance of a 'dark blue' T. maxima. Compare this weak reflectance to that of the 'light blue' clam in Figure 4. Also interesting is the distinct 'crown' reflection at ~575nm, 600nm and 650nm- the typical spectral signature of zooxanthellae. Why do reflectances shown in Figures 3 and 4 lack this pronounced feature?

light (200-300 µmol·m²·sec, or 10,000-15,000 lux, is generally sufficient).

ZOOXANTHELLAE CLADES FOUND IN GIANT CLAMS

As we near the closing of our discussion, we should examine the 'types' of zooxanthellae known to infect *Tridacna* clams. Reasons for including this information are two-fold. First, it establishes that clams of the same species can contain different zooxanthellae 'types' (clades). It also suggests that animals in the listings could possibly have the same light requirements.

As to the real question - Is there a genetic link between a particular clam recognizing a specific symbiont clade and a need for photoprotection via optical manipulations?

A3 - Found in a *Tridacna* clam (species unreported, Baille et al., 2000), *Tridacna crocea*, *T. maxima*, *T. derasa*, *T. gigas*, and another 'giant clam' (*Hippopus hippopus*; LaJeunesse, 2001). Clade A3 is tolerant of higher light levels (Hennige et al., 2006). Known hosts include the jellyfish *Cassiopeia mertensii* from Hawaii (LaJeunesse, 2001; LaJeunesse et al., 2004), *Montastrea faveolata* (Belize, across a depth range of 2 to 8m), a Belizean stony coral (*Siderastrea intersepta*, @ 8-15m; Warner et al., 2006), the anemone *Condylactis gigantea*, stony corals *Acropora palmata*, shallow-water *Acropora cervicornis*, and *Stephanocoenia michelini*. A3 zooxanthellae are known to produce 1 ultraviolet-absorbing compound - the MAA mycosporine-glycine (Banaszak et al., 2006).

C1 - Found in *Tridacna derasa* (1-8m); *T. gigas* (1-8m) and *T. maxima* (1-8m). Clade C1 is considered a 'generalist' zooxanthellae in that it infects a large number of photosynthetic hosts in the Pacific as well as the Atlantic, and is distributed over a wide variety of depths. Thus, corals and clams containing this clade could be considered highly adaptive in that they can tolerate high light but are probably best suited for lower light intensities. Clade C1 (along with C3, C21, C3d, C1c and C45) is believed to be an ancestral type from which other clades evolved (LaJeunesse, 2004). *Acropora cervicornis* (Baker et al., 1997), *Acropora divaricata*, *A. humilis*, *A. hyacinthus*, *A. longicyathus* (from the GBR; van Oppen et al., 2001), *Acropora palifera* (from Taiwan, Chen et al., 2005), *Acropora sarmentosa* , *A. tenuis* (GBR; Van Oppen et al., 2001), *Astreopora* (GBR, LaJeunesse et al., 2003), *Astreopora myriophthalma* (Taiwan; Chen et al., 2005), Caribbean anemones *Bartholomea* and *Condylactis* spp. (LaJeunesse et al., 2003), Great Barrier Reef 'corallimorpharia' and *Coscinaraea*, *Coscinaraea wellsi* and *Cycloseris vaughani* from Hawaii (LaJeunesse et al., 2004), *Cyphastrea* (LaJeunesse et. al., 2003), *Cyphastrea chalcidicum* (van Oppen, 2005), Atlantic and Pacific *Discosoma* spp. (LaJeunesse, 2005), *Echinophyllia orpheensis*, *Echinophyllia lamellosa* (Chen, 2005), Caribbean *Eunicea* (LaJeunesse et. al., 2003), *Euphyllia ancora*, *Euphyllia glabrescens* (Chen, 2005), *Favia* (LaJeunesse et. al., 2003), *Favia favus* and *Favites abdita* from Taiwan (Chen, 2005), *Fungia* (LaJeunesse et. al., 2003), *Fungia crassa* (van Oppen, 2005), *Galaxea*, *Goniastrea* (LaJeunesse et. al., 2003), *Goniastrea rectiformis* (Chen, 2005), *Goniopora* (LaJeunesse et. al., 2003), *Goniopora columba*, *Goniopora lobata* (Chen, 2005), *Herpolitha*, *Hydnophora* (LaJeunesse et. al., 2003), *Hydnophora excessa* (Chen, 2005), *Icilogorgia*, *Lebruna*, *Leptastrea* (LaJeunesse et. al., 2003), *Leptoria phrygia* (Chen, 2005), *Leptoseris incrustans* (LaJeunesse, 2004), *Linuche*, *Lobophytum*, *Merulina* (LaJeunesse et. al., 2003), *Merulina ampliata* (Chen, 2005), *Merulina scrabicula* (van Oppen, 2005), *Millepora* sp. (LaJeunesse et. al., 2003), *Montipora aequituberculata* (Chen, 2005), *Montipora cactus* from Indonesia (van Oppen, 2004), *Montipora cactus*, *Montipora curta* from Taiwan (Chen, 2005), *Montipora confusa* (van Oppen, 2004), *Montipora digitata*, *Montipora effluorescens*, *Montipora hispida*, *Montipora* sp., *Montipora spongodes*, *Montipora undata* from Taiwan (Chen, 2005), *Mycedium* (LaJeunesse et. al., 2003), *Mycedium elephantotus* (Chen, 2005), *Pachyseris*, *Paulastrea*, Caribbean *Palythoa*, Hawaiian *Palythoa* (LaJeunesse et. al., 2003), *Pavona desucata*, *Pavona frondifera*, *Pavona varians*, *Pavona venosa* (Chen, 2005), the 'bubble' coral *Plerogyra* (LaJeunesse et. al., 2003), *Plesiastrea verispora* (Chen, 2005), gorgonians *Plexaura* and *Plumigorgia* (LaJeunesse et. al., 2003), Taiwanese *Pocillopora damicornis* (Chen, 2005), *Polyphyllia*, *Porites* sp. (LaJeunesse et. al., 2003), shallow-water *Porites cylindrica*, *Porites lutea*, *Porites solida* (from Taiwan; Chen, 2006), GBR *Psammocora* (LaJeunesse et. al., 2003), *Pseudosiderastrea tayamai* (Chen, 2005), *Rhodactis*, *Rumphella*, *Sarcophyton*, Pacific *Scolymia*, *Siderastrea*, *Sinularia* (LaJeunesse et. al., 2003), *Stylocoeniella guentheri* (Chen, 2005), *Stylophora* sp. ((LaJeunesse et. al., 2003), *Stylophora pistillata* (Chen, 2005), *Turbinaria* sp. (LaJeunesse et. al., 2003), *Turbinaria mesenteria* (Chen, 2005), Pacific and Caribbean *Zoanthus* spp. (LaJeunesse et. al., 2003).

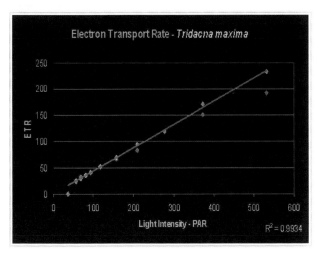

Figure 6. Rate of photosynthesis (Electron Transport Rate, or ETR) of a Tridacna maxima clam under an artificial light source.

CLAM COLORATION - IS IT CAMOUFLAGE?

Reflection of ultraviolet radiation could serve as a photoprotective measure to both host and symbiont, but is a poor idea for camouflage since many fishes can see well into the ultraviolet radiation range. Of course, the same applies to visible radiation. It would seem that clam mantle coloration is just the opposite of the best camouflage strategy - that of invisibility, such as offered by transparency, where background light is transmitted through tissues. Further, the apparent self-protection reaction made possible by clams' photoreceptors (primitive 'eyes') to shadows is well known - the sudden closing of the valves, where water is forced out of internal cavities (usually enough to scare away predator fishes, such as *Thalassoma* wrasse spp. This, naturally, does not exclude camouflage's potential of predator avoidance, if you will. However, some researchers believe mantle coloration acting as camouflage to be a remote possibility).

There is also the possibility that physical qualities of the mantle could enhance photosynthesis. However, there is very little evidence supporting this hypothesis and it will not be discussed here.

I present this information for those truly interested in pursuit of answers. Unfortunately, I can no longer work on this since NELHA donated their *Tridacna* clams to the Waikiki Aquarium.

It should be apparent that we have a fairly good understanding of how clams' mantles are colorful, but a very poor one of why they appear this way.

This is an excellent project for a dedicated hobbyist to undertake. Quality spectrometers are becoming increasing affordable as diffraction gratings find their way into different applications, and a fair number of instruments are now in hobbyists' hands. Those hobbyists willing to expend their time and money could be rewarded with unlocking mysteries of clam coloration - how they do it, why they do it - and perhaps turning those less-than-desirable specimens into 'killer clams'.

I will be glad to assist in any way possible. Contact me at RiddleLabs@aol.com.

REFERENCES

1. Alo, M., 2005. Survivorship, growth and pigmentation responses of the marine ornamental invertebrate *Tridacna maxima* to varied irradiance levels in two different culture systems. Master's Thesis, University of Florida. 79 pp.

2. Baillie, B., C. Belda-Baillie and T. Maruyama, 2000. Conspecificity and Indo-Pacific distribution of *Symbiodinium* genotypes (Dinophyceae) from giant clams. J. Phycol. 36:1153-1161.

3. Baker, A. and R. Rowan, 1997. Diversity of symbiotic dinoflagellates (zooxanthellae) in scleractinian corals of the Caribbean and eastern Pacific. Proc. 8th Int. Coral Reef Symp., Panama. 2: 1301-1306.

4. Brocco, S., 1977. The ultrastructure of the epidermis, dermis, iridophores, leucophores and chromatophores of *Octopus dolfleini martini* (Cephalopod: Octopoda) Ph.D. Thesis, University of Washington, Seattle.

5. Burton, C., undated. Mantle colouration variation and genetic diversity in Lizard Island giant clams (*Tridacna gigas*). 14-23.

6. Chen, C., Y-W Yang, N. Wei, W-S Tsai and L-S Fang, 2005. Symbiont diversity in scleractinian corals from tropical reefs and sub-tropical non-reef communities in Taiwan. Coral Reefs, 24(1): 11-22.

7. Fankboner, P., 1971. Intracellular digestion of symbiotic zooxanthellae by host amoebocytes in giant clams (Bivalvia: Tridacnidae), with a note on the nutritional role of the hypertrophied siphonal epidermis. Bio. Bull. 141: 222-234.

8. Farmer, M., W. Fitt and R. Trench, 2001. Morphology of the symbiosis between *Corculum cardissa* (Mollusca: Bivalvia) and *Symbiodinium corculorum* (Dinophycae). Biol. Bull., 200: 336-343.

9. Fatherree, J., 2006. *Giant Clams in the Sea and the Aquarium: The Biology, Identification, and Aquarium Husbandry of Tridacnid Clams.* Liquid Medium, Tampa, Fla. 227 pp.

10. Griffiths, D., H. Winsor and T. Luong-Van, 1992. Iridophores in the mantle of giant clams. Aust. J. Zool., 40: 319-326.

11. Hennige, S., D. Suggett, M. Warner and D. Smith, 2006. Photoacclimation of *Symbiodinium* revisited: Variation of strategies with thermal tolerance? Natural Environment Research Council, University of Essex.

12. Hirose, E., K. Iwai and T. Maruyama, 2006. Establishment of the photosymbiosis in the early ontogeny of three giant clams. Mar. Biol., 148(3).

13. Johnsen, S. and H. Sosik, 2003. Cryptic coloration and mirrored sides as camouflage strategies in near-surface pelagic habitats: Implications for foraging and predator avoidance. Limnol. Oceanogr. 48(3): 1277-1288.

14. Klumpp, D. and J. Lucas, 1994. Nutritional ecology of the giant clams *Tridacna tevoroa* and *T. derasa* from

Tonga: Influence of light on filter-feeding and photosynthesis. Mar. Ecol. Prog. Ser., 107: 147-156.

15. Knop, D., 1996. *Giant Clams: A Comprehensive Guide to the Identification and Care of Tridacnid Clams.* Dähne Verlag, Ettlingen. 255 pp.

16. LaJeunesse, T., R. Bhagooli, M. Hidaka, L. de Vantier, T. Done, G. Schmidt, W. Fitt and O. Hoegh-Guldberg, 2004b. Closely related Symbiodinium species differ in relative dominance in coral reef host communities across environmental latitudinal and Biogeographical gradients. Mar. Ecol. Prog. Ser., 284: 147-161.

17. Yoshihisa, K., undated. Organization and development of reflecting platelets in iridophores of the giant clam *Tridacna crocea* Lamarck: Developmental biology.

18. Zoo. Sci., 7(1):63-72.

FEATURE ARTICLE

MONTIPORA DIGITATA: A STONY CORAL FOR ALL HOBBYISTS

By Dana Riddle

These animals are generally hardy in captivity and can grow rather quickly, making them attractive to beginning and intermediate reefkeepers.

Published January 2008, Advanced Aquarist's Online Magazine   © Pomacanthus Publications, LLC

Keywords: Coloration, Coral, Dana Riddle, Feature Article, Lighting, Water Circulation
Link to original article: http://www.advancedaquarist.com/2008/1/aafeature2

This *Montipora* species is a good choice for those hobbyists wanting to make the jump to small-polyp stony (SPS) corals. Their appearance is soft and velvet-like when their polyps are extended. These animals are generally hardy in captivity and can grow rather quickly, making them attractive to beginning and intermediate reefkeepers. *Montipora digitata* specimens can lend a numbers of colors to an aquarium, as they can be brown, orange, purple, pink or a combination of colors. The single-color specimens are usually readily available and relatively inexpensive. Unusually colored specimens are often in high demand and command premium prices. In short, *M. digitata* is a coral that can be appreciated by beginning and advanced hobbyists.

Common Name: Velvet Coral

Family: Acroporidae

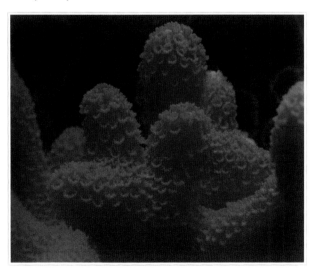

Genus: *Montipora* (L. - *mons*- mountain, and *pora* - pore; describing elaborations and porous nature of the corallum).

Species: *Montipora digitata*, which can be confused with *M. samarensis*.

Geographical Range and Common Habitat: Shallow waters of the Indo-Pacific and Red Sea.

Growth Forms: Colonies are digitate (finger-like) or arborescent (tree-like) with branches that may fuse together (technically called anatomosing branching).

Known Symbionts: Zooxanthellae (Symbiodinium sp.) including any one of the following: Clade* C1 (a 'generalist' clade with ability to adapt to a wide variety of depths and light conditions), or C15 (thermally-tolerant), or Clade C73 (from shallow water, and possibly an example of a clade co-evolving with this *Montipora* species).

*A 'clade' is a grouping of organisms based on phylogenetic similarities while sharing a common ancestor.

LIGHT REQUIREMENTS

Zooxanthellae photosynthesis is dependent upon many factors, and lighting is an important link in this chain of factors. Providing sufficient lighting while ignoring other parameters (such as water motion and water chemistry) can result in low rates of photosynthesis. Details of these other factors are detailed below. With this in mind, let's begin our look at types of zooxanthellae known hosted by *M. digitata*.

In order to understand the lighting requirements of *M. digitata* specimens, we should examine the types ('clades') of symbiotic dinoflagellates found within their tissues.

There are 3 clades known to infect *M. digitata*, one of these is a 'generalist' zooxanthellae tolerant of high and low light. C15 is noted as being tolerant of higher temperatures. Little is known about Clade C73 other than it seems to be found only in *Montipora digitata* specimens from shallow water (LaJeunesse, 2005).

It is assumed that *Montipora digitata* specimens harbor only one zooxanthella clade at a time - there is no contrary evidence to my knowledge. However, current technology used to genetically fingerprint zooxanthellae do not 'see' clades when their numbers are only 5% or so of the total population. If *M. digitata* contains two or more clades, then 'reshuffling' (where one clade becomes dominant, but temperature and other factors could play a role) according to environmental conditions (most likely lighting - either due to depth or seasonal changes) could explain the host's abundance. Vertical zonation (where light is rapidly attenuated with increasing depth) is thought to be explained by the type zooxanthellae hosted by the coral animal (Iglesias-Prieto et al., 2004).

This listing is presented under the presumption that each of these zooxanthellae clades has a genetically-imprinted photoadaption range and is the dominant symbiont; hence the following groupings of corals would probably do well under the same lighting regime as long as other environmental conditions are correct.

C1: Clade C1 is considered a 'generalist' zooxanthellae in that it infects a large number of coral genera hosts in the Pacific as well as the Atlantic, and is distributed over a wide variety of depths. Thus, corals containing this clade could be considered highly adaptive to light intensities. They can tolerate high light *but are probably best suited for lower light intensities.* Clade C1 (along with C3, C21, C3d, C1c and C45) is believed to be an ancestral type from which other clades evolved (LaJeunesse, 2004). If we subscribe to the theory that all C1 zooxanthellae have the same photoadaptive capabilities, then these photosynthetic animals would do well under the same lighting conditions: *Acropora cervicornis* (Baker et al., 1997), *Acropora divaricata, A. humilis, A. hyacinthus, A. longicyathus* (from the GBR; van Oppen et al., 2001), *Acropora palifera* (from Taiwan, Chen et al., 2005), *Acropora sarmentosa , A. tenuis* (GBR; Van Oppen et al., 2001), *Astreopora* (GBR, LaJeunesse et al., 2003), *Astreopora myriophthalma* (Taiwan; Chen et al., 2005), Caribbean anemones *Bartholomea* and *Condylactis* spp. (LaJeunesse et al., 2003), Great Barrier Reef 'corallimorpharia' and *Coscinaraea, Coscinaraea wellsi* and *Cycloseris vaughani* from Hawaii (LaJeunesse et al., 2004), *Cyphastrea* (LaJeunesse et. al., 2003), *Cyphastrea chalcidicum* (van Oppen, 2005), Atlantic and Pacific *Discosoma* spp. (LaJeunesse, 2005), *Echinophyllia orpheensis, Echinophyllia lamellosa* (Chen, 2005), Caribbean *Eunicea* (LaJeunesse et. al., 2003), *Euphyllia ancora, Euphyllia glabrescens* (Chen, 2005), *Favia* (LaJeunesse et. al., 2003), *Favia favus* and *Favites abdita* from Taiwan (Chen, 2005), *Fungia* (LaJeunesse et. al., 2003), *Fungia crassa* (van Oppen, 2005), *Galaxea, Goniastrea*

(LaJeunesse et. al., 2003), *Goniastrea rectiformis* (Chen, 2005), *Goniopora* (LaJeunesse et. al., 2003), *Goniopora columba, Goniopora lobata* (Chen, 2005), *Herpolitha, Hydnophora* (LaJeunesse et. al., 2003), *Hydnophora excessa* (Chen, 2005), *Icilogorgia, Lebruna, Leptastrea* (LaJeunesse et. al., 2003), *Leptoria phrygia* (Chen, 2005), *Leptoseris incrustans* (LaJeunesse, 2004), *Linuche, Lobophytum, Merulina* (LaJeunesse et. al., 2003), *Merulina ampliata* (Chen, 2005), *Merulina scrabicula* (van Oppen, 2005), *Millepora* sp. (LaJeunesse et. al., 2003), *Montipora aequituberculata* (Chen, 2005), *Montipora cactus* from Indonesia (van Oppen, 2004), *Montipora cactus, Montipora curta* from Taiwan (Chen, 2005), *Montipora confusa* (van Oppen, 2004), *Montipora effluorescens, Montipora hispida, Montipora* sp., *Montipora spongodes, Montipora undata* from Taiwan (Chen, 2005), *Mycedium* (LaJeunesse et. al., 2003), *Mycedium elephantotus* (Chen, 2005), *Pachyseris, Paulastrea*, Caribbean *Palythoa*, Hawaiian *Palythoa* (LaJeunesse et. al., 2003), *Pavona desucata, Pavona frondifera, Pavona varians, Pavona venosa* (Chen, 2005), the 'bubble' coral *Plerogyra* (LaJeunesse et. al., 2003), *Plesiastrea verispora* (Chen, 2005), gorgonians *Plexaura* and *Plumigorgia* (LaJeunesse et. al., 2003), Taiwanese *Pocillopora damicornis* (Chen, 2005), *Polyphyllia, Porites* sp. (LaJeunesse et. al., 2003), shallow-water *Porites cylindrica, Porites lutea, Porites solida* (from Taiwan; Chen, 2006), GBR *Psammocora* (LaJeunesse et. al., 2003), *Pseudosiderastrea tayamai* (Chen, 2005), *Rhodactis, Rumphella, Sarcophyton*, Pacific *Scolymia, Siderastrea, Sinularia* (LaJeunesse et. al., 2003), *Stylocoeniella guentheri* (Chen, 2005), *Stylophora* sp. (LaJeunesse et. al., 2003), *Stylophora pistillata* (Chen, 2005), a giant clam (*Tridacna* sp.), *Turbinaria* sp. (LaJeunesse et. al., 2003), *Turbinaria mesenteria* (Chen, 2005), Pacific and Caribbean *Zoanthus* spp. (LaJeunesse et. al., 2003).

C15: Limited to the Indo-Pacific and considered thermally tolerant and often found in *Porites* corals. It is often found in Pacific *Porites* spp., though obviously not exclusive of other genera. For instance, C15 is also found in *Aglaophenia, Heteroxenia* (western Pacific, both sampled at 1.0 -15.m LaJeunesse et al., 2003), *Montipora* (GBR, Pochon, 2004), *Pocillopora damicornis* (0.3-8.0m, Kenya, Visram and Douglas, 2006), *Porites* sp. from various Pacific locations (LaJeunesse et. al., 2003 and Pochon et al., 2004), *Porites brighami* (at 20m in Hawaii, LaJeunesse et al., 2003); *Porites compressa* (Hawaii, 15-25m, LaJeunesse et al., 2003), *Porites cylindrica* (GBR, LaJeunesse et al., 2003), *Porites evermanni* (now *P. lutea*, Hawaii, 5.0-20.0m, LaJeunesse, 2004), *Porites lobata* (Hawaii, 2-20m, LaJeunesse, 2003), *Porites lutea* (purple variant, 1.5m, Hawaii, LaJeunesse et al., unpublished). C15 is possibly a variant of Clade C3 (LaJeunesse, 2005).

(As a footnote, a Hawaiian *Porites compressa* specimen was transplanted from depth to about 1m - it retained its C15 zooxanthellae even years after the move. What does this suggest about fidelity of a particular zooxanthellae clade to its host coral?)

PAM fluorometry work found onset of photosaturation ranging from 250-400 µmol ·m²·sec (~12,500 - 20,000 lux) and onset of photoinhibition ranging from ~350 to ~750 µmol·m²·sec (~17,500 - 37,500 lux) in a Hawaiian *Porites lobata* and *Porites lutea* specimens, respectively (ITS 2 'DNA fingerprinting' analysis on *P. lutea* by LaJeunesse et al., unpublished; PAM fluorometry by Riddle, unpublished).

C73: Apparently found only in *Montipora digitata* specimens in very shallow water (0.5m, Eastern Pacific, LaJeunesse et. al., 2003).

AQUARIUM LIGHTING CONDITIONS

I've been fortunate in having had the opportunity to view many reef aquaria across the country. On many of these trips, I carried a PAR meter (a Li-Cor 189 with cosine-corrected submersible sensor) with me and collected the following information.

Orange *M. digitata* specimens were observed to be tolerant of a wide range of lighting conditions (up to 700 µmol·m²·sec in one instance) but did well in lower light intensity ranging from 144 µmol·m²·sec (provided by an Iwasaki 400w 6500K metal halide lamp), to 150 µmol·m²·sec (PFO LEDs; see Figures 2-5) to 200-223 µmol·m²·sec, and, finally, 565 µmol·m²·sec.

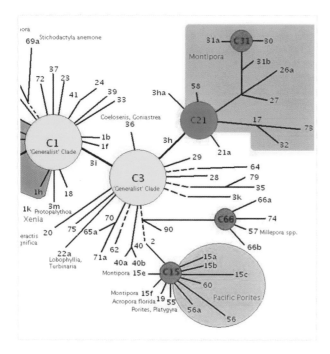

Figure 1. A diagram depicting adaptive radiations of zooxanthellae clades. Montipora digitata specimens are known to contain C1 (generalist), C15 (resistant to high temperature) and C73 clades. Note - the orange shading represents clades found only in Montipora species, although some are descended from clade C15. After LaJeunesse 2005.

Purple specimens were less common than orange ones. PAR values for successful maintenance of this variant was seen at 240-265 µmol·m²·sec (generated by a 175w 6500K metal halide lamp and actinic-white VHO fluorescent lamps).

A green *M. digitata* was doing well at a light intensity of 240 µ·mol·m²·sec (produced by a 175w 6500K metal halide and actinic-white VHO fluorescent lamp combination). Another green specimen was seen in light intensity of 550µ·mol·m²·sec.

Blue and pink specimens were not common. The former was growing (and maintaining coloration) at 200 µ·mol·m²·sec (a 400-watt Venture 'daylight' metal halide lamp) and the latter was doing nicely at 360 µmol·m²·sec.

Note: For those having a submersible lux meter, be aware that it is possible to convert PAR to lux. Each lamp will have a different conversion factor, but a very general rule of thumb is to divide lux by 50 to arrive at a *crude* estimate of PAR.

WATER MOTION

Water motion is difficult to quantify so most hobbyists must rely upon visual indicators, with polyp expansion and movement probably the most common. Interestingly, too much and too little water motion can cause corals to retract polyps. Too much will of course deform the polyp and perhaps cause shearing or tearing of soft tissues. On the other hand, a coral can recognize too little flow and after a prolonged period of little water movement, it realizes it is not catching any food and will retract polyps in order to conserve energy (Sebens, 1997). (Too much lighting will also cause some corals to contract their polyps to protect themselves and their zooxanthellae from excessive light. This is sometimes indicated by expansion of shaded polyps while those exposed to light are retracted.)

Fortunately, providing sufficient water motion is not the challenge it once was. Some of the newer propeller pumps on the market can potentially provide sufficient water movement along with low electrical consumption (see Riddle, 2007 for details).

Correct water motion is indicated by polyps gently rocking in the currents.

GROWTH SEQUENCE

The following photos (Figures 2 -5) show growth of a *Montipora digitata* over the course of 12 months.

OTHER PARAMETERS

Hobbyists should pay close attention to calcium and alkalinity concentrations. Calcium, of course, is important for skeletal growth, and concentrations should be maintained in the 400-450 mg/l range. Alkalinity (reported as $CaCO_3$) is very important as well - it is the inorganic carbon source for photosynthesis and is also used for skeletal growth. Alkalinity should be maintained at 160 mg/l or ~3.25 meq/l. Addition of

bicarbonates (in the form of any of the commercially-available 'alkalinity boosters') may promote growth in corals even in the presence of relatively high nutrient concentrations (Marubini, 1999).

COLORATION

Velvet corals can be very colorful, with blue, green, orange, pink (sometimes called 'super purple' or 'rose') and purple colonies (sometimes referred to as 'grape') being quite common, in addition to the brown morphs.

Orange colonies can sometimes become pinkish when maintained under intense lighting (probably due to loss of photopigments when zooxanthellae bleach). Orange and

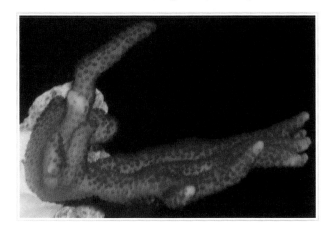

Figure 2. The epoxy holding this coral to the substrate has barely cured on Day 1.

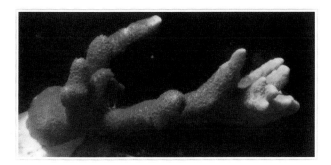

Figure 3. Ninety days after arrival. The coral has adapted to its new home and is starting to encrust its base as well as extend its branches.

Figure 5. Lateral branching has slowed, with most growth seen at the coral's base. Some branches have been accidentally broken off during routine tank maintenance.

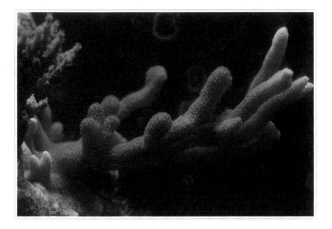

*Figure 4. Who says SPS corals can't grow under LED lamps? This one is (and many others are) at a light intensity of 150 **μmol·m²·sec.***

Figure 6. The Superman digitata (although its irregular shape and thin branches suggest it is possibly M. samarensis). It is an attractive animal, no matter what the identification. Photo courtesy Steven Reyes.

green coloration is almost certainly due to fluorescent pigments within the coral tissues. There are two types of fluorescent pigments that could cause the orange coloration - the first is a fluorescent protein (Fluorescent Pigment, or FP 575; the maximum fluorescent emission is 575nm - reddish-orange); the other is a photopigment (phycoerythrin) found in cyanobacteria living in symbiosis with the coral host (Mazel et al., 2004). The spectral signature of the fluorescent emission of FP-575 and phycoerythrin are practically identical and the emission's shape will not distinguish between the two.

'Rose' and purple colorations are probably due to non-fluorescent chromoproteins. These pigments (assuming they are indeed distinct from one another) appear as they do since they preferentially reflect red and blue wavelengths. The status of the blue pigment is, to me, uncertain. It could be either fluorescent or non-fluorescent.

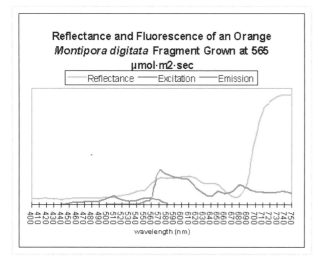

Figure 7. An example of fluorescence influencing apparent coloration. A fluorescent pigment, with maximum emission at ~575nm, lends an orange-red color to the light reflected by the coral. The fluorescent pigment is maximally excited by green light at about 508nm. Mazel, unpublished data, from an aquarium specimen supplied by the author.

Figure 8. This M. digitata variant contains a non-fluorescent purple chromoprotein.

COLORATION AND DOMINANCE

Interestingly, differently colored corals we identify as *M. digitata* can be (but are not always) highly competitive. The lowly brown morph can be attacked and their tissues destroyed by purple, orange and green morphs. Those specimens colored forest green are dominant over the other three morphs, but orange *digitatas* beat up on purple ones. We have to wonder why these corals of the same species do not always recognize each other as 'self' (perhaps DNA fingerprinting will someday tell us these coral morphs are different species). For the moment, realize that these corals can be competitive, so place them with plenty of room for growth.

Many thanks to Steve Ruddy of Coral Reef Ecosystems (www.coralreefecosystems.com) for his continuing support in preparation of this and other articles.

REFERENCES

1. Baillie, B., C. Belda-Baillie and T. Maruyama, 2000. Conspecificity and Indo-Pacific distribution of *Symbiodinium* genotypes (Dinophyceae) from giant clams. J. Phycol. 36:1153-1161.

2. Baker, A. and R. Rowan, 1997. Diversity of symbiotic dinoflagellates (zooxanthellae) in scleractinian corals of the Caribbean and eastern Pacific. Proc. 8th Int. Coral Reef Symp., Panama. 2: 1301-1306.

3. Chen, C., Y-W Yang, N. Wei, W-S Tsai and L-S Fang, 2005. Symbiont diversity in scleractinian corals from tropical reefs and sub-tropical non-reef communities in Taiwan. Coral Reefs, 24(1): 11-22.

4. Hennige, S., D. Suggett, M. Warner and D. Smith, 2006. Photoacclimation of *Symbiodinium* revisited: Variation of strategies with thermal tolerance? Natural Environment Research Council, University of Essex.

5. Iglesias-Prieto, R. V. Beltrán, T. LaJeunesse, H. Reyes-Bonilla, and P. Thomé, 2004. Different algal symbionts explain the vertical distribution of dominant reef corals in the eastern Pacific. Proc. R. Soc. Lond. B., 271:1751-1763.

6. LaJeunesse, T., W. Loh, R. vanWoesik, O. Hoegh-Guldberg, G. Schmidt and W. Fitt, 2003. Low symbionts diversity in southern Great Barrier Reef corals, relative to those in the Caribbean. Limnol. Oceanogr., 48(5):2046-2054.

7. LaJeunesse, T., R. Bhagooli, M. Hidaka, L. de Vantier, T. Done, G. Schmidt, W. Fitt and O. Hoegh-Guldberg, 2004. Closely related *Symbiodinium* species differ in relative dominance in coral reef host communities across

environmental latitudinal and biogeographical gradients. Mar. Ecol. Prog. Ser., 284: 147-161.

8. LaJeunesse, T, 2005. "Species" radiations of symbiotic dinoflagellates in the Atlantic and Indo-Pacific since the Miocene-Pliocene transition. Mol. Biol. Evol. 22(3): 570-581.

9. Marubini, F. and B. Thake, 1999. Bicarbonate addition promotes coral growth. Limnol.

10. Oceanogr., 44(3): 716-720.

11. Mazel, C., M. Lesser, M. Gorbunov and P. Falkowski, 2004. Discovery of nitrogen-fixing cyanobacteria in corals. Science, 305: 997-1000.

12. Pochon, X., T. LaJeunesse, and J. Pawlowski, 2004. Biogeographical partitioning and host specialization among foraminiferan dinoflagellates symbionts (*Symbiodinium*: Dinophyta). Mar. Biol., 146:17-27.

13. Riddle, D., 2007. Product Review: Water Motion Devices: Sea Flo's Maxi-Jet Modification Kits. In press, www.advancedaquarist.com

14. Sebens, K., 1997. Adaptive responses to water flow: Morphology, energetics, and distribution of reef corals. Proc. 8th Int. Coral Reef Symp., Panama. 2: 1053-1058.

15. Van Oppen, M., F. Palstra, A. Piquet and D. Miller, 2001. Patterns of coral-dinoflagellate associations in *Acropora*: Significance of local availability and physiology of *Symbiodinium* strains and host-symbiont selectivity. Proc. R. Soc. Lond B., 268: 1759-1767.

16. Van Oppen, M., J. Mieog, C. Sánchez, and K. Fabricius, 2005. Diversity of algal endosymbionts (zooxanthellae) in tropical octocorals: the roles of geography and host relationships. Mol. Ecol., 14: 2403-2417.

17. Visram, S. and A. Douglas, 2006. Molecular diversity of symbiotic algae (zooxanthellae) in scleractinian corals of Kenya. Coral Reefs, 25: 172-176.

AQUARIUM FISH

LARGE ANGELS IN THE HOME AQUARIUM, PART 1

By Jim McDavid

The information in this article is by large the result of my 22+ years of experience observing these animals in my own tanks, as well as tracking the results obtained by other hobbyists during that time.

Published January 2008, Advanced Aquarist's Online Magazine

© Pomacanthus Publications, LLC

Keywords: Angelfish, Aquarium Fish, Fish, Jim McDavid
Link to original article: http://www.advancedaquarist.com/2008/1/fish

Thinking of purchasing an Angelfish? Then this article is just for you. Similarly, if you've attempted to keep one of these magnificent animals in the past only to encounter problems, then the next few pages should help tremendously. Of all the fish that can be found on a tropical coral reef, there is nothing more majestic than angelfish. Indeed, if my experience over the past few decades dealing with and helping people in this hobby is any indication, this group of fish is near the top of the list in popularity. Although definitely not for everyone, this doesn't stop just about every marine aquarist from lusting after and trying their hand at keeping one of these beauties in his or her living room at some point or another in his/her fish keeping careers. The results as with any species can run the gamut, but there are concerns with these genera that I think warrant a detailed look.

The information in this article is by large the result of my 22+ years of experience observing these animals in my own tanks, as well as tracking the results obtained by other hobbyists during that time. I've had plenty of time to learn what does and does not work, both under my care and that of others. Success with these fish cannot be measured in months, or a few years. These fish can live for over 20 years in captivity; therefore only long-term results are salient when discussing what is best for their well-being. For the most part, this article is not the result of research, but hard earned empirical knowledge.

ON WITH IT THEN!

Just like the freshwater ones right?

Not exactly, in fact not even close. Freshwater angelfish belong to a group of secondary division freshwater fish (close lineage to marine fish) known as the cichlids, which also contain popular aquarium fish such as the Oscar and Firemouth. While both the marine and freshwater angels belong to the order perciformes, and share a vague, tall bodied, laterally compressed similarity, the practical resemblance ends there.

A resplendent *Pomacanthus imperator* adult. Photo by Teresa Zuber-bühler, http://www.starfish.ch/.

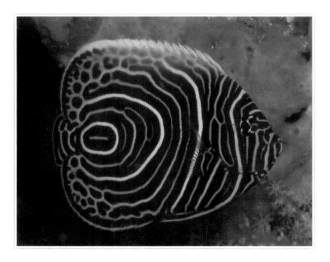

Pomacanthus imperator in it's juvenile colors. Photo by Teresa Zuber-bühler, http://www.starfish.ch/.

Marine angels can be the length of your little finger or as large as 24 inches. They can be muted, garish, or anything in between. They are intelligent, and like the groupers and triggers that I've written about previously, they have loads of charisma and personality. The large angels that we will be discussing here are also rather robust as adults, despite a somewhat delicate, often butterfly-like nature when young.

WHAT DO I NEED TO KNOW?

Plenty! This article will be in 2 parts, and a little long-winded compared to the previous two on hinds and triggers, simply because there is much more than needs to be said. When considering purchasing one of these fish, you have to know your stuff, and you have to be prepared! These animals are by most measures one of the less forgiving families available to the marine fish keeper, and this unforgiving nature manifests itself in a variety of ways, including space requirements, nutritional requirements, temperamental considerations, and usually a combination of the three. This of course varies drastically with genus and species. There is too much variation and too many idiosyncrasies within this family to impart all necessary information here, so this article will not, and cannot be the extent of your research. However, I'll attempt to give an overview of the family, and the must do's and don'ts in order to help you keep these fish successfully. With regards to specific species, I'm going to speak in terms of what the hobbyist is likely to encounter with regard to hardiness and temperament for that species. Nothing is all the time, and you may have a stroke of luck with normally fragile species, or have a string of bad luck with a species that is generally trouble free.

The most important thing to keep in mind with regard to marine angels is that they do not suffer a lazy keeper easily - they are for advanced keepers with the resources to give them

Pomacanthus asfur - juvenile.

what they require to thrive. In the grand scheme of things, when compared to many other fish species that are available, they are decidedly on the delicate side. This tendency is understated not only in most articles and books in my opinion, but by many keepers as well. This I believe is because many mistake a living fish, with a thriving fish in resplendent health. They see a fish swimming around still after a year, or 4 years, and assume all is well. Often in fact this apparently healthy fish is heading towards doom, even though it may not show outward symptoms of disease or stress. Below I will examine further why this is, and how to mitigate the potential problems. For now it's enough to say that the keeper who neglects his initial research, fails to quarantine his new arrival, fails to give his charge the proper nutrition, the proper space, or fails to perform adequate maintenance on the tank itself is asking for problems. So, let's get down to business and figure this family out!

DO I HAVE THE SPACE?

As the title of this article indicates, by home aquarium standards these are large fish. This is a subjective term of course, and adult size varies from 6" to 20" or so in the wild depending on species. While adult size in the wild doesn't necessarily translate into size attained in the home aquarium under average conditions (more on this below) you can easily choose a species that will be very at home in your 80 gallon, or very, VERY cramped in a 200 gallon tank if you're not careful. So the first thing you need to determine is what species your tank will accommodate in the real estate department. Given the diversity of the family, and the varying growth rates and sizes of various species, coupled with conditions that vary greatly from one living room to the next, generalizations are difficult at best here. To further complicate this matter, some angels will attain a size close to their wild adult maximum under the right conditions, while others almost never reach full size in most living room tanks, even relatively large ones. As a general rule, and I stress that this is a generalization, most larger species can be expected to eventually attain half to three quarters of their maximum wild adult size under *very* favorable conditions. Most of the time, growth also slows as size increases, and appears to all but stop at various sizes depending on species and conditions at hand. This is due to stunting, and is a problem not dealt with in most publications with regards to this family.

The fact that minimum tank size is often grossly understated for most species in some trusted sources doesn't help matters either. I will stress the previous point by saying that some very popular, current and often-referenced material is preposterously off the mark with regard to tank requirements for these fish, including just about every reference you'll find on fish retailer websites. In short, the tank sizes given insure a stressed and possibly stunted animal, and therefore the accompanying health issues and shorter life span that comes along with it. A German Shepard will live in a 10' by10' room for years, and he might look just fine for the

A juvenile French Angel, P. paru.

Pomacanthus semicirculatus - adult. Photo by Teresa Zuberbühler, http://www.starfish.ch/.

most part during that time, but would you subject the animal to this? I'm betting you wouldn't. The conditions many keepers subject their fish to, often from the guidance of local fish stores, books, or fellow keepers posting in online forums is tantamount to exactly this.

What happens when you keep an angel in a tank that is too small? In short, you induce psychological and physical stress that has profound effects on the growth, color, immune response, and life span of the fish. In a physiological sense, cramped surrounding encourages stunting, which in extreme cases affects muscle and organ development, and leads to a dead fish well before it's lifespan is reached. Minimally, a tank that is too small prohibits these fish from reaching their full majesty not only with regard to size, but some species will not attain full adult coloration, or the adult colors will be lackluster compared to wild specimens. (Diet plays into this too, more on that later).

It's unfortunate that many aquarists do not appreciate the psychological stress that cramped surroundings create. Some species adapt to a confined environment with no apparent ill effects, at least not in the first years of life. Angels do not fall into this category however. Aside from the buildup of growth limiting substances that cramped surroundings encourage, psychological stress stunts growth in a huge way as well. More importantly in the short term -it breaks down the immune response, which will invariably lead to disease. While often we see disease almost immediately due to this stress, these effects are not always apparent at first, and make take weeks, months or even years to become evident, again depending on species and circumstances. A tank might be too small because of the size, or eventual size of the angel, or it might be too small because of tank mates that you've chosen to keep with your angel. Forcing an angel to cohabitate with aggressive species, especially without allowing enough room

for the angel to escape the aggressor's attentions is a recipe for trouble. In any case, the results will be the same for the angelfish eventually. Further, what would be an acceptable sized tank for a 10" trigger is not necessarily an acceptably sized tank for a 10" angelfish. This is simply because the Pomacanthids are generally more prone to the psychological stress that comes with going from the infinite ocean to the confines of a glass box. Remember, an angelfish in the wild often maintains a territory as large as the lot that your house is sitting on! In short, they need more physical space than you're probably used to providing, and certainly more than most wishful thinking in current literature indicates.

So what does all of this mean in actual practice? While some of the *Chaetedontoplus* species will live long term in quarters as small as 80 gallons, most *Holocanthus* and *Pomacanthus* species require *at least* a 250 to 300 gallon tank to live a proper life span in optimum health. If this sounds ridiculous, think of the size difference between a tennis court and an 8' aquarium. I think asking the fish to adapt to the 300 gallon tank is quit enough, don't you?

Let's look at a popular, easily obtained species - the Koran Angelfish, *Pomacanthus semicirculatus*. This species attains a maximum adult size of 15" or so in the wild. Now, most literature will tell you that you need anywhere from a 100 to 135 gallon tank as a minimum to maintain this species. Not so fellow fish keepers! Will a juvenile Koran live in a 135-gallon tank for quite some time? He sure will. Will he live for 20 years, reach his full adult size and thrive? Most definitely not - he'll most likely become stunted and eventually, sick. A more appropriate long term home for this species would be in the 200-gallon range, or even better, 300 gallons. Having said this, this is one of the species that will suffer least from such treatment. Other species that are often lumped into the "minimum 135 gallon tank" category will suffer to a greater extent, both in ways that are, and are not readily apparent, and often simply wither and die for reasons typically unbeknownst to the keeper. To see the Emperor or Queen angel sited as needing such meager quarters is just ridiculous. An adult Queen angel, by the time fin trailers are measured pushes 2 feet, a 135-gallon tank is typically 18" wide! The Annularis Angel pushes a foot in length, yet many would have you house it in a 100 or 120 gallon. The Emperor Angel attains almost 18" - again, the idea of a 135-gallon tank is just silly.

The justification that the fish will not attain adult size in captivity, and therefore not require such a large tank is erroneous and indicative of poor husbandry philosophy. The health of the fish kept under such methodology will suffer sooner or later. There are fish that do not suffer *as* greatly from such an approach (within reason) such as the triggerfish, or many grouper species. While a genus or species being generally forgiving in this regard should not be interpreted as license to cramp them into tight quarters, the Pomacanthids offer no such level of forgiveness. They eventually and invariably show faded color, and/or withering health, and begin a long, (or not so long) downward spiral. If that all sounds discouraging, no worries, the good news is that you can split the difference between a small inland sea in your living room, and a tank that is too small to allow for a long and healthy life for your angelfish. The bottom line here is that you will have greater success the more room you provide from the get-go, even beyond the sizes I'm about to list. This means that despite it's small size, a 3" juvenile Queen angel will do much better in the long run *starting out* in a 180 gallon tank than it will an 80 gallon tank, even though from a space perspective, 80 gallons would seem large enough for the time being, and certainly would be for a 3" Hawkfish. Remember, we're concerned just as much about the psychological effect of the environment at this point, and by extension we are managing the stress level, immune response, growth rate and color of our specimen. When upgrading to something larger, do so before he's starting to look too small for the 180 gallon, say around 6" or so. To reiterate, artificially stunting these fish by keeping them in inadequate quarters is not appropriate husbandry practice, despite how common this practice is, whether it be from ignorance, or lack of space, or limited finances. While the above statement moves a majority of aquarists out of the realm of being able to keep these fish, considering the frequency with which these fish die under the care of well meaning but ill-equipped hobbyists - I think this is justified. This family is without a doubt for advanced keepers in multiple respects. Just because a fish is collected and imported, does not mean it's appropriate for your living room. The aquarist must be, above all things, conscious of the well being of the animals he/she keeps.

As stated before, these fish generally do not grow quickly, even under the best of circumstances, but some species will buck this slow growth tendency, even in less than adequate surroundings, such as Pomacanthus paru, the French Angelfish. This species will not only grow large, it will do it rather quickly, often going from the size of a half dollar to the size of a dinner plate in a year. While I haven't personally seen any other species grow quite this quickly, that doesn't mean it's not possible. By large though, fish belonging to this family are relatively slow growers in captivity when provided with typical accommodations, and for the most part they will not reach full adult size in tanks that are available or affordable to most hobbyists.

HOW DO I SELECT A HEALTHY SPECIMEN?

As with any marine fish, selecting your specimen is where your success or failure in keeping the animal begins. This is easier said than done of course, as the fish has been through quite an ordeal by the time it reaches your local retailer. All things being equal, the general effect of this ordeal varies from one genus or species to another. As mentioned above, the Pomacanthids are among the most sensitive species of fish to stress. The rigors associated with capture (often with cyanide), being held with little or no food, then being shipped halfway around the world in a bag is taxing to even the most robust species.

So, what do you look for? In short, a flawless, alert looking specimen. This means no sunken regions on the body, either on the dorsal or ventral regions. Fins should be intact, with no light or discolored patches on the eyes, fins or body. There should be no sores, pits or lesions of any kind along the lateral line, or anywhere on the fish. Angels often turn sideways to maneuver through holes or crevices in rocks or coral - aside from this exception, the fish should be swimming upright at all times. The specimen should show awareness of your presence, even if this means it insists on hiding behind something to avoid you, which is quite common with some species. The fish should of course show good color!

As with many species, you should also avoid specimens that are too small. Anything under 1.5" is not likely to be sturdy enough, or eat enough to enable it's survival beyond a week or two. Likewise, avoid larger specimens above 6" or so, as they are unlikely to adapt to captive foods and conditions. Always ask to see the little guy eat, but be aware that many specimens will be much too stressed to take any food in the store's holding tanks. Still, if given the choice between two identical, healthy fish, take the one that eats -it will ease the acclimation process when you finally get him home.

ONE MORE THING... LOCATION, LOCATION, LOCATION!

Specifically, the location that your angel fish to be was collected from. Unfortunately, the use of Cyanide to collect marine fish is still prevalent in many regions. Fish that are stunned, or "juiced" with cyanide during collection, and survive the initial exposure (many die outright) have been shown to have an extremely high mortality rate 55.9% to 61% 40 days post-importation. (Jay Hemdal pers comm.) Worse, the fish often appears normal, even spectacular when viewed at the fish store and may even eat well, only to "crash" a few weeks, or even months later for *apparently* no reason. I have seen at least 2 authors call into question the validity of studies attempting to prove the long-term effects of cyanide on marine fishes, and I commend any effort to add to our knowledge base. However at the same time they do acknowledge that concentrated exposure to cyanide is most definitely deadly to marine organisms, and there are other more recent studies that validate delayed mortality after cyanide exposure. Even if the specific long-term physiological effects of cyanide are still unclear on fish that initially survive exposure, it's clear that cyanide is a poison, and in high concentrations it kills fish outright. In my opinion, the need to debate the issue ends there. When dealing with toxins, there are very few examples of "X-amount kills instantly, but Y amount has no ill effect". It's the belief of this author based on 22 years of observation at all levels of the hobby, that at least some seemingly inexplicable deaths post-capture are caused by cyanide poisoning. My advice is to let others poke holes in published graphs and charts, and do your best to stay away from cyanide caught fish - period. At the very least, the additional physiological stress and negative health effects that this method most likely brings on are not something our angel friends suffer easily. My own empirical data on Pomocanthids caught in regions such as the Philippines where cyanide fishing is rampant supports this contention.

Where does this leave you? For starters, from time to time captive reared angles are available from online dealers. These are usually captured larvae that are reared in pens or tanks, and are most suitable for the aquarium. At the time of this writing, I've been unable to verify the legitimacy of the current captive reared offerings out there, so proceed with caution. Investigate thoroughly before purchasing! Lastly, and most importantly, you can arm yourself with research as to where cyanide fishing takes place, which locations are cyanide free, and where your prospective new aquarium inhabitant hails from. This way not only can you be sure for instance to avoid an Emperor angel that was collected in the Philippines, if the store employee tells you he's from Mexico, you know you're not getting accurate info, and to steer clear of that fish. Any reputable dealer will know where his fish come from!

A good place for information on locality for just about any fish species is www.wetwebmedia.com and a bit more technical, www.fishbase.org. Up to date information regarding where cyanide fishing is taking place, and what areas are safe is a bit harder to come by. The following is a list of localities that are known more or less safe from cyanide use.

The Red Sea, Australia, the Cook Islands, Sri Lanka, East Africa and Fiji (Jay Hemdal pers comm.), as well as Papua New Guinea, Mexico and Tonga, (Gresham Hendee, pers comm.)

This is not necessarily a complete list, nor am I contending that every fish from everywhere else is doomed to die from cyanide poisoning. I've purchased plenty of fish from "unsafe" zones and did just fine with them. The point is that you need the variables on your side, and ending up with a "juiced" fish is a good one to eliminate, especially with this family. Cyanide fishing is the most rampant now in Indonesia/Bali, with the Philippines coming in a close second. (Steve Robinson, pers comm).

One final note on cyanide, and that is the damage this practice causes not only to the environment, but also to the indigenous peoples in the regions where this practice occurs. Most fishermen are not tropical fish catchers, yet they all lose when habitat is destroyed by cyanide fishing - resulting in poverty and genuine suffering for these populations. (Steve Robinson, pers comm.) As aquarists, we are the least of the victims. For these reasons alone we should strive to avoid purchasing fish collected with this toxin.

Next issue, we'll look at further husbandry requirements, including acclimation, compatibility and stocking methods, as well as diet and species profiles.

The Queen Angel, Holocanthus ciliaris.

LATERAL LINES

WATER FLOW PART 1: WHERE TO BEGIN

By Adam Blundell M.S.

How can a hobbyist decide how to set up their tank if they don't have an idea on how the water will move in the tank?

Published January 2008, Advanced Aquarist's Online Magazine

Keywords: Adam Blundell M.S., Flow, Laminar Flow, Lateral Lines, Water Circulation
Link to original article: http://www.advancedaquarist.com/2008/1/lines

Hello and welcome to the Water Flow series. This series of articles will be my best attempt to take real world scientific information, and put that into helpful hobbyists terms. That isn't to say that the scientific information isn't hobbyist friendly, only to say that I receive emails and suggestions for topics that often address water flow issues.

My final "goal" for this series to answer some basic questions. I get emails all the frickin' time asking me questions like "what kind of pumps should I use", "are brand X pumps worth the money", "what is the best kind of flow", "what is this random flow and linear flow I keep hearing about"....

I'm at a loss for words. How can tell someone what pump to buy when I don't know a thing about their desires? More importantly how can a hobbyist decide how to set up their tank if they don't have an idea on how the water will move in the tank?

SETTING UP A SALT WATER AQUARIUM

Before you ever put water in your aquarium make sure you know how you are going to move that water around! You wouldn't believe how many people (most likely including you, the reader) set up their aquariums and then start to think about how the water is going to move around. Well, for your next aquarium (lets face it everyone sets up another) lets try to tackle this issue before hand.

Is it a reef tank? Do you have a sump? How will the water produce gas exchange? How will the water carry nutrients to the filtration system? Is this a biotope? Is this a planted aquarium? WHAT TYPE OF FLOW DO YOU WANT?

DEFINING THE TERMINOLOGY

I love semantics. I'm not sure why but terminology in general is just fun. Maybe it is the challenge of working with something that is almost always wrong. Regardless of the

Invertebrate nano tank.

Whether you plan to set up a small invertebrate tank or a seven hundred gallon aquarium, you will need to think about water movement and flow design.

reason, I do think it is important for hobbyists to first grasp these terms and know how they relate to their aquarium.

RANDOM FLOW

I hear this term about 10 times per day. Let me be clear, you do NOT want truly random flow in your aquarium. Example- you take 10 powerheads and stick them in your 75 gallon tank, just hanging their by the cords. You turn them all on and let them blow around. This means, that just by random chance, everyone once in a blue moon, completely random, all those powerheads for a moment will be near the surface facing straight up blowing water out of the tank and all over the lights. It also means that every once in a while the powerheads will blow directly into the sand all together at one time. It also means that all the powerheads would face directly onto your frogspawn and blow all the tissue right off. Hey, if it is random it is bound to happen at some point. The key to defining Random Flow is that by definition it is NOT predictable.

CHAOTIC FLOW

This is what people describe when they usually say Random Flow. Chaotic Flow means that the moving water will make contact with water moving in a different direction. Example- you take two powerheads on opposite sides of the aquarium and you face them both towards the middle. At the middle of the aquarium the two bodies of fluid run into each other and the momentum is dissipated by pushing water in different directions. This is certainly NOT random. In fact it is very predictable. If you see an aquarium like this and look at how the water is moving, you can predict how the water will be moving 5 minutes later, 10 hours later, and even 2 weeks later. It will be moving just like it is right then and there in front of you.

ALTERNATING FLOW

This flow is characterized by changing the direction, speed, volume, or some other aspect of the water flow. Example- the most common example I can think of is the rotating output devices like a Sea Swirl. If you aren't familiar with them I'll just simply state that they basically take water from a powerhead and push it through an outlet. However, unlike a standard powerhead the Sea Swirl sweeps that outlet horizontally back and forth changing the direction that the water is coming out. Now, lets say you have a few of these in your tank. They continually move back and forth and change where the water is going. This creates some Chaotic Flow, but that Chaotic Flow is changing... in fact that is why it is Alternating Flow. This is once again NOT Random Flow. I can look at an aquarium with several Sea Swirls. I can time how long it takes each of them to move back and forth. Then, I can calculate where they will be pointing in 10 minutes, in 10 hours, in 10 weeks. This is certainly NOT random but is in fact very predictable.

LAMINAR FLOW

Water flowing in one direction is termed laminar flow. It also describes the idea of bulk water flow in that direction. Example- having all the water in your tank moving from the left side to the right side. This could be done by pumping in a lot of water on the left side, and having an overflow on the right side where the water leaves the tank. Thus all the water is slowly moving from left to right. Until recently this wasn't used, but some adventurous hobbyists have really had fun with this. Another Example- having all the water flow around the aquarium in a circular motion. To get this idea imagine sticking your arm in a 5 gallon bucket and swirling the water around in a circle. If you did that in an aquarium the water would always be flowing in one direction in relation to any fixed item (like a coral).

The aquarium shown here uses two closed loop systems. The inlets for each closed loop are on the opposite sides of the aquarium from the outlets. Therefore as one closed loop is running it drains water from one side of the tank and pumps it into the other. All the water is flowing in one direction (lets say from left to right). Then 4 hours later that closed loop

This SeaSwirl is a device which rotates the output of a pump. This causes an alternating flow pattern.

turns off and a second closed loop turns on. This is plumbed in the opposite direction so now all the water moves from right to left for the next 4 hours. This is Alternating Laminar Flow... pretty cool!

SLOSHING FLOW / TIDAL FLOW

This type of flow has been nearly non existent in the hobby until recently. This type of flow is characterized by pushing a very large volume (maybe the entire tank volume) in one direction for a short time (lets say 2 seconds) and then pushing it all back in the other direction. This is usually very predictable. Example- Having the entire aquarium sitting on a Teeter-Totter (seesaw) so one side move up, and then down, and then up, and then down (as the other side moves opposite). Another Example- having a piston on the side of the aquarium pushing in, then pulling out, then pushing in, then pulling out. Either way would cause all the water to move back and forth.

SURGE FLOW

This is characterized by moving the bulk of the water up and then down, then up, and then down. Example- dropping a five gallon bucket of water into your 75 gallon aquarium all at one time, then pulling back out an entire 5 gallon bucket. This is seen in tide pools as a wave crashes in and the water all "surges" up filling the pools, then drains back out. This happens over and over with each passing wave. It also takes place on reefs where strong currents and strong winds cause large waves. A scuba diver may notice this as they are literally picked up, then set down, then picked up, then set down by the force of the water around them. As a side note, it is a blast to witness this under water. Nothing is cooler than seeing a whole school of yellow tangs swimming by as they get lifted 4 feet up into the water column, and then are pushed back down with each passing wave. Note: this is actually done in a circular motion.

STAGNANT FLOW

This is really the lack of water flow. Most aquarists are trying to avoid this, but some aquariums are actually designed to minimize water flow. Delicate animals (say jellyfish) or cold-water systems are often made to prevent water flow.

CIRCULAR FLOW

Describes the vertical movement of water in a circular pattern (remember horizontal circular flow is a type of laminar flow). Example- most kreisel tanks are designed to keep items slowly moving in a circle. This is often done to produce a "suspended" environment. The most common examples include jellyfish aquariums and larval rearing aquariums.

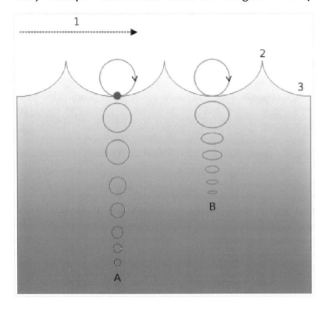

Photo Courtesy of Wikipedia

CONCLUSION

Water flow is a huge topic. For now the goal of this article is to get people thinking of terminology and how to properly describe water flow. There are many ways to move water and many directions/speeds/volumes for it to go. To conclude, keep this in mind as we move forward in describing water flow.

AUTHOR INFORMATION

Adam Blundell M.S. works in Marine Ecology, and in Pathology for the University of Utah. He is also Director of The Aquatic & Terrestrial Research Team, a group which utilizes research projects to bring together hobbyists and scientists. His vision is to see this type of collaboration lead to further advancements in aquarium husbandry. While not in the lab Adam provides services for of one of the Nation's largest hobbyist clubs, the Wasatch Marine Aquarium Society (www.utahreefs.com). Adam has earned a BS in Marine Biology and an MS in the Natural Resource and Health fields. Adam can be contacted at adamblundell@hotmail.com.

FEATURE ARTICLE

Granular Activated Carbon, Part 2: Modeling of Operational Parameters for Dissolved Organic Carbon Removal from Marine Aquaria

By Ken S. Feldman, Lauren F. Vernese, Karl T. Mueller, Kelly Maers

Chemistry Department, The Pennsylvania State University. In Part 2, the authors will discuss the results of their research and make some recommendations to the aquarist on its usage.

Published February 2008, Advanced Aquarist's Online Magazine

© Pomacanthus Publications, LLC

Keywords: Feature Article, Filtration, Karl T. Mueller, Ken S. Feldman, Lauren F. Vernese, Water Quality, Water Testing, Kelly Maers, GAC, Granular Activated Carbon

Link to original article: http://www.advancedaquarist.com/2008/2/aafeature1

RESULTS AND DISCUSSION

USING THE LANGMUIR ISOTHERM MODEL TO CALCULATE THE TOTAL BINDING CAPACITY OF HYDROCARBON2 (HC2)

Solutions of basic blue 3 dye (BB3) and, independently, fluorescein disodium (FL) in 35 ppt salinity salt water were prepared by adding 30 mg of dye to 1.20 L of salt water (from Instant Ocean salt mix and distilled water, 77 °F). 100.0 mL portions of each dye solution were placed in 250 mL flasks, and so each flask initially contained 2.5 mg of dye and the overall dye concentration was 25 mg/L. A carefully weighed amount of HC2 was added to each flask. The amounts added ranged between 10 mg and 100 mg as indicated in Table 1. Each flask was tightly stoppered and clamped onto a shaker apparatus that continuously agitated the flasks to ensure good contact between the solution and the HC2 sample. The dye concentration in each flask was assayed every 3 - 5 days by spectrophotometric measurement using a Beckman DU70 Spectrophotometer. The BB3 sample dye concentrations were measured at 645 nm, and the fluorescein solutions were recorded at 490 nm (nm = nanometer, a measure of spectral wavelength). The experiment was continued until sequential measurements did not exhibit much change in the amount of dye present (i.e. the HC2 was saturated and could not absorb any more dye). This criterion was met in the BB3 run at 17 days, whereas the fluorescein samples reached equilibrium after 14 days. The experimentally measured dye absorptions are given in Table 1. The key Langmuir model parameters 1/x and 1/C (Eq. (5)) can be derived from these experimental quantities (Table 1). 1/C is just the inverse of the dye concentration at the end of the experiment (= equilibrium), and this dye concentration can be derived by simply multiplying the initial dye concentration (= 25 mg/L) by the ratio A_{eq}/A_0, where A_{eq} and A_0 are the dye absorptions of the solution at the end of the experiment and at the beginning, respectively. The quantity 1/x is calculated by dividing the amount of HC2 used by the amount of dye absorbed (= (2.5 mg)(1-A_{eq}/A_0)). Graphing 1/c vs. 1/x then gives the desired quantity, the binding capacity (x_m) of HC2 for these dyes, as the inverse of the Y-intercept. By this analysis, HC2's binding capacity for BB3 in seawater is 61 ± 7 mg/gm, and for fluorescein is 45 ± 2 mg/gm. Note that the Y-intercept values from Figure 3 are reported in units of mg of HC2/mg of dye, so the derived x_m value was multiplied by 0.001 to arrive at the mg of dye/gm of HC2 values noted above. For subsequent analyses, it will become convenient to just average these values to derive a "general" binding capacity for dyes by HC2; $x_{m(ave)} \sim 53$ mg/gm.

RATE OF DYE REMOVAL AS A FUNCTION OF HC2 AMOUNT

The first series of dye removal experiments utilized constant amounts of both BB3 and fluorescein, and the amount of GAC was varied. We expected that the calculated k values would be invariant with respect to the amount of GAC used (see the discussion associated with Eq. (3)), and so these experiments will provide a good test of our model and its assumptions. The experimental set-up is simple, and follows one used by other authors. A five-gallon bucket with a small aperture in the top was filled with 4.0 gallons of freshly prepared 35 ppt salinity salt water, and 243 mg of basic blue 3 (**7**) and 268 mg of fluorescein disodium (**8**) were added (16 and 18 ppm, respectively). These two dyes were run simultaneously since their spectral signatures do not overlap. The Phosban reactor was charged with the indicated amount of pre-washed Hydrocarbon2 GAC (see Table 2), and an Eheim1048 pump was used to remove water from the bucket, push it through the Phosban reactor, and then return it to the bucket in a closed loop arrangement. The pump was adjusted to a flow rate of 49 gph (0.81 gpm). Samples of the reservoir water were removed at specific time intervals, typically every 5 - 15 min over a 120 - 180 min time course, and these samples were assayed for dye content with the Beckman DU70 UV/VIS spectrophotometer. As with the Langmuir isotherm experiments, the blue dye signal was monitored at 645 nm, and the fluorescein signal was monitored at 490 nm. No effort was made to adjust the solution temperature, which typically increased from 72 to 75 °F during the run. If the GAC column in the Phosban reactor began to separate due to the vigorous water flow, the cylinder was gently tapped until the GAC particles repacked into a single column. Control experiments (dye + salt water/no GAC) demonstrated that the dyes did not decompose over the experimental time regime.

Figure 4 below shows the amount of dye remaining (as the quantity ($[dye]_t/[dye]_0$)) as time progresses for five different amounts of HC2: 25 gm, 50 gm, 75 gm, 100 gm, 150 gm, and 200 gm. Each individual experiment was replicated 2-3 times, but only a single representative data set is shown on the graphs for simplicity of presentation. These HC2 amounts span a range from about 6 to 50 gm/gal, and correspond to filling the Phosban reactor from 0.8" to 6.5" in height with the Hydrocarbon2. Some useful interconversions are:

(16) Grams of HC2 = 31 • height of the HC2 column, in inches

(17) Grams of HC2 = 81 • cups of the HC2

Inspection of the graphs indicate that indeed, the amount of blue dye (left) and fluorescein (right) remaining decreases over time, and that the rate at which the amounts decrease depends on the amount of GAC present. The mathematic treatment derived in Eq. (13) can be used to process these raw data into the desired quantity, k, the rate constant for dye removal (Table 2). Since both BB3 and fluorescein were run together, we can only report an averaged rate constant for them both. This simplification is in line with the expectation that in an aquarium setting, the DOC that GAC removes is quite heterogeneous, and average values for a compilation of compounds are probably more valuable than the rate constant value for any particular compound. The rate constants shown in Table 2 are the average values from the 2-3 independent runs for each set of unique experiments. In addition, the r^2 values for the data are given; these numbers reflect how accurately the mathematical model fits the data. Any value of r^2 greater 0.9 is good, and any r^2 values over 0.98 indicated an exceptionally solid correlation between the model and the data.

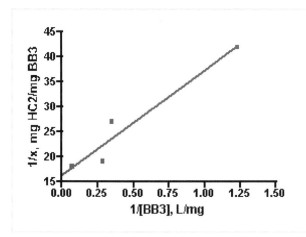

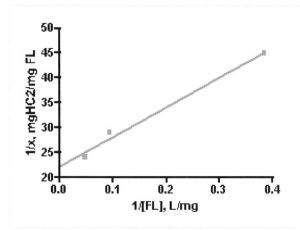

Figure 3. Graphical representation of the Langmuir isotherm experiment. BB3 is on the top ($r^2 = 0.94$), and fluorescein is on the bottom ($r^2 = 0.99$).

Table 1. Experimental data and derived quantities for the Langmuir isotherm-based calculation of the binding capacity of HC2.

HC2 (mg)	A_0	A_{eq}	1/C (L/mg)	1/x (mg HC2/mg dye absorbed)
0	2.77			
20.1		1.56	0.071	18
39.8		0.39	0.28	19
60.1		0.32	0.35	27
100.4		0.090	1.20	42
0	2.30			
10.4		1.90	0.048	24
41.3		0.98	0.094	29
100.7		0.24	0.38	45

As discussed earlier, all of the calculated k's should be identical, since k is independent of the amount of GAC present. The fact that they are not requires some interpretation. The rate constant values for each dye when GAC ≥ 75 gm do indeed approach this criterion, lending confidence to the mathematical model for GAC-based dye removal in this GAC range. However, the rate constants k for the 25 and 50 gm of GAC runs are anomalously small. A possible explanation for this discrepancy emerges upon consideration of the actual manner in which the GAC packs into a bed in the Phosban reactor. It is possible, for example, that at the low HC2 loadings (25 and 50 gms), the shallowness of the GAC bed (< 1" for the 25 gm runs) allows channeling of the current, which in turn leads to GAC dead spots and diminished opportunities for dye binding. As the GAC amount increases, the bed becomes thicker, channeling is reduced, and more of the GAC charge can be utilized in dye binding. In this scenario, the higher loadings of HC2, which correspond to the more realistic GAC bed depths of 2.5 - 6.5", operate normally, and would fall under the purview of a typical Phosban charge in an aquarium setting. The k values between 75 and 200 gms of HC2 vary from 21 to 31 L/mol-min, a spread of about 20% (ave = 26 ± 5 L/mol-min). Given the assumptions used and all of the other possible experimental variables, this level of variation is not very surprising, and it is a reminder that we will likely only be able to draw approximate and not numerically precise conclusions from this analysis. However, one early conclusion can be drawn from these data: using less that 75 gm of GAC (< 2.5 inches) in a Phosban reactor is not an effective way to utilize GAC for impurity removal.

The time required to remove 90% of the dye (t_{90}, see Eq. (14) and the accompanying discussion) can be calculated for these experiments as well, see Table 2. These t_{90} values are specific to the conditions of the dye removal experiment (i.e., functions of flow rate and volume, mass of HC2, and the starting dye concentration). By plotting the t_{90} values as a function of the amount of HC2, the complex relationship between the quantity of HC2 and the rate of dye removal is revealed. These data are presented in Figure 5. It is apparent from inspection of Figure 5 that once a charge of 75 gm of HC2 (or greater) is used, the t_{90} values do not change much. Since the t_{90} values are a function of the rate constant k, and k does not change much in this HC2 range, this observation is not surprising. One interpretation of this trend is that when HC2 amounts above the 75 gm threshold are used, a large excess of HC2 binding sites are available compared to the amount of dye present, and so the dye molecules always "see" binding sites. This hypothesis is buttressed by the fact that 511 mg of dye in total is used in each experiment, and with an average binding capacity of 53 mgs of dye per gram of HC2 (from the calculated x_m above), only about 10 grams of HC2, in principle, is required to sop up all of the dye. Of course, since there is a great heterogeneity of binding sites, it would take a long time (recall the Langmuir binding experiments took over 14 days to reach equilibrium) to saturate all of the slow-binding sites. And so, it appears empirically that in the region above 75 grams of HC2, there are enough fast-binding sites to absorb the dye over the course of the 2-3 hour experiment. It is likely that in an aquarium, the fast binding sites are responsible for most of the absorption as well.

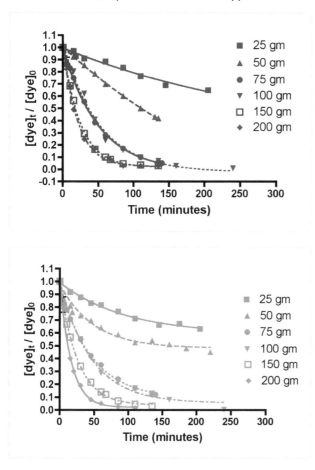

Figure 4. Basic Blue 3 (7) (top) and fluorescein (8) (bottom) removal by Hydrocarbon2 GAC as a function of GAC amount.

Table 2. Figures of merit for the removal of Basic Blue 3 and Fluorescein (combined) by varying amounts of HC2; flow rate = 49 gph.

		Amount of HC2, gms					
		25	50	75	100	150	200
Basic Blue 3 and Fluorescein	k (L/mol-min)	9.6±0.6	13±0.7	27±0.5	21±1	31±2	28±1
	r^2	0.97	0.99	0.99	0.98	0.98	0.99
	t_{90} (hr)	22	7.1	2.2	2.2	0.99	0.81

Rate of Dye Removal as a Function of Dye Structure and of Flow Rate

The next series of experiments probed two independent questions:

1. How does the chemical structure of the dye molecule influence its rate of removal by HC2?

2. How do dye removal rates respond to changes in the flow rate through the Phosban reactor?

The first question was examined by choosing one arbitrary set of experimental parameters (flow = 49 gph, 100 gm of Hydrocarbon2, 15-21 ppm of each dye molecule in a volume of 4 gallons) and measuring the decrease in dye absorption for the four dyes chosen, Basic Blue 3 (**7**) and Fluorescein (**8**) combined, Acid Yellow 76 (**9**) and Chlorophyllin (**10**). The choice of a 100 gram Hydrocarbon2 charge should put these experiments in the "constant k" regime of dye removal (cf. Table 2) where channeling through the GAC is not important. The Basic Blue 3 and Fluorescein 100 gm Hydrocarbon2 results are already described in Section 2.2. The remaining two dyes, **9** and **10**, were run separately since there was insufficient spectral dispersion to make meaningful measurements in mixtures. In addition, both **9** and **10** were not soluble at the 15 ppm level in 35 ppt salt water. Therefore, these two dyes were examined in pure distilled water. This change in media raises obvious concerns about the relevance of the data acquired to questions of reef tank DOC removal. In order to address these concerns, a mixture of Basic Blue 3 (15.9 ppm) and Fluorescein (17.5 ppm) in *pure distilled water* was subjected to a HC2 removal run at 72 gph with 50 gm of HC2 (this issue was probed before we realized the benefits of using an HC2 amount greater than 75 gms). The measured rate constant for dye removal under these circumstances (k = 5.7 ± 0.3 L/mol-min) does differ from the same values obtained in

salt water under identical experimental conditions (k = 4.1 ± 0.2 L/mol-min), and so some caution is necessary in interpreting the dye-to-dye comparison data. However, the discrepancy is not large, and so it will not affect the overall tenor of the conclusions.

A second independent series of dye removal experiments was conducted at a higher flow rate, 72 gph. These flow rate values (49 and 72 gph) span the range of suggested flow rates supplied with the Phosban reactor. The data are presented in Figure 6 and Table 3.

The question of dye removal rate as a function of dye structure can be addressed in a general sense by considering the graphs depicted in Figure 7. It is clear from inspection of these graphs that the rate of dye removal does vary as per the dye structure. This variation can be quantified by application of Eq. (13) as described in the Mathematical Modeling section, and the values of the derived rate constants are presented in Table 3. The differences in rates of removal are

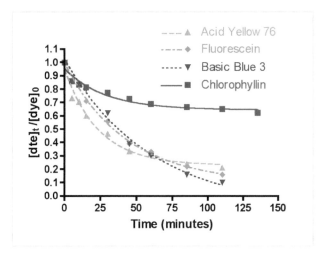

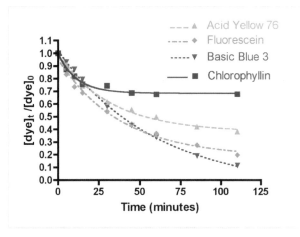

Figure 6. Basic Blue 3, Fluorescein, Acid Yellow 76 and chlorophyllin removal as a function of time. Top: 49 gph.; Bottom: 72 gph. (100 gms of Hydrocarbon2, 15-21 ppm dye each).

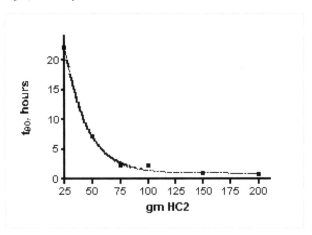

Figure 5. t₉₀ values for dye removal as a function of the amount of HC2 used.

not large, however, and vary no more that a factor of 10 between fastest (Basic Blue 3/Fluorescein) and slowest (Chlorophyllin).

The experimental observation that the rate constants for dye removal, k, *decreased* at the faster flow with all of the dyes was unexpected. Intuitively, an *increase* in the rate constant for dye removal might be expected to result from a situation in which more dye-containing solution passes through the GAC bed per unit time (i.e., faster flow rate). How can this discrepancy be rationalized? In fact, it is typical for flow-through reactor experiments such as the one used in these studies to find that mass transfer of the solute (= dye molecules in this case) from the bulk solution to the adsorption site is actually the slow, or rate-limiting, step. Since the rate constant can be thought of as a probability of adsorption as the solution passes through the GAC layer, the residence time of a given dye molecule becomes important. If the residence time is long compared with the time it takes for the dye molecule to find its adsorption site, then the k value will be high. On the other hand, if the residence time is short compared to the time it takes for the dye to find its adsorption site, then the k value will be smaller. Residence time scales inversely with flow rate, so it is possible that we have entered a regime where the faster flow (= less residence time) lead to lower k's. Some experimental evidence that supports this conclusion can be found in Figure 7, where the k values scale inversely with the molecular weight of the dyes. This behavior is consistent with a scenario where mass transfer in solution, which also scales inversely with increasing molecular weight, is a significant factor in the overall kinetics. That is, the more a molecule weighs, the slower is its transit from point A to point B in solution, and so it benefits (= larger k) from a longer residence time in the GAC bed (= slower flow rate).

Is it possible to delve deeper into these rate vs. structure differences and arrive at some correlation between the rate constant for dye removal and some measurable molecular parameter? If such a relationship can be discerned, then these model dye experiments may have some predictive

value in terms of removal efficiencies for the types of compounds that have been proposed as components of DOC in the marine environment. We examined the correlation between dye removal rate constants k and three molecular parameters: molecular weight, molecular volume, and molecular surface area of the dye. The former value is just the sum of the weights of the component atoms. The latter two values were calculated by using a commercially available computational chemistry program called *Spartan* [Spartan'04], one of the standard tools of chemists who work with complex organic molecules. The data are plotted in Figure 8. As can be seen by inspection of these graphs, there is significant correlation between each of the molecular parameters and the rate constant for dye removal, k. Perhaps a larger data set of structurally different dyes might have yielded even more compelling relationships, but at the very least, there does appear to be a trend among these data sets: molecules with smaller molecular weights/volumes/surface areas appear to be removed faster by HC2. Thus, GAC might be better at removing the smaller molecular metabolites, colored or uncolored, that are inevitably produced in marine tanks compared to the larger biomacromolecules (or large fragments thereof), such as proteins, polynucleic acids, and oligosaccharides that also are present. As discussed earlier, this k dependence on size may be largely attributed to the inverse relationship between molecular weight and mass transfer in solution.

LEACHING EXPERIMENTS: DOES SATURATED GAC RELEASE BOUND DYES?

How well do the dyes stick to the GAC particles? Do the dyes (and by inference, DOC's) leach back out into solution over time? Actually, just such leaching in the context of equilibrium binding is a requirement for application of the Langmuir isotherm model to measuring dye saturation points. In the context of aquarium chemistry, this concern becomes particularly relevant if the GAC in an aquarium setting is not changed out prior to saturating. At that point, will it serve as a DOC source, slowly polluting the aquarium water?

This question was examined by recovering the used HC2 from Chlorophyllin and Basic Blue 3 adsorption experiments, washing it with distilled water, and then resuspending it in the Phosban reactor. Distilled water was added to the reservoir and the Phosban reactor in the usual amounts (4.0 gallons), and the Eheim pump was turned on to 49 gph. The dye

Table 3. Figures of merit for four different dyes upon removal by 100 gms of Hydrocarbon2 at two different flow rates.

dye		flow rate (gph)	
		49	72
Basic Blue 3 andFluorescein	k (L/mol-min)	21±1	18.0±0.3
	r^2	0.98	0.99
	t_{90} (hours)	2.2	2.4
Acid Yellow 76	k (L/mol-min)	14.1±0.6	7.7±1
	r^2	0.97	0.92
	t_{90} (hours)	3.0	5.4
Chlorophyllin	k (L/mol-min)	2.6±0.3	2.1±0.4
	r^2	0.94	0.80
	t_{90} (hours)	16	20

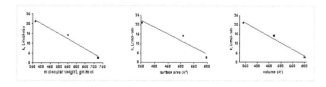

Figure 7. Rate constant, k, for the different dyes vs. measurable molecular parameters.

content of the reservoir was measured at the indicated time intervals (Figure 8). For these experiments, the $[dye]_0$ measurement was taken a few minutes after adding the dye-saturated HC2 to the pure water. Therefore, the $[dye]_t/[dye]_0$ ratio should increase over time, as more dye diffuses out of the HC2. From these data, it appears that both Chlorophyllin and Basic Blue 3 leach out in observable and significant quantities over the course of several hours. The Chlorophyllin concentration ultimately diminishes, but based upon the color changes observed at long experimental times, it is possible that this species is undergoing some type of chemical destruction (oxidation? demetalation of the porphyrin core?) in competition with HC2 binding. Extrapolating from these dye results to DOC in the aquarium requires the usual caveats, of course, but these observations are suggestive of the fact that organics may not stay stuck to GAC over time. This tentative conclusion raises the concern that keeping saturated, or spent, GAC in the system past its useful life may be problematic. Is there a way to "guestimate" when the GAC is saturated? Section 3.2 will address this point.

These leaching results do not negate the assumption underlying the kinetic analysis described in the Mathematical Modeling section, as long as the rate of removal data were recorded under an experimental protocol were the Hydrocarbon2 was not saturated. Given that the experiments were conducted under a regime where a large excess of HC2 binding sites compared with dye were evident (at least for ≥ 75 gms of HC2), it does not appear that saturation of the HC2 samples was achieved, and hence dye leaching during the trials is not likely to compromise the data.

GAC COMPARISON: HYDROCARBON2 VS. BLACK DIAMOND

A brief comparison of two different GAC's, Hydrocarbon2 from Two Little Fishes and Black Diamond from Marineland,

was pursued. For these trials, a 50 gm charge of GAC was used, the flow was set at 49 gph, and all four dyes were examined. The choice of a 50 gram GAC charge was made prior to the discovery that GAC amounts below 75 gm led to suboptimal rate constants (cf. Table 2). Therefore, it is not appropriate to compare directly the rate constants reported in Table 4 below, which were derived from the 50 gm GAC charges, with the maximal values from Table 1 derived from the 75 - 200 gm Hydrocarbon2 charges. Nevertheless, the *relative* rate constants for the different dyes from these 50 gram GAC experiments should be directly comparable, and the conclusions drawn from these comparisons should be unaffected by the channeling problems posited earlier with the < 75 gm Hydrocarbon2 charges.

Figure 9 displays the change in concentration of the four dyes as time increases for both Black Diamond and Hydrocarbon2. As noted earlier, Basic Blue 3, Acid Yellow 76 and Fluorescein all behave similarly to each other, but chlorophyllin is adsorbed by Black Diamond no better than it is by Hydrocarbon2. However, there is a conspicuously steeper drop-off in dye concentration for the other three dyes with

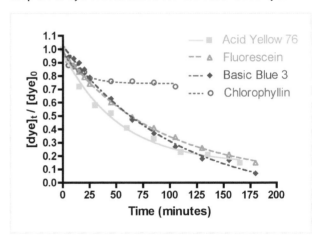

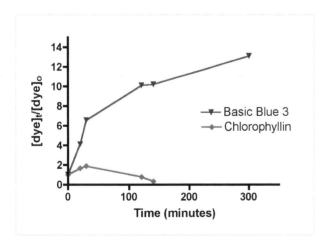

Figure 8. Leaching of both Basic Blue 3 and Chlorophyllin from Hydrocarbon2 infused with the dyes.

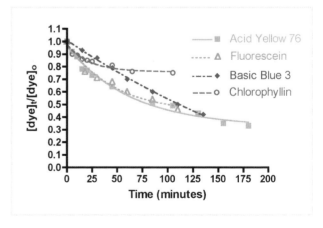

Figure 9. Dye removal by Black Diamond (top) and Hydrocarbon2 (bottom) at 49 gph flow, using 50 gm of GAC.

Black Diamond compared to Hydrocarbon2. This steeper drop-off is reflective of a larger rate constant for dye removal, and these differences can be quantified using Eq. (13), as shown in Table 4.

For the three dyes that do seem to be susceptible to significant adsorption by GAC (Acid Yellow 76, and Fluorescein/Basic Blue 3 combined), the rate constants k for dye removal are approximately twice as large with Black Diamond as they are with Hydrocarbon2. Correspondingly, the derived t_{90} values with Black Diamond are about half of those with Hydrocarbon2. These data lead to the clear conclusion that Black Diamond removes these dyes more rapidly than Hydrocarbon2, and by inference, DOC in general. Whether the factor-of-two difference with the dyes translates to a similar ratio with authentic DOC removal in a marine tank is unknown, but it seems likely that the large advantage enjoyed by Black Diamond for dye removal will lead to enhanced rates of organic clearance for the aquarist.

AQUARIUM APPLICATIONS

HOW MUCH GAC SHOULD I USE?

The answer to this question really depends on what the goal is. There are arguments for removing impurities rapidly (clearing a toxic substance) and for removing them slowly (don't shock the corals with more light penetration), and so no one best GAC amount will fit all circumstances. Nevertheless, the data presented below (Figure 10) might be useful in establishing guidelines for selecting the appropriate amount of GAC for a given situation. These graphs illustrate the calculated time (in hours) required to *cut the amount of DOC by 90%* as a function of the mass of HC2 used, the tank water volume, and *the amount of DOC assumed to be initially present*.

What is the justification for the assumption that certain amounts of DOC are present? More succinctly, "Just how much DOC is in reef tank water?" Due to a lack of adequate

assay methods at present, this quantity, while crucial to any DOC removal technology, can only be approximated. A reef tank has a certain amount of DOC present as a consequence of a balance between DOC production and DOC removal (by any method), but how can that amount be quantified?

Commercially available DOC measurement kits are uniformly disappointing in that they only detect a small class of organic substances. As part of an ongoing study of protein skimmer efficiency in removing proteins and other DOC from aquarium tank water, we are exploring an oxidation-based assay procedure for DOC quantification that utilizes commercially available protein measurement kits. Although it is beyond the scope of this article to elaborate on this procedure (see coming attractions: "Quantitative Evaluation of Protein Skimmer Performance"), our preliminary assays of both skimmed-and-GAC-treated and unskimmed/no-GAC marine tank water reveal DOC levels on the order of 0.5 - 1 ppm for GAC/skimmed tanks and 5-10 ppm for no-GAC/unskimmed tanks. Specifically, oxidizable organic levels from three skimmed and GAC-treated reef tanks and one fish-only tank are: 0.40 ppm, 0.42 ppm, 1.3 ppm, and 1.3 ppm. Similarly the oxidizable organic levels in two unskimmed/no-GAC reef tanks (soft corals, invertebrates and a few fish) are: 4.5 and 8.5 ppm. Since our assay only detects oxidizable organics, it is likely to underestimate the actual amount of DOCs, but probably not by a great amount. That is, the oxidizing agent employed in the assay is powerful enough to oxidize (and hence detect) molecules from many of the compound classes illustrated in Figure 1. We plan to employ this assay with specific members of these molecular classes to test this assumption, but those studies remain for the future. This admittedly small sample size will be taken as representative for the purpose of the calculations below. To incorporate these oxidizable organic concentration values in the calculations, we will use as arbitrary starting points the values of 1.0 ppm of DOC and 7.5 ppm of DOC to represent "cleaner" and "dirtier" tanks, respectively. It will be of some interest to obtain samples of aquarium water out of a wide range of tanks from the greater reefkeeping community to expand upon this data set and see if consensus values emerge for oxidizable organics that correlate to different husbandry techniques, or to determine if the oxidizable organic level varies significantly, for example, when the lights are on or off, or during the period after a tank feeding. Those studies are in the future. Of course, continual replenishment of DOC's by active biological processes (at an unknown rate) would ensure that DOC removal would never be complete! However, it is only necessary to remove DOC at a rate commensurate with, or faster than, the rate of DOC production in order to bring the DOC levels down to some arbitrarily low value.

The same mathematical approach discussed in Section 1.4 can be used to address the more interesting question for aquarists: how long will it take to remove, say, 90% of the DOC from the initial starting point of either 1 ppm or 7.5 ppm? In this case, Eq. (14) is used, but with new values for the water

Table 4. Figures of merit for the comparison of HC2 and Black Diamond GAC's, using 50 gm of GAC, 49 GPH flow rate.

dye		GAC	
		HC2	Black Diamond
Basic Blue 3 and Fluorescein	k (L/mol-min)	13±0.7	28±1
	r^2	0.99	0.99
	t_{90} (hours)	7.1	3.3
Acid Yellow 76	k (L/mol-min)	11.9±0.7	23±1
	r^2	0.97	0.98
	t_{90} (hours)	7.3	3.8
Chlorophyllin	k (L/mol-min)	3.7±0.4	3.9±0.7
	r^2	0.79	0.83
	t_{90} (hours)	23	21.6

volume and the initial concentration of the DOC (equivalent to 1 and 7.5 ppm, respectively, of an average 400 molecular weight compound). The values of m and k are those extracted from the BB3/Fluorescein removal experiments - hence, the value of the dye system as a model for DOC removal in an aquarium. An average x_m value of 53 mg of DOC/gm of GAC is used, which is based solely on the BB3/Fluorescein Langmuir isotherm experiments. It is possible, even likely, that other dyes (or more generally, other organic structures that are components of DOC) have different saturation values. The measurement of a larger collection of x_m values corresponding to a range of plausibly DOC-like molecules will have to await further experimentation. Nevertheless, we have correlated k and x_m values only for the BB3/Fluorescein dyes, and so we will confine our further analysis to these inputs. The results are displayed in Figure 10, with the 1 ppm DOC data on the left, and the 7.5 ppm DOC data on the right.

The curves in these graphs can be fitted to the expressions shown in Eqs. (18 - 27) below, where t_{90} is the time, in days, required to deplete the DOC level to 10% of its original value, for a given amount of HC2 (indicated by "gm"). These mathematical relationships are strictly empirical and should not be extrapolated beyond the HC2 data range. Note that in the 7.5 ppm DOC case, the 200 gallon water volume contains too much DOC to be 90% absorbed by amounts of HC2 less than ~ 100g.

(18) (1 ppm DOC, 75 gallon) $t_{90} = 3.7e^{(-0.008 \cdot (gm))} - 0.2$, $r^2 = 0.92$

(19) (1 ppm DOC, 100 gallon) $t_{90} = 5.1e^{(-0.0081 \cdot (gm))} - 0.3$, $r^2 = 0.93$

(20) (1 ppm DOC, 125 gallon) $t_{90} = 6.5e^{(-0.0084 \cdot (gm))} - 0.3$, $r^2 = 0.93$

(21) (1 ppm DOC, 150 gallon) $t_{90} = 8.0e^{(-0.0084 \cdot (gm))} - 0.4$, $r^2 = 0.93$

(22) (1 ppm DOC, 200 gallon) $t_{90} = 11.4e^{(-0.013 \cdot (gm))} + 1.2$, $r^2 = 0.89$

(23) (7.5 ppm DOC, 75 gallon) $t_{90} = 6.7e^{(-0.012 \cdot (gm))} + 0.04$, $r^2 = 0.96$

(24) (7.5 ppm, 100 gallon) $t_{90} = 14e^{(-0.016 \cdot (gm))} + 0.3$, $r^2 = 0.98$

(25) (7.5 ppm DOC, 125 gallon) $t_{90} = 41.2e^{(-0.023 \cdot (gm))} + 0.74$, $r^2 = 0.99$

(26) (7.5 ppm DOC, 150 gallon) $t_{90} = 1441e^{(-0.055 \cdot (gm))} + 1.8$, $R^2 = 0.99$

(27) (7.5 ppm DOC, 200 gallon) $t_{90} = 8001e^{(-0.056 \cdot (gm))} + 2.3$, $r^2 = 0.99$

How might an aquarist use this information to answer the question "How much GAC should I use?" The aquarist will have to estimate the water volume of the system (for an accurate and simple way to calculate system water volumes, see http://www.reefkeeping.com/issues/2006-04/pr/index.php, Experiment 3), and then make a guess as to whether their tank has a low level of DOC's (~ 1 ppm in a system with adequate nutrient removal) or a high level (~ 7.5 ppm in a system with poor/absent nutrient removal). For example, a system with 150 gallons of total water volume that is adequately skimmed (or subjected to other effective nutrient removal, assume [DOC] = 1 ppm) would be characterized by the aqua curve on the left-hand graph in Figure 10. By interpolating from that curve (or, more quantitatively, by using the expression of Eq. (21)), an aquarist can conclude that a 200 gram charge of HC2 should remove about 90% of the DOC in approximately 1.1 days, but a 75 gram portion of HC2 would take approximately 3.9 days to achieve the same result.

Of course, DOC is continually being introduced via feeding and metabolic processes, and so the ultimate question of how much GAC to use in order to deplete the DOC concentration to some arbitrarily low target value in the aquarium requires knowledge of the rate of DOC production and not just the rate of DOC removal. Since this former quantity is not measurable by any simple means, only half an answer is possible at this point in the analysis (however, see Section 3.2). Of course, using a larger charge of HC2 would be more likely to allow the aquarist to "keep ahead" of the DOC production rate.

WHEN SHOULD I CHANGE MY GAC?

The useful lifetime of a GAC charge will depend on a host of factors, including the amount of GAC employed, the tank water volume, and the steady-state level of DOCs present. For the purpose of these calculations, we define a quantity, t_{90}, as the time when 90% of the GAC's DOC absorption capacity has been utilized. Using the experimentally determined k values from Table 2, the 53 mg-of-dye/gm-of-HC2 saturation value derived from Table 1, and an arbitrary starting DOC concentration (either 1 ppm or 7.5 ppm as per the discussion in

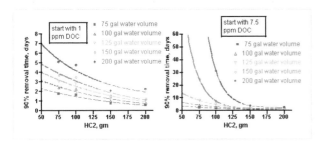

Figure 10. Calculated time for removal of 90% of DOC at starting points of 1 ppm DOC (left) and 7.5 ppm (right), as a function of tank water volume and amount of HC2 used.

Section 3.1), the KinTekSim program can decipher the kinetics of Eq. (15) and calculate the concentrations of [DOC] and [GAC$_{bs}$] as a function of time, when both [PoOP] and k_1 are user-defined inputs. One important test of any kinetics simulation approach for extracting useful information from complex systems is the ability to reproduce experimental data with fidelity. Towards this end, we examined the simulated removal of DOC from tank water with the DOC input mechanism turned off ([PoOP]•k_1 set to 0). This test simulation is equivalent to the simple Eq. (1) case, and the calculated output of [DOC] as a function of time matched closely the experimental data shown in Figure 4, at least for the 3 cases examined: 50, 100, and 200 gms of HC2 in the 4 gallon volume of the experimental reservoir.

For the initial [DOC] = 1 ppm series, we examined [PoOP]•k_1 values spanning the range of 0.1 ppm/day to 1 ppm/day for a 100 gallon water volume and a 100 gm HC2 charge (chosen to be in the middle of the water volume and GAC amount ranges), and recorded the calculated average DOC levels during the time t = 0 days to t = t$_{90}$ days. The goal of this exercise was to iterate through the [PoOP]•k_1 values until readings for [DOC]$_{ave}$ fell into the experimental range of ~ 0.5 - 1.0 ppm observed in actual marine tanks (see section 3.1).

The range of [PoOP]•k_1 values that met this criterion centered around 0.2 ppm/day, and so for the range [PoOP]•k_1 = 0.15 - 0.35 ppm/day, we expanded our calculations to include "extreme" values of tank water and GAC used, in the hopes of capturing the full spread of [DOC] amounts that might emerge from these simulations. These data are recorded in Table 5. A similar approach was employed for the dirtier tank, using [DOC] = 7.5 ppm as the starting point. These latter calculations required substantially greater DOC introduction to achieve the [DOC]$_{ave}$ » 4 - 8 ppm level, and the relevant [PoOP]•k_1 values turned out to be an order-of-magnitude higher that in the cleaner tank case where the initial [DOC] = 1 ppm. Is this a realistic outcome? It is important to recognize that the aquarium water which measured ~ 4 - 8 ppm of oxidizable organics with our protein assay was taken from unskimmed tanks, whereas the water that measured 0.5 - 1 ppm of oxidizable organics was taken from skimmed tanks. Our simulations do not account for any other methods of nutrient removal besides GAC, so skimming or water changes are not recognized. Therefore, in order to elevate [DOC]$_{ave}$ to the ~ 4 - 8 ppm level characteristic of the unskimmed ("dirty") tanks for these simulations, we cannot remove less DOC (as implied by the absence of skimming) and so we must increase the rate of DOC introduction (larger [PoOP]•k_1).

Since all of the calculated [DOC]$_{ave}$ values in Table 5 fall within the experimental ranges of measured tank oxidizable organic levels, which values do we choose to continue on with the simulations? Since the tank water assay detects only oxidizable organics, it seemed prudent to choose a higher end value to account for the undetected non-oxidizable components of DOC. For this reason, we selected [PoOP]•k_1 = 0.30 ppm/day at 1 ppm of starting DOC as the input rate of DOC production for the remaining simulations, and [PoOP]•k_1 = 3.0 ppm/day for the simulations starting with 7.5 ppm of DOC. Once a [PoOP]•k_1 value is chosen, it must be used for all of the other tank-volume/GAC-amount variations examined in the respective 1 ppm or 7.5 ppm DOC series, as [PoOP]•k_1 will not scale with either water volume or GAC mass. This constraint leads to some spread in the data, as not every volume/GAC pairing will be best described by [PoOP]•k_1 = 0.30 ppm/day.

The influence of the specific [PoOP]•k_1 value on the desired calculated quantity, t$_{90}$, can be seen from inspection of the data in Figure 11. These graphs depict the calculated DOC and GAC$_{bs}$ concentrations as a function of time for a 100gallon/100 gm HC2 simulation, at different [PoOP]•k_1 values (upper: 1 ppm starting DOC. lower: 7.5 ppm starting DOC). The intersections of the GAC$_{bs}$ lines with the t$_{90}$ lines indicate the time required to saturate 90% of the HC2 with DOC. Quantitatively, for the 1 ppm starting DOC series (upper graph): for [PoOP]•k_1 = 0.25 ppm/day, t$_{90}$ = 49 days; for [PoOP]•k_1 = 0.30 ppm/day, t$_{90}$ = 41 days, and for [PoOP]•k_1 = 0.35 ppm/day, t$_{90}$ = 36 days. So, if we guessed wrong for the [PoOP]•k_1 value by 17%, we introduce a spread of about 14% into the final t$_{90}$ values. That is, a spread in [DOC]$_{ave}$ of 0.75 - 0.98 ppm (from Table 5) correlates to t$_{90}$ values of 36 - 49 days, or for the 100gallon/100gm case, the GAC will be 90% saturated at around 41 ± 6 days. Similarly, for the 7.5 ppm starting DOC series (lower graph), the following t$_{90}$ values can be gleaned: for [PoOP]•k_1 = 2.0 ppm/day, t$_{90}$ = 5.0 days; for [PoOP]•k_1 = 3.0 ppm/day, t$_{90}$ = 3.9 days, and for [PoOP]•k_1 = 4.0 ppm/day, t$_{90}$ = 3.3 days. Once again, estimating [PoOP]•k_1

Table 5. The variation in calculated average DOC concentration ([DOC]$_{ave}$) and terminal DOC concentration ([DOC] at t$_{90}$; i.e., when the HC2 is 90% saturated) as a function of starting [DOC] and DOC generation rate [PoOP]•k_1. The [DOC]$_{ave}$ values were averaged over 5 sets of experimental inputs (gallons of tank water/gms of HC2): 75 /50, 75/200, 100/100, 200/50, and 200/200.

Starting [DOC] = 1.0 ppm			Starting [DOC] = 7.5 ppm		
[PoOP]•k_1 ppm/day	[DOC]$_{ave}$ ppm	[DOC] at t$_{90}$ ppm	[PoOP]•k_1 ppm/day	[DOC]$_{ave}$ ppm	[DOC] at t$_{90}$, ppm
0.15	0.57	1.2	1.0	3.7	4.5
0.20	0.65	1.3	2.0	5.1	6.8
0.25	0.75	1.5	3.0	6.6	8.5
0.30	0.87	1.7	4.0	7.1	10.1
0.35	0.98	2.0	5.0	7.9	11.7

incorrectly by 33% leads to an 18 - 28% error in the calculated t_{90} values. These potential errors carry much less significance in the starting [DOC] = 7.5 ppm case compared with the starting [DOC] = 1 ppm series, since the t_{90} values are so short. Basically, the HC2 saturates in just a few days, and it will likely matter little to the aquarist working under these conditions whether the exact saturation time is 3 days or 5 days. Given all of the assumptions that undergird this simulation, a conservative approach to interpreting these output values would seem prudent, and would require these rather large error bars. This lack of precision may be disquieting, but it is important to emphasize that the simulation results are clearly not consistent with, for example, a scenario where t_{90} values of 10 days or 100 days are calculated ([DOC] = 1 ppm case). This spread in the data is typical of kinetics simulations where the input parameters are uncertain. As a last point, note how the DOC concentration begins to rise significantly when the GAC is 90% saturated - this behavior is entirely consistent with the physical reality of the tank getting dirtier via DOC production when the DOC removal mechanism shuts down.

An interesting observation to emerge from these simulations is that, at least for the 100 gallon water volume/100 gm of HC2 case described by Table 5 and Figure 11, the GAC saturation times vary tremendously depending upon the clean/dirty state of the tank water. Under conditions of aggressive DOC removal (skimming, water changes, GAC use), the GAC charge should last over a month, but under more passive nutrient removal husbandry (no skimming? no frequent water changes?), the GAC charge will be depleted in just a few days.

Extension of these simulations to a range of tank water volumes and GAC amounts will provide the aquarist with

suggestions for GAC depletion times over a range of realistic usage scenarios. Using the [PoOP]•k_1 values of 0.3/ day and 3.0/day for the 1 ppm and 7.5 ppm of [DOC] cases, respectively, simulations covering tank volumes of 75 - 200 gallons and HC2 amounts of 50 - 200 gm leads to the family of linear relationships that are shown in Figure 12 (starting [DOC] = 1 ppm on the left side, and starting [DOC] = 7.5 ppm on the right side). Each line represents a different tank water volume, and expresses the relationship between the amount of HC2 used (X-axis) and the corresponding time-of-use until the HC2 is 90% saturated (Y-axis). These relationships can be expressed by the mathematical formulae Eq. (28) - Eq. (37) below. In principle, all of these lines should pass through the origin of the graph (t_{90} = 0 when there is no HC2 present). However, the best-fit lines have small and positive Y-axis intercepts. This deviation from ideality is again a reminder of the role that assumptions and experimental error plays in any laboratory enterprise. Fortunately, for this case, the non-zero Y-intercepts only amount to < 10% of the final t_{90} readings. These mathematical relationships are strictly empirical and should not be extrapolated beyond the HC2 data range.

(28) (1 ppm DOC, 75 gallon) $t_{90} = 0.51 \cdot (gm) + 3.7$, $r^2 = 0.99$

(29) (1 ppm DOC, 100 gallon) $t_{90} = 0.37 \cdot (gm) + 5.2$, $r^2 = 0.99$

(30) (1 ppm DOC, 125 gallon) $t_{90} = 0.27 \cdot (gm) + 8.3$, $r^2 = 0.99$

(31) (1 ppm DOC, 150 gallon) $t_{90} = 0.23 \cdot (gm) + 6.2$, $r^2 = 0.99$

(32) (1 ppm DOC, 200 gallon) $t_{90} = 0.16 \cdot (gm) + 7.6$, $r^2 = 0.97$

(33) (7.5 ppm DOC, 75 gallon) $t_{90} = 0.046 \cdot (gm) + 0.22$, $r^2 = 0.99$

(34) (7.5 ppm, 100 gallon) $t_{90} = 0.032 \cdot (gm) + 0.57$, $r^2 = 0.99$

(35) (7.5 ppm DOC, 125 gallon) $t_{90} = 0.021 \cdot (gm) + 1.2$, $r^2 = 0.98$

(36) (7.5 ppm DOC, 150 gallon) $t_{90} = 0.016 \cdot (gm) + 1.3$, $R^2 = 0.94$

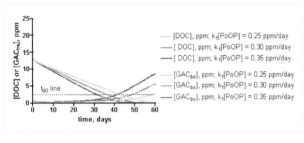

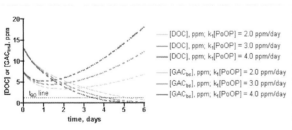

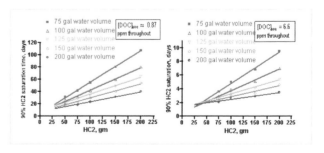

Figure 11. Examples of the KinTekSim output for a 100 gallon/100gm of HC2 simulation, using different values of the input parameter [PoOP]•k_1. Upper graph: 1.0 ppm DOC starting point. Lower graph: 7.5 ppm starting point.

Figure 12. Calculated time to saturate 90% of the available HC2 binding sites as a function of amount of HC2, tank water volume, and starting DOC concentration (1 ppm (left) and 7.5 ppm (right)).

(37) (7.5 ppm DOC, 200 gallon) $t_{90} = 0.010 \bullet (gm) + 2.6$, $r^2 = 0.93$

How might an aquarist use this information to answer the question "When should I change my GAC?" Much as with the "How much GAC?" question addressed in Section 3.1, the aquarist will have to estimate the water volume of the system, and then make a guess as to whether their tank has a low level of DOC's (~ 1 ppm in a system with adequate nutrient removal) or a high level (~ 7.5 ppm in a system with poor/absent nutrient removal). For example, a system with 150 gallons of total water volume that is adequately skimmed (or subjected to other effective nutrient removal, [DOC] ≤ 1 ppm) would be characterized by the aqua line on the left-hand graph in Figure 12. By interpolating from that line (or, more quantitatively, by using the expression of Eq. (31)), an aquarist can conclude that a 100 gram charge of HC2, for example, should be replaced in approximately 29 days, whereas a 200 gram portion of HC2 would last approximately 52 days before it became saturated with DOC's. In a similar manner, an aquarist running an unskimmed (i.e., [DOC] at approximately 7.5 ppm) 75 gallon tank could use the magenta line in the right-hand graph of Figure 12 (or Eq. (33)) to estimate that a 100 gm HC2 charge will become saturated with DOC's in approximately 4.8 days, and a 200 gm portion of HC2 would last about 9 days. Clearly, very nutrient rich tanks will require better means of DOC export than only GAC-based removal!

CONCLUSIONS

Aquarists who choose to use granular activated carbon (GAC) to aid in water purification are faced with two over-arching questions: "How much GAC should I use?", and "When should I replace my GAC?". Through a combination of experimentation using dyes as surrogates for dissolved organic carbon (DOC) and computer simulations of the DOC introduction/removal process, we can suggest tentative answers to these questions (Figures 10 and 12). The answers depend on three aquarist input quantities: the amount of DOC present, the amount of GAC used, and the tank water volume. The latter two metrics are easy to come by, but quantifying the amount of DOC present must still await reliable assay kits. Nevertheless, data from a small sampling of tanks provides guidance on this point, as both low-nutrient (~ 0.5 - 1 ppm of measurable oxidizable organics) and high-nutrient (~ 4 - 8 ppm of measurable oxidizable organics) water samples seem to correlate with either the presence or absence of an efficient protein skimmer. Certainly, a broader survey of marine tanks in the future will help refine these numbers.

In the final analysis, this study presents results that are based on model systems and not real operational marine tanks. We have made a case for the extrapolation of these model system conclusions to marine aquariums, but ultimately each aquarist will have to find their own comfort level regarding the validity of this connection.

ACKNOWLEDGMENT

We thank the Pennsylvania State University, the PSU Center for Environmental Kinetics Analysis (National Science Foundation grant # CHE-0431328) and du Pont de Nemours and Company for their financial support of this work.

REFERENCES

1. Alberts, B.; Johnson, A.; Lewis, J.; Raff, M.; Roberts, K.; Walter, P. 2002. Molecular Biology of the Cell, 4th Ed. Garland Science, Taylor and Francis Group, Boca Raton, Florida.

2. Bansal, R. C.; Goyal, M. 2005. Activated Carbon Adsorption. Taylor and Francis Group, Boca Raton, Florida.

3. Baup, S.; Jaffre, C.; Wolbert, D.; LaPlanche, A. 2000. "Adsorption of Pesticides onto Granular Activated Carbon: Determination of Surface Diffusivities Using Simple batch Experiments." Adsorption, 6, 219-228.

4. Bingman, C. A. 1996. "Aquatic Humic Acids." Aquarium Frontiers, 3, 11-14.

5. Callot, H. J.; Ocampo, R. 2000. Porphyrin Handbook. Kadish, K. M.; Smith, K. M.; Guilard, R., Eds., Academic Press, San Diego, California, 349-398.

6. Cerreta. 2006. "Experiment: Is All Granular Activated Carbon (GAC) Created Equally?" Reef Central Chemistry Forum.

7. Cheremisinoff, N. P.; Cheremisinoff, P. N. 1993. Carbon Adsorption for Pollution Control. PTR Prentice Hall, Englewood Cliffs, New Jersey.

8. Chien, J.-Y. 1948. "Kinetic Analysis of Irreversible Consecutive Reactions." J. Am. Chem. Soc., 70, 2256-2261.

9. Francois, R. 1990. "Marine Sedimentary Humic Substances: Structure, Genesis, and Properties." Rev. Aquatic Sci., 3, 41-80.

10. Ganguly, S. K.; Goswami, A. N. 1996. "Surface Diffusion Kinetics in the Adsorption of Acetic Acid on Activated Carbon." Separations Sci. Tech., 31, 1267-1278.

11. Gillam, A. H.; Wilson, M. A. 1986. "Structural Analysis of Aquatic Humic Substances by NMR Spectroscopy." ACS Symposium Series: Organic Marine Geochemistry, 305, 128-141.

12. Harker, R. 1998. "Granular Activated Carbon in the Reef Tank: Fact, Folklore and Its Effectiveness in Removing Gelbstoff -Parts 1 and 2." Aquarium Frontiers, May and

June issues. http://www.reefs.org/library/aquarium_frontiers/index.html.

13. Harvey, G. R.; Boran, D. A.; Chesal, L. A.; Tokar, J. M. 1983. "The Structure of Marine Fulvic and Humic Acids." Marine Chem. 12, 119-132. For a commentary on the conclusions drawn in this article, and a rebuttal, see: Laane, R. W. P. M. 1984. "Comment on the Structure of Marine Fulvic and Humic Acids." Marine. Chem. 15, 85-87, and Harvey, G. R. Reply: Comment on the Structure of marine Fulvic and Humic Acid." Marine Chem. 15, 89-90.

14. Homes-Farley, R. 2004 "Organic Compounds in the Reef Aquarium." Reefkeeping, 10, http://www.reefkeeping.com/issues/2004-10/rhf/index.php.

15. Hovanec, T. 1993. "All About Activated Carbon." Aquarium Fish Magazine, 5, 54-63.

16. Khan, A. R.; Ataullah, R.; Al-Haddad, A. 1997. "Equilibrium Adsorption Studies of Some Aromatic Pollutants from Dilute Aqueous Solutions on Activated Carbon at Different Temperatures." J. Colloid Interface Sci. 194, 154-165.

17. Lliopoulos, A.; Reclos, J. G.; Reclos, G. J. 2002. "Activated Carbon." Fresh Water and Marine Aquarium, January issue.

18. Kvech, S.; Tull, E. 1997. "Activated Carbon." Water Treatment Primer, Civil Engineering Department, Virginia Tech, http://ewr.cee.vt.edu/environmental/teach/wtprimer/carbon/sketcarb.html.

19. Noll, K. E.; Gouranis, V.; Hou, W. S. 1992. Adsorption Technology for Air and Water Pollution Control. Lewis Publishers, Chelsea, Michigan.

20. Rashid, M. A. 1985. Geochemistry of Marine Humic Compounds. Springer-Verlag, New York, New York.

21. Romankevich, E. A. 1984. Geochemistry of Organic Matter in the Ocean. Springer-Verlag, New York, New York.

22. Sardessai, S.; Wahidullah, S. 1998. "Structural Characteristics of Marine Sedimentary Humic Acids by CP/MAS 13C NMR Spectroscopy." Oceanologica Acta, 21, 543-550.

23. Schiemer, G. 1997. "About Activated Carbon." Aquarium Frontiers, July issue.

24. Singh, S.; Yenkie, M. K. N. 2006. "Scavenging of Priority Organic Pollutants from Aqueous Waste Using Granular Activated Carbon." J. Chinese Chem. Soc. 2006, 53, 325-334.

25. Spartan'04. Wavefunction, Inc. Irvine, CA.

26. Suzuki, M. 2001. "Activated Carbon Adsorption for Treatment of Agrochemicals in Water." Environmental Monitoring and Governance in the East Asian Hydrosphere Symposium Abstracts, http://landbase.hq.unu.edu/Symposia/2001Symposium/abstracts/06Suzuki.htm.

27. Walker, G. M.; Weatherley, L. R. 2000. "Prediction of Bisolute Dye Adsorption Isotherms on Activated Carbon." Trans. Institut. Chem. Eng., 78, 219-223.

28. Walker, G. M.; Weatherly, L. R. 1999. "Kinetics of Acid Dye Adsorption on GAC." Water Res. 33, 1895-1899.

FEATURE ARTICLE

SUPER CORALS - SUPERMAN MONTIPORA

By Dana Riddle

The following article will examine some husbandry techniques for this exotic coral.

Published February 2008, Advanced Aquarist's Online Magazine

© Pomacanthus Publications, LLC

Keywords: Coloration, Coral, Dana Riddle, Feature Article
Link to original article: http://www.advancedaquarist.com/2008/2/aafeature2

Only a few corals can match this coral's startling contrast of colors, making the Superman *Montipora* a highly desirable animal for display reef aquaria. As can be expected, the demand for this coral ensures a premium price.

The following article will examine some husbandry techniques for this exotic coral. Since many of us are not particularly interested in how information within this article was obtained, I'll present the pertinent data first and will save the nitty-gritty technical details and methods for the end of this article.

Again, bear in mind that the details below are from a limited number of specimens, and other *Montipora* species may bear a resemblance to *M. danae* (be sure of the coral's ID!).

Common Name: Superman

Family: Acroporidae

Genus: *Montipora*

Variously described as these species: *Montipora danae* (which can be confused with *M. verrucosa, M. verruculosus and M. palawanensis.* The latter two species are uncommon and restricted to a smaller geographical area than the two former species). Also described in advertisements as *M. tuberculosa.* The coral in Figure 1 is likely *M. danae* as its immersed corallites are widely spaced between hillocky coenosteum verrucae (or tuberculae) and partially fused ridges. Identification is based on results obtained by using Veron's *Coral ID* software. See Comments below for basis of identification.

Geographical Range: Indian and Pacific Oceans and possibly the Red Sea.

Known Symbiont Types: *Symbiodinium* species, including Clades C2, C31, C+ and C·.

LIGHT REQUIREMENTS

Reef hobbyists, as a group, have the correct concept about lighting - it is an important factor in successful reefkeeping and probably the most expensive routine maintenance item in terms of electricity consumption. Yet relatively few own or

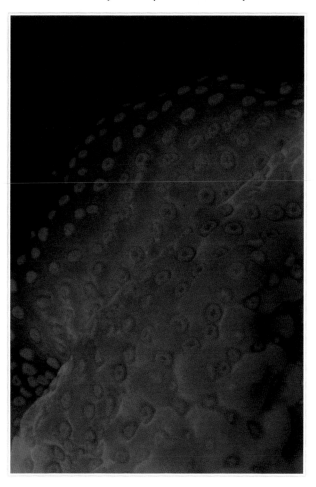

Figure 1. A Superman Montipora.

use any sort of light meter. This is probably due to the fact that so little is known about light requirements of photosynthetic invertebrates. However, there are instruments available to determine how much light is actually required. As this information becomes available, we can arm ourselves with this knowledge and can potentially begin to put our reef aquaria on energy diets. In short, a light meter is a good investment.

At a minimum, hobbyists should have (or have access to) a lux meter with a submersible sensor or, even better, a quantum meter for measuring Photosynthetically Active Radiation (PAR, reported in units of micro Mol photons per square meter per second, or µmol photons·m²·sec, but usually just µmol·m²·sec. Maximum PAR in the tropics at noon on a cloudless day can be as high as 2,200 µmol·m²·sec).

Although either of these instruments is relatively expensive, the price of a quality meter has dropped dramatically over the last decade or so. No longer is it necessary to spend over $1,000 for a PAR meter - quite adequate units are available for ~$250.

I have to wonder what state the hobby would be in if we treated many of the established parameters in the manner many treat light intensity. What if we were advised to maintain either a high or low pH? Alkalinity? Phosphorus? Calcium?

With that said, how does light does a Superman *Montipora* require? Instead of saying 'not much' or 'a lot', we can estimate the light requirements via the technique of non-invasive fluorometry. What does that mean? It simply means that we can, with proper instrumentation, observe how energy flows in the photosynthetic process. This energy flow is called the 'Electron Transport Rate' (or ETR for short). The higher the ETR, the higher the rate of photosynthesis. Here, we report 'relative ETR' (rETR) since absorption of light by photopigments within zooxanthellae was not measured.

It is a common misconception that reef aquaria cannot have too much light. To the contrary, evidence suggests many corals actually photo-saturate (where the rate of photosynthesis - the rETR - does not increase with increasing light intensity. For examples, see Ulstrap et al., 2006, where the SPS coral *Pocillopora damicornis* becomes photo-inhibited at ~450 µmol·m²·sec).

Photoinhibition is possible. Photoinhibition is the phenomenon of reduced photosynthesis where available light exceeds that needed for maximum photosynthesis. In these cases, zooxanthellae are trying to protect themselves from photodestruction via dumping excess energy as chlorophyll fluorescence in a process called photochemical quenching. In addition, xanthophyll pigments within zooxanthellae can absorb blue light and dissipate this energy as non-radiant heat that is called non-photochemical quenching. So, what amount of light is sufficient for growth and coloration of the Superman coral?

Figure 2 demonstrates the rate of photosynthesis of one Superman specimen under various light intensities. For those arguing that these numbers represent only a snapshot of one coral's zooxanthellae after photoacclimation (which, of course, they do), I suggest that they've missed the point! The point is not so much that these rETRs are representative of zooxanthellae photosynthetic activity after photoacclimation to a given amount of light - it is the fact that the zooxanthellae have the ability to adapt to this particular amount of light!

If we assume that calcification rates are linked to rates of photosynthesis, then Figure 2 takes on added meaning. Examination of Figure 2 suggests photosynthesis (and hence calcification and growth) would theoretically be about the same at 250 µmol·m²·sec and 500 µmol·m²·sec. However, bleaching of a Superman specimen has been noted at a light intensity of only 300 µmol·m²·sec (and a photoperiod of 11 hours. It seems certain that light - and not temperature, ultraviolet radiation, or any other 'nasty' factor - is responsible for the bleaching. This observation certainly deserves further investigation).

The bottom line - analyses suggest these two *M. danae* specimens and their zooxanthellae seem to prefer lower light conditions, where intensity is only 100 - 200 µmol·m²·sec.

KNOWN SYMBIONTS

Recent 'fingerprinting' of zooxanthellae DNA has revealed a large number of sub-species or 'clades'. There are several known 'types' of zooxanthellae found in *Montipora danae*, including Clade C2 (based on ITS2 analyses, Van Oppen, 2004; 2005), C31 (LaJeunesse, 2004; Okinawa, Japan, 1-10m), C+ and C· (ITS1; Van Oppen, 2004).

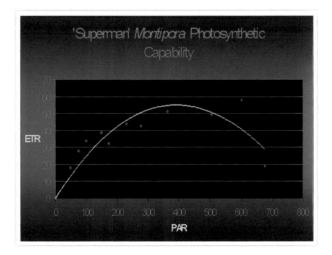

Figure 2. Photosynthetic activity (relative Electron Transport Rate, or rETR shown by the yellow line) of one Superman Montipora specimen. In this case, maximum photosynthesis occurs at a PAR value of ~400 µmol·m²·sec. Increasing light intensity above this point is counterproductive as photoinhibition occurs (as indicated by reduced rETR).

Figure 3. Appearance of the Superman Montipora when illuminated by a warm-white fluorescent lamp. The non-fluorescent chromoprotein reflects blue and red light, making the coral appear violet/purple.

Clade C2: This zooxanthellae clade is found largely in Family Acroporidae corals (*Acropora, Montipora*, among others) including *Acropora aspera, Acropora cerealis* (GBR, Van Oppen, 2001), *Acropora cervicornis* (Caribbean 2.0-17.0m, Baker et al., 1997), *Acropora cuneata* (Van Oppen et al., 2005), *Acropora florida, Acropora gemmifera, Acropora intermedia, Acropora longicyathus, Acropora loripes, Acropora millepora, Acropora nastua, Acropora spathulata, Acropora tenuis, Acropora valida* (GBR, Van Oppen, 2001),*Montipora aequituberculata, Montipora capricornis, Montipora danae, Montipora florida* (from Indonesia, Van Oppen, 2005 based on ITS2 fingerprint). Clade C2 has also been reported from *Pavona varians* (Van Oppen, 2005), *Goniastrea rectiformis* (Van Oppen, 2005), zooxanthellae collected and cultured from the clam *Hippopus* (LaJeunesse, 2003), and *Pocillopora damicornis* (two locations in Taiwan, 0-5.0m, Chen et al., 2005). C2 is believed to have adaptively radiated from Clade C3 (a 'generalist' zooxanthella).

It is an interesting notion that corals containing Clade C2 could possibly have the same range of photoacclimation. Photoacclimation in most zooxanthellae is not infinite in range, although it seems certain that some 'types' of *Symbiodinium* have more latitude in adjusting to light intensity than others. This is an important concept - zonation of certain corals has been linked to light intensity (Iglesias-Prieto et al., 2003), though factors such as temperature tolerance and others also play roles.

Clade C31: So far, Clade C31 seems to be most common in *Montipora* specimens. It has been found in *Montipora danae* specimens (Okinawa, Japan, 1-10m; LaJeunesse, 2004) as well as *Montipora* species (western and Central Pacific 2-20m; LaJeunesse et. al., 2003); *Montipora capitata* (Hawaii, 1-5m, LaJeunesse, 2004) and *Montipora patula* (Hawaii, 20m, LaJeunesse, 2004). C31 is believed to have evolved from Clade C21. Clade C31 has also been found in *Montastraea annularis* (Belize, 8m; Warner et al., 2006).

A pulse amplitude modulation (PAM) analysis of photosynthetic capacity of a shallow-water Hawaiian *Montipora capitata* (believed to contain Clade 31) found onset of photosaturation at ~135 µmol photons·m²·sec (~6,750 lux).

47

Photoinhibition is thought to occur at ~250 μmol photons·m²·sec (Riddle, in press).

Based on the information about coral species and associated depth presented by researchers (above), it appears that Clade C31 zooxanthellae probably tolerate, if not prefer, lower light intensity.

Clade C+: Isolated from the Pacific stony coral *Montipora danae* (van Oppen 2004) in combination with Clade C2 (Van Oppen, 2004) and *Plesiastrea verispora* (Magalon et al., 2007).

Clade C·: This zooxanthella is believed to have co-evolved with *Montipora* species, but sometimes found in *Porites attenuata* and *Porites cylindrica*. *Montipora* species containing Clade C· include *Montipora aequituberculata, M. altasepta, M. angulata, M. cactus, M. capitata, M. crassituberculata, M. danae, M. delicatula, M. digitata, M. gaimardi, M. hispida, M. hoffmeisteri, M. mollis, M. peltiformis, M. spongodes, M. stellata, M. turtlensis, M. undata,* and *M. verrucosa* (van Oppen et al., 2004). This clade is presently known to be distributed from Indonesia southward to the Great Barrier Reef. One has to wonder if this clade has high fidelity to *Montipora* spp. and is one of those listed in LaJeunesse's more-or-less concurrent paper (namely Clades C17, C26a, C27, C30, C31, C31a, C31b, C32, C58 and C73). Van Oppen's IDs are based on ITS1 sequences (while LaJeunesse's - and many others'- are based on ITS2 fingerprinting).

Figure 4. The same coral in Figure 3. Note the considerable growth that has occurred over 4 months time under 'low light' conditions - only 100 μ-mol·m²·sec, although much of the non-fluorescent purple coloration has disappeared.

POSSIBILITIES OF 'SYMBIONT SHUFFLING'

Are the clades listed above the only zooxanthellae inhabiting *Montipora danae*? Probably not. But it is the best information currently available; however, new laboratory techniques will undoubtedly change our view.

Warming of the earth's oceans has generated much interest in how corals and their zooxanthellae respond to environmental conditions. Researchers are identifying the possibility of 'symbiont shuffling' where one zooxanthella clade loses its dominance due to unfavorable conditions (excess light, UV, temperature, etc.) and is replaced by a second clade that finds the new environment as hospitable and thus becomes dominant.

Much of the recent research work involves techniques that cannot detect zooxanthellae populations when they are less than 5-10% of the total population (although Mieog et al., 2007, report a technique with 100-fold increased sensitivity. Future results using this technique should prove quite interesting). Only one case to my knowledge demonstrates two clades living simultaneously in a *M. danae* specimen (C2 and C+; Van Oppen, 2004).

Zooxanthellae inhabiting *Montipora* specimens likely have a high fidelity for their host (and vice versa); In fact some clades are believed to have co-evolved with their host coral. In addition, *Montipora* larvae acquire their symbionts directly from the parental colony - the eggs are infected by zooxanthellae from the parent - in a process called maternal acquisition (not all corals behave in this manner - many larvae obtain symbionts from the water column). In either case, acroporid corals seem to have a preference for specific zooxanthella clade(s) (van Oppen, 2004).

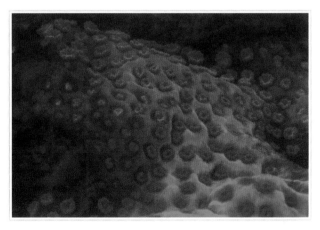

Figure 5. A closer view of the coral pictured in Figures 3 and 4. A high kelvin lamp will showcase the blue, green and orange fluorescent pigments.

CORAL PIGMENTATION - WHAT COLOR DO YOU DESIRE?

Coloration of the Superman coral is dependent upon the type of light and here's why: Analyses of fluorescence have revealed the presence of at least six pigments within the Superman *Montipora*. The major pigment is found within coral tissues and fluoresces at a peak of 489nm (blue-green). Their reddish color of the polyps is due to fluorescence peaking at 611nm (see Figure 6). Other minor fluorescent pigments are seen at 546, 567, 587, and 617, with possible fluorescent spikes at 491, 520 and 540nm. There is also an unidentified non-fluorescent chromoprotein at can make the coral appear blue or purple (depending upon the spectrum of the illumination source).

Note that other *M. danae* specimens can contain different pigments. For instance, Salih et al. (2006) identified two additional fluorescent pigments. Fluorescent emissions are seen at 483 and 495nm. Excitation wavelengths include UV-A, violet and blue wavelengths (see Figure 7).

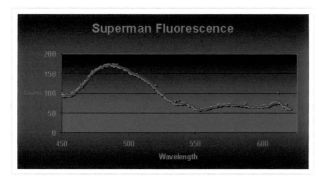

Figure 6. Fluorescent emission of a Superman coral reveals a major peak at 489nm. The reddish polyps fluoresce strongly at 611nm.

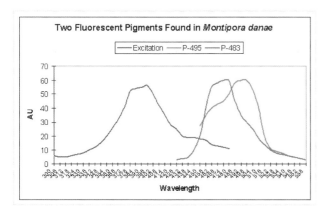

Figure 7. Two other fluorescent pigments from a Montipora danae specimen. After Salih et al., 2006.

Figure 7 is useful in understanding which wavelengths will make this coral fluoresce in the blue-green range. Although ultraviolet light will induce fluorescence, the maximum excitation wavelength is in the violet portion of the spectrum.

The purple chromoprotein seems to be expressed as a result of light intensity (although other 'proper' conditions in aquaria are also required). At light intensity of about 100 $\mu mol \cdot m^2 \cdot sec$, the purple coloration is barely seen, but growth is good (see Figure 4). The bluish chromoprotein can become the apparent dominant pigment at ~175 $\mu mol \cdot m^2 \cdot sec$.

While non-fluorescent coloration seems dependent upon light, the fluorescent orange seen in the polyps and the blue-green 'body' pigments (produced by the coral animal and not zooxanthellae) are usually seem except when the light intensity is too high (and the coral bleaches) or when light is too low (and the zooxanthellae/host suffer from light deprivation. Though strictly speculation on my part, the host probably stops producing pigments as an energy-saving measure).

WATER MOTION

This coral's 'bumpy' surface (called tuberculae or verrucae, depending upon their size relative to corallites) indicates this animal requires 'good' water flow. These tuberculae act as 'speed bumps' to laminar water flow and create turbulence, which is not surprising as these corals are often found on upper reef slopes. Slowing of water velocity by these bumps prevents deformation of polyp shape and allows the coral to feed.

Fortunately, creating sufficient water movement is quite easy with some of the newer propeller pumps and other devices (see Riddle, 2007).

OTHER AQUARIUM CONDITIONS

The Superman *Montipora* fares well when other physical and chemical conditions in an aquarium are within 'reasonable' ranges. To avoid potential overheating of coral specimens, water temperature should not exceed 80° F when using metal halide lamps (see Riddle, 2006 for details). Although a link to coloration in aquaria conditions needs to be established, alkalinity and its potential relationship to coral tissue pH (Battad et al., 2007) under lighted conditions could also play a role in coral coloration.

METHODS AND MATERIALS

Rates of photosynthesis were determined with a Walz 'Teaching PAM' Chlorophyll Fluorometer (Effeltrich, Germany) equipped with a fiber optic cord. A fluorometer is basically a 'photosynthesis meter' and exploits measurements of chlorophyll fluorescence in order to determine rates of photosynthesis (in terms of 'relative electron transport rate' or rETR between Photosystem I and Photosystem II within zooxanthellae. Since pigment absorption of light was not measured, the ETR is considered to be relative). Corals were maintained in total darkness for at least one hour before initial measurements were made in order to allow Photosystem reaction centers to 'open'. The external actinic light source was a 400-watt Iwasaki 6,500K metal halide lamp that was shielded for ultraviolet radiation by a clear acrylic material. Intensity was adjusted upwards by moving the light source closer to the coral (which was contained in a 3-gallon plastic container). Light intensity (Photosynthetically Active Radiation, or PAR) was measured with an Apogee QMSS quantum meter and a submersible, cosine-corrected sensor. Water motion was provided by a magnetic stirrer and a 3" stir bar.

After the dark-adaptation period, minimum chlorophyll fluorescence (Fo) was determined with weak light (<1 μmol·m²·sec) generated by the instrument's internal actinic lamp. Increasing the intensity of the internal actinic lamp to provide a saturating light pulse determined Maximum Fluorescence (Fm). The metal halide lamp was then turned on and allowed to warm up until PAR values stabilized (15-20 minutes). Chlorophyll fluorescence values were determined and the light intensity increased. The coral's zooxanthellae were allowed to adjust to the new light intensity for 15 minutes and another chlorophyll fluorescence measurement was made. The PAM meter calculated Photosynthetic Yield, which was simply multiplied by the appropriate PAR measurement in order to estimate the 'relative Electron Transport Rate' or rETR. This is a valid method for observing photosynthetic trends.

Fluorescence was determined with an Ocean Optics USB-2000-FL fiber optic spectrometer (Dunedin, Florida) using an 18-watt black light (maximum emission at 365nm) as the excitation source. Light was collected with a cosine-corrected CC-3 lens.

Photographs were taken with a Canon Rebel XTi digital camera (10.1 megapixels) equipped with two stacked teleconverters and a 60mm macro lens.

COMMENTS ON BASIS OF IDENTIFICATION

Veron (2000) states: "The identification of aquarium-raised corals is a difficult and sometimes impossible task... They may also assume growth forms which are sometimes seen in the wild, but usually only in deep water that may be unusual for the species." With that said, hobbyists are cautioned that information contained within this article was obtained from two aquarium-grown specimens, and, although best efforts have been made to identify these animals, limitations of the software lend a degree of uncertainly as to the exact coral species.

In an effort to identify these corals, twenty-seven identification points, including those observed from two living and one skeletal remains, were entered into Veron's *Coral ID* software. These observations for data entry were made from examinations of enlarged photographs of living corals and microscopic examinations of a skeleton.

To properly identify a coral, its geographic origin should be known, and in these cases, the collection point(s) is not known. Assuming these corals originated from the central Indo-Pacific Ocean (including Indonesia, Philippines and Solomon Islands), the software determined identity as *Montipora danae* or *M. undata*, with the software's 'Best Bet' option signaling *M. danae* as the proper identification.

While changing the location data point (and retaining all others), the identification consistently included *M. danae*. For instance, entering Oceanic West Pacific (including Fiji) the software also returned two possibilities - *Montipora danae* and *M. undata*. Similar results were listed for SW Indian Ocean. Central Pacific (including Tonga) suggested only one possibility - *M. danae*.

These are the other identification criteria (those items in italics were determined by microscopic exams):

- Multiple mouths and corallites

- Attached to the substrate (as opposed to free-living)

- Hemispherical, sub-massive or encrusting growth forms

- Branching absent

- Calice width less than 1mm

- Corallite centers distinct

- Corallites separate individuals

- Immersed corallites

Figure 8. Distinctly different skeletal growth forms within millimeters of each other. To the right, linear elaborations typical of many Montipora specimens are dominant. To the left, the skeleton flattens to a rather featureless, flattened growth pattern.

- Neither axial nor central corallite

- Corallites widely spaced (more than twice the diameter of the corallite opening)

- Tentacles expanded by day

- Tentacle length <10mm

- Partial skeletal masking

- Daytime tissue projection <1mm

- Extra-thecal skeleton present

- Extra-thecal surface perforated

- Linear elaborations present

- Linear elaborations greater than calice diameter

- *Columella absent*

- *Costae absent*

- *Septa not fused*

- *2 cycles septa*

- *Septa not exsert*

- *Septal margin not smooth*

- *Paliform structures absent*

Many thanks to Steve Ruddy of Coral Reef Ecosystems (www.coralreefecosystems.com) for his assistance in preparation of this article.

REFERENCES

1. Baker, A., 2003. Flexibility and specificity in coral/algal symbiosis: Diversity, ecology and biogeography of *Symbiodinium*. Annu. Rev. Ecol. Syst., 34:661-689.

2. Battad, J., P. Wilmann, S. Olsen, E. Byres, S. Smith, S. Dove, K. Turcic, R. Devenish, J. Rossjohn and M. Prescott, 2007. A structural basis for the pH-dependent increase in fluorescence efficiency of chromoproteins. J. Mol. Biol.

3. Chen, C., Y-W Yang, N. Wei, W-S Tsai and L-S Fang, 2005. Symbiont diversity in scleractinian corals from tropical reefs and sub-tropical non-reef communities in Taiwan. Coral Reefs, 24(1): 11-22.

4. Iglesias-Prieto, R., V. Beltran, T. LaJeunesse, H. Reyes-Bonilla and P. Thome, 2004. Different algal symbionts explain the vertical distribution of dominant reef corals in the eastern Pacific. Proc. R. Soc. Lond. B, 271:1757-1763.

5. LaJeunesse, T., W. Loh, R. van Woesik, O. Hoegh-Guldberg, G. Schmidt and W. Fitt, 2003. Low symbiont diversity in southern Great Barrier Reef corals, relative to those of the Caribbean. Limnol. Oceanogr., 48(5):2046-2054.

6. LaJeunesse, T., R. Bhagooli, M. Hidaka, L. deVantier, T. Done, G. Schmidt, W. Fitt and O. Hoegh-Guldberg, 2004. Closely related *Symbiodinium* spp. differ in relative dominance in coral reef host communities across environmental, latitudinal and biogeographic gradients. Mar. Ecol. Prog. Ser., 284:147-161.2004.

7. LaJeunesse, T., D. Thornhill, E. Cox, F. Stanton, W. Fitt and G. Schmidt, 2004. High diversity and host specificity observed among symbiotic dinoflagellates in reef coral communities from Hawaii. Coral Reefs, 23:596-603.

8. Magalon, H., J.-F. Flot and E. Baudry, 2007. Molecular identification of symbiotic dinoflagellates in Pacific corals in the genus *Pocillopora*. Coral reefs, 26:551-558.

9. Mieog, J., M. van Oppen, N. Cantin, W. Stam and J. Olsen, 2007. Real-time PCR reveals a high incidence of *Symbiodinium* clade D at low levels in four scleractinian corals across the Great Barrier Reef: implications for symbiont shuffling. Coral Reefs, 26:449-457

10. Riddle, D., 2006. Temperature and the reef aquarium. Advanced Aquarist Online. http://www.advancedaquarist.com/2006/2/aafeature2/

11. Riddle, D., 2007. Product Review: Water motion devices: Sea Flo's Maxi-Jet modification kits. http://www.advancedaquarist.com/2007/12/review1

12. Salih, A., G. Cox, R. Syymczak, S. Coles, A. Baird, A. Dunstan, G. Cocco, J. Mills and A. Larkum, 2006. The role of host-based color and fluorescent pigments in photoprotection and in reducing bleaching stress in corals. Proc. 10th Coral Reef Symp., Okinawa, Japan.

13. Ulstrap, K., P. Ralph, A. Larkum and M. Kuhl, 2006. Intra-colony variability in light acclimation of zooxanthellae in coral tissues of *Pocillopora damicornis*. Mar. Biol., 149:1325-1335.

14. Van Oppen, M., F. Palstra, A. Piquet and D. Miller, 2001. Patterns of coral-dinoflagellate associations in *Acropora*: Significance of local availability and physiology of *Symbiodinium* strains and host-symbiont selectivity. Proc. R. Soc. Lond B., 268: 1759-1767.

15. Van Oppen, M., 2004. Mode of zooxanthella transmission does not affect zooxanthella diversity in Acroporid corals. Mar. Biol., 144:1-7.

16. Van Oppen, M., A. Mahiny, and T. Done, 2005. Geographical distribution of zooxanthella types of three coral species of the Great Barrier Reef sampled after the 2002 bleaching events. Coral Reefs, in press.

17. Veron, J., 2000. *Corals of the World.* Australian Institute of Marine Science, Townsville.

18. Veron, J., 2002. *Coral ID: An electronic key to the zooxanthellate scleractinian corals of the world.* (software). Australian Institute of Marine Science and CCR Qld Pty Ltd. University of Queensland, Australia.

19. Warner, M., T. LaJeunesse, J. Robinson and R. Thur, 2006. The ecological distribution and comparative photobiology of symbiotic dinoflagellates from reef corals in Belize: Potential implications for coral bleaching. Limnol. Oceanogr., 51(4):1887-1897.

FEATURE ARTICLE

ALGAE: SOMETIMES BOTH BEAUTIFUL AND USEFUL

By Christopher Paparo

Too often marine macro algae are only considered to be part of an aquarium's filtration system.

Published February 2008, Advanced Aquarist's Online Magazine

© Pomacanthus Publications, LLC

Keywords: Algae, Christopher Paparo, Feature Article, Filtration
Link to original article: http://www.advancedaquarist.com/2008/2/aafeature3

Just the mere mention of the word algae in a room of aquarists will send them running for their scrub pads. Algae are the nemesis of most aquarists, from pesky diatom algae covering our décor in a brown film, to the nearly impossible to eradicate hair algae. Not all algae should be despised however; many types are extremely useful and some can be quite beautiful.

Most of us are familiar with the ornamental species common to the trade, such as *Caulerpa* and *Chaetomorpha*. Occasionally species of *Codium, Halimeda, Acetabularia,* and some miscellaneous red species will show up at your local fish shop attached to a piece of base rock. But how many of us have wandered the local shoreline in search of algae for our aquariums?

Living on Long Island, I am fortunate to be minutes away from the bay or ocean. A short walk along the shoreline at

This is the macro algae tank I care for at Atlantis Marine World and will go into more detail on the care of such a tank in a future article.

low tide will expose you to a wide variety of algae. Many of the species, being temperate in range, will tolerate a wide range of temperatures, including those of a reef environment. Knowing what to look for will enable you to collect algae for your home aquarium.

There are three phyla of algae; Chlorophyta (green), Chrysophyta (brown) and Rhodophyta (red). Each of these phyla has unique characteristics causing them to be found at different depths of the water column.

Chlorophyta, the green algae, need more light than the other phyla and will be found higher in the water column. Of the greens, *Ulva lactuca*, or better known as sea lettuce, is probably the most abundant and widely known. Growing in large, thin sheets, it is unmistakable. Ranging from subarctic to tropical environments world wide, it can be found growing among the rocks of an inlet, to the calm waters of the back bay. It is frequently found thriving in areas of high nutrients.

A species similar to *Ulva lactuca* is *Ulva intestinalis* (formerly, *Enteromorpha intestinalis*). This green alga shares the same environment as *Ulva lactuca* but grows in long narrow tubes. This growth form allows it to survive in areas that might be too turbulent for the delicate sheets of *U. lactuca* to grow. As with many plants and even some animals (i.e., corals), morphology will vary with environmental conditions. In areas of high current or wave action, it tends to grow in very narrow tubes, almost as if it was hair algae, while growing in wider tubes in calm conditions. Large blades growing in such a turbulent area would only be broken off before the alga gets a chance to grow. Like *U. lactuca*, *U. intestinalis* has a worldwide range.

Arriving to the east coast of America from the Pacific in 1957, *Codium fragile* is an invasive green alga that is quite abundant. Commonly called Dead Man's Fingers or Green Fleece, *C.fragile* grows in ropelike spongy branches, and when exposed at low tide, it looks like fingers. *C.fragile* is unique as it is a long single cell that is made up of many nuclei but no cell wall dividing them. Being able to reproduce by fragmentation has allowed it to spread easily through out the east coast of North America. This invasive species has been very destructive to shellfish beds, especially oysters. Upon attaching to a shellfish, wave action causes the shellfish to be "uprooted" and the currents wash it ashore. This species is commonly found in calm, protected waters. Locally, I tend to find it attached to some of our more common epibenthic mollusks such as Cockles and Slipper Shells.

Chrysophyta, the brown algae, tend to grow much larger than the greens. Some of The most common brown algae of the intertidal zone belong to the genus, *Fucus*. Fucus can tolerate exposure to a wide range of environmental conditions. Being exposed at low tide, it is subject to freezing in winter months, and to extreme heat and dehydration in the summer. To adapt to these harsh conditions, *Fucus* has thick rubbery blades allowing the algae to retain moisture while it is exposed. The blades of *Fucus* have many air bladders that provide buoyancy for the blades. This buoyancy allows the blades to sway in the currents removing any detritus that has

settled during the low tide. Algae growing in high surge areas will have fewer bladders as the current will keep the blades moving. Growing mostly in cooler waters, it has a worldwide distribution.

Another type of brown algae found on our shorelines is kelp. When talking about kelp, we think of the giant kelp forests of cold-temperate waters such as the California coast, New England, and western South America. Some species, such as *Macrocystis pyrifera*, can grow at a rate of 30 cm a day and can reach a length of 60 meters. Like *Fucus*, giant kelp has air bladders that keep it suspended in the water column. On the east coast of North America, our species of kelp, *Laminaria agardhii*, is much different than *M.pyrifera*. Under ideal conditions, it can grow 2 cm a day, growing to 3 meters in length. Looking like a large lasagna noodle, it has one large blade, a stipe (similar to a stem), and a large holdfast. Similar in appearance to roots of vascular plants, the holdfast's sole purpose is for attachment, there is no nutrient uptake. Growing in areas of strong surges, the holdfast is important to keeping the alga from washing away. Unlike *M.pyrifera*, *L.agardhii* has no air bladders. It depends on strong currents

Rocky intertidal zone at Orient Point, NY

Ulva lactuca

to keep it suspended in the water column. Long Island is the southern most part of *Laminaria's* range, and can only be found in the winter months.

The last group of algae you will find while walking the beach are the Rhodophyta or red algae. Red algae contain a pigment called phycoerythrin. This pigment absorbs blue light and reflects red light, giving the algae its red color. Being that blue light penetrates deeper in the water column, red algae tend to be found growing at greater depths. This can make it a little more difficult to collect as you might need to get your feet wet to find a suitable specimen. An abundant and well-known red seaweed in our local waters is *Chondrus chrispus*, better know as Irish Moss. *C.chrispus* is commercially

harvested for use in the food industry. Carrageen is an extract of *Chondrus* that is used as a thickener in soups and dairy products.

Codium fragile with a red algae growing as an epiphyte.

Fucus sp.

Laminaria agardhii

Ulva intestinalis

One red algae, although not a macro algae, is encrusting coralline algae. Common to the tropics, encrusting coralline algae is absent from Long Island waters. As you move north away from Long Island, encrusting coralline algae becomes

The holdfast of Laminaria.

Chondrus chrispus

common once again. Even though encrusting red corallines are absent, we do have a macro coralline alga, *Corallina officinalis*, better know as coral weed. Unlike the encrusting species, it grows as fan-like tuffs reaching only a couple inches in length. When found washed up on the beach, it is white in color and will crumble in you hand when you pick it up.

Two other species of red algae commonly found around Long Island and ranging to the tropics are, *Agardhiella tenera* and *Gracilaria foliifera*. Both species are delicately branched and their color can vary from a bright red to almost brown. They can be found attached to rocks or shells, but are more commonly found free floating. They seem to prefer calm waters where they are less likely to be washed ashore.

Too often marine macro algae are only considered to be part of an aquarium's filtration system. They are tucked deeply away in a refugium under ones aquarium, never to be shown as proudly as the main tank. Many of these algae are extremely beautiful, and deserve their own display. Although they do pose some challenges in keeping them, it can be done and I will share with you how to keep them in a future article.

Agardhiella tenera

FEATURE ARTICLE

WEST ATLANTIC STONY CORALS PART 2: SPS CORALS CONTINUED AND FAVIID CORALS

By Jake Adams

Jake continues his series on Atlantic stony corals.

Published February 2008, Advanced Aquarist's Online Magazine

© Pomacanthus Publications, LLC

Keywords: Atlantic, Coral, Feature Article, Jake Adams
Link to original article: http://www.advancedaquarist.com/2008/2/aafeature4

Siderastrea is a genus of small polyped stony corals which is also known as starlet coral. The three species are most often colored pale to dark brown but they can be vivid pink or blue in shallow water. In ideal reef conditions *Siderastrea siderea* commonly grows to two feet in diameter and it sometimes grows to twice that size. The genus grows into massive, encrusting or hemispherical shapes.

S. radians is the most durable Siderea species and it perhaps the most extreme stony coral in the Atlantic Ocean. It is the only coral which can be found growing high in the littoral zone, in inter-tidal pools which can experience very high temperatures. Although these colonies are pale and stunted, they still occur at great abundance in these stressful environments. In shallow water, *S. radians* is mostly brown but it can be difficult to distinguish from the similar yet slightly smaller polyp *S. siderea. S. radians* is frequently brought into the aquarium trade on Florida aquacultured live rock.

S. stellata are typically smaller encrusting or hemispherical colonies which occur at intermediate depth. The species has the larger, more recessed corallites of the *Siderea* species. The corallites have a polygonal shape with bright corallite walls, giving the coral a noticeable honeycomb pattern. The species is rarely very large and not very abundant.

S. siderea is largest and most abundant member of the genus. It is more common in shallow water where it will be encrusting to submassive when small and hemispherical when it is large. In some environments it will often develop a brilliant pink or blue color, especially on the side which is receiving the most light. The corallites of *S. siderea* are of intermediate size for the genus, they are slightly recessed and they appear as little pits on the surface of the colony.

Madracis occurs in both the Atlantic and Pacific Oceans and it is represented in the tropical West Atlantic by no fewer than five species. The *Madracis* genus belongs to the Pocilloporid

The reef scene depicts four West Atlantic coral species which are covered in this article: Siderastrea siderea at left, Diploria labyrinthiformis in the middle, Montastrea annularis at right and Diploria strigosa at bottom center. Aldo Croquer.

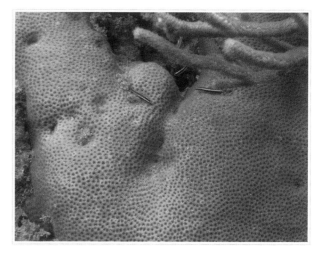

The inch-long neon gobies are frequently seen perching on Siderastrea siderea colonies.

family which makes it closely related to familiar aquarium corals such as *Stylophora* and *Seriatopora*. Like its Pacific counterparts *Madracis* grows into various branching shapes but there are also a few species which are cryptic and encrusting. The polyps are very small and often extended during the day, giving *Madracis* species a fuzzy appearance.

M. mirabilis grows into thin, pale yellow branches which is why it is called yellow pencil coral. In its marginal, deepwater habitat *M. mirabilis* occurs as small isolated patches but it is most abundant in shallow water where it forms large, sometimes extensive monotypic stands. The open nature of the skeleton provides refuge for a host of cryptic and commensal creatures which densely colonize *M. mirabilis* colonies, leaving just a few inches of living tissue at the tips.

M. decactis and *M. formosa* are corals with very similar growth forms but they are identified by minute skeletal features. *M. decactis* is paler in color, usually olive or tan, with short bulbous branches and ten primary septa visible in the corallites. *M. formosa* is darker in color, often dark brown with pale corallite centers and eight primary septa visible in the corallites. *M. formosa* colonies are also larger with broad, slightly flattened branches. Both species co-occur at intermediate to great depths but *M. decactis* is generally more common than *M. formosa*.

FAVIIDS

Favia fragum is a fast growing yet short-lived coral species. The brown, tan or orange colonies are crustose or hemispherical and they rarely grow much larger than a couple of inches across. The polyp mouth is recessed into the skeleton but the corallite itself can be exert from the surrounding skeleton. *F. fragum* goes by the name of golf ball coral and it is can

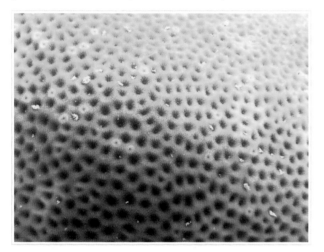

Siderastrea radians has a pitted, uneventful surface.

Under ideal reef conditions Siderastrea siderea can grow to massive sizes. This large spherical colony was over four feet in diameter.

Siderea stellata has a unique honeycomb appearance

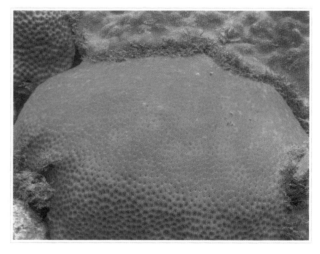

When growing in shallow water Siderastrea siderea can develop very brilliant coloration.

sometimes found growing on Florida aquacultured rock. It can be found in shallow water habitats above about twenty feet and it is particularly abundant in backreefs and other environments with slightly reduced wave action. This coral can resemble small colonies of *Dichocoenia stokesi* but that species has much more exert corallites and more noticeable septa around the corallite walls.

Colpolphyllia natans grows to the largest size of all massive corals in the tropical West Atlantic Ocean. *C. natans* commonly grows to over six feet across with some of the largest individuals reaching twice that size. The surface of the coral colony has wide meandering grooves with darker colored ridges. The skeleton is so porous that it can float once dried out which has led to some archeological confusion in the past when specimens of this species were found far from any

modern tropical coral reefs (Korniker and Squires 1962). This genus is one which was found to have a significant enough divergence from the Faviid family lineage to suggest being placed in a separate family (Fukami et al 2006).

Diploria is an abundant and important reef-building coral genus on West Atlantic reefs. The genus contains only three species which grow into diverse forms but they are easily distinguished based on the size and density of their grooves. Ancient *Diploria* fossil skeletons are the source of the famous Florida Keystone. The three species of *Diplora* co-occur together in all environments but they have separate peaks of abundance based on depth. The long continuous valleys of *Diploria* species most resemble *Leptoria* and Australian *Goniastrea* species which are available in the aquarium trade,

The extended polyps of this Madracis mirabilis make it appear fuzzy. Nate Kwiatek.

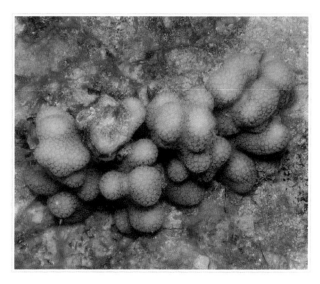

Madracis decactis has somewhat bulbous branch tips.

Madracis mirabilis can form extensive stands in shallow water. Nate Kwiatek.

The branches of Madracis formosa have somewhat flattened ends.

D. clivosa is the least common of the *Diploria* species. It is only found in shallow water habitats above fifteen feet where there is a generous amount of water motion. The color is usually pale brown or olive but very occasionally it can have brilliant green grooves with contrasting dark brown ridges. *D. clivosa* colonies grow encrusting or hemispherical shapes with small, tightly meandering grooves and a knobby irregular surface.

D. labyrinthiformis is a very fleshy species with deep meandering corallite valleys. The width of the corallite valleys varies greatly between specimens but the species is easily recognized by the presence of a noticeable groove on the ridge between the valleys. Even during the day the polyp tentacles are often visible protruding slightly through the narrow valleys. *C. labyrinthiformis* most often grows into hemispherical shapes on the seaward part of reefs. Although the species

can occur at all but the shallowest depths, it is most abundant *Diploria* species on intermediate to deeper reefs. Colors of *D. labyrinthiformis* are most often pale tan, grey or olive with the occasional specimen being pastel yellow or green.

D. strigosa is the most common *Diploria* species on many West Atlantic reef habitats. The species is frequently a dominant coral of shallow water reefs where large hemispherical colonies often grow to over three feet in diameter. The meandering continuous corallite valleys are regular in appearance and evenly spaced. Corallite valleys are mostly perpendicular to the colony edge, often with brightly colored grooves which contrast with the darker colored ridges. *D. strigosa* is a frequent host of *Spirobranchus* featherduster worms and some older colonies become veritable featherduster condominiums. The species is most abundant at shallow to intermediate depths.

Favia fragum rarely grows much larger than the size of the pictured specimen.

C. natans sometimes has exceptionally brilliant color.

This C. natans has a striking pattern.

In shallow, high energy reef environments, D. strigosa often grows into a spherical shape.

Manicina areolata is a Faviid but because of the puffy appearance of the fleshy tissue it often resembles a Mussid. Although this species doesn't usually get much larger than a few inches across, in certain shallow backreef and lagoonal habitats it can occur at densities well above a dozen individuals per square meter. Juvenile Manicina corals begin life as a conical oval shaped polyp which is attached to a substrate by a central stalk. The most common areolata growth form has tighter valleys and it will maintain an elliptical outline with a conical base that can remain attached or become free-living and lying in the substrate. The less common mayori growth form has wider valleys and it grows to a larger size with a flattened underside. Although nearly all Atlantic stony corals are unavailable in the aquarium trade, this species is an exception. Manicina frequently grows out on cultured live rock from the Tampa Bay area and it is available from dealers who request this coral along with their rock. The free living form

of Manicina greatly resembles the common Trachyphyllia coral.

Montastrea is a prominent genus of Atlantic corals which also occurs in the Pacific Ocean. The genus is the second most important contributor to the reef building process after Acropora. The genus contains four recognized species although there is some evidence to suggest that the larger polyped M. cavernosa may comprise more than one species.

M. annularis is a fast growing coral which forms large aggregations of lobed colonies in shallow water. Although the individual lobes of M. annularis are usually no more five to six inches across, the aggregations may form large single species stands. In deeper water the lobes become cylindrical columns with live tissue mostly on the topside of the columns. The surface is relatively smooth overall with the color usually

The common appearance of the narrow-grooved D. clivosa growing in shallow water.

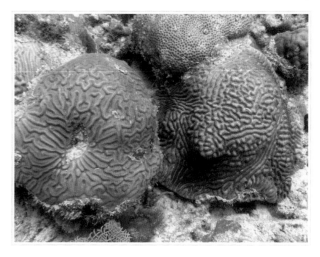
This image taken in shallow water shows D. labyrinthiformis on the left and D. clivosa on the right.

This is an exceptionally brilliant specimen of D. clivosa growing at about 15 feet deep.

This specimen of D. labyrinthiformis has particularly wide grooves.

appearing tan, creamy brown or green. The species was long thought to contain three distinct growth forms but those have since become reclassified into three separate species. The small polyps of *Montastrea* species in the annularis complex can resemble the *Cyphastrea* species of the Pacific Ocean.

M. faveolata is a small polyped *Montastrea* which is common on a wide range of reef habitats but it is most abundant at intermediate depths. The colonies are encrusting or hemispherical when small becoming mound-shaped and plating at the edges when large. Huge, thousand year-old colonies can grow to over a dozen feet across. The surface is mostly smooth, appearing grey or tan, sometimes with bright green or yellow colored polyps.

M. franksi is the deepwater representative of the small polyped *Montastrea* species. *M franksi* usually grows encrusting, hemispherical or plating with a bumpy nodulous surface which is unlike any other *Montastrea* species. The tissue is pale brown or grey overall with irregular, lighter colored patches and orange to reddish polyps. *M. franksi* colonies do not grow to nearly the size of the other *Montastrea* species.

M. cavernosa is the large polyp representative of *Montastrea* in the Atlantic Ocean. The colonies grow into massive boulder or hemispherical shapes at intermediate, becoming increasingly plating with depth. *M. cavernosa* is a highly variable species which occurs in many colors including red, pink, brown and blueish with green, yellow or white polyp interiors. The corallites are strongly exerted from the surrounding skeleton with two distinct forms which have different abundance distributions separated by depth. The small polyped

An exceptionally large D. labyrinthiformis growing at intermediate depth. Aldo Croquer.

D. strigosa frequently hosts featherduster worms and old colonies may accumulate an abundance of them over time.

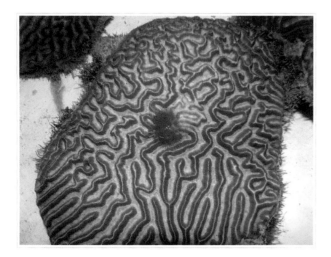

D. strigosa occasionally has beautiful blue meandering corallite valleys.

This image taken in shallow water shows D. clivosa on the left and D. strigosa on the right.

form has cone-shaped corallites, is more abundant in shallow water and it usually has polyps extended during the day. The larger polyp form has button shaped corallites, it is more abundant in deeper water and the polyps are rarely extended during the day. One morphological study found enough differences between the two forms which could not be explained by environmental factors to suggest further investigation into the taxonomic status of the species (Amaral 1994).

The next article will conclude the coverage of West Atlantic corals with the large polyp stony corals and it will also cover the fire corals and some of the non-reefal corals.

REFERENCE:

1. Amaral. F. D. Morphological variation in the reef coral *Montastrea cavernosa* in Brazil. Coral Reefs. Volume 13, Number 2 / May, 1994.

2. Fukami, Hironobu, Ann F. Budd, G. Paulay, A. Solé-Cava, C. Allen Chen, K. Iwao & N. Knowlton. 2004. Conventional taxonomy obscures deep divergence between Pacific and Atlantic corals. Nature 427: 832-835.

3. Humann, Paul and Ned DeLoach. 2002. Reef Coral Identification. New World Publications Inc. Jacksonville, Florida.

These Manicina were both brought into the trade on Florida aquacultured live rock.

A large colony of M. annularis growing in the shallow water of a wave-washed fore-reef

An example of an individual lobe of M. annularis

This huge mound of M. faveolata is not even close to the maximum size of M. faveolata.

A small isolated lobe of colorful M. faveolata.

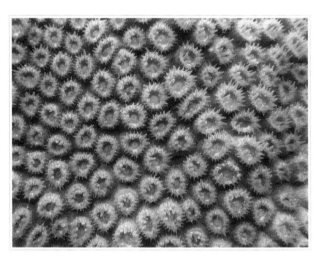

Like most smaller polyped M. cavernosa, this coral has polyps extended during the day.

The irregular surface of this coral identifies it as M. franksi.

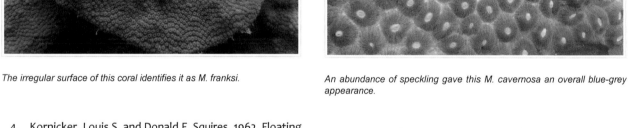

An abundance of speckling gave this M. cavernosa an overall blue-grey appearance.

4. Kornicker, Louis S. and Donald F. Squires. 1962. Floating Corals: A Possible Source of Erroneous Distribution Data. *Limnology and Oceanography*, Vol. 7, No. 4 pp. 447-452

5. Lesser, Michael P., Charles H Mazel, Maxim Y Gorbunov, Paul G Flakowski. 2004. Discovery of nitrogen-fixing bacteria in corals. Science. Vol 305: 995-1000.

6. Wood, Elizabeth. 1983. Corals of the World. T.F.H.

PRODUCT REVIEW

LIGHTING FOR REEF AQUARIA: TIPS ON TAKING LIGHT MEASUREMENTS

By Dana Riddle

Hobbyists using a light-measuring device for the first time will probably be surprised at how rapidly the light field can change within an aquarium.

Published February 2008, Advanced Aquarist's Online Magazine

Keywords: Dana Riddle, Light Meter, Lighting, Product Review, Quantum Meter, Sunlight, UV
Link to original article: http://www.advancedaquarist.com/2008/2/review

Proper lighting is one of several critical parameters in successful reef keeping. If there is not enough light, photosynthetic creatures will slowly perish. On the other hand, many corals (or, more correctly, their symbiotic algae called zooxanthellae) can not tolerate conditions of 'high' light and might not thrive. Excessive light is potentially harmful to symbiotic invertebrates but is also wasteful and needlessly expensive. Many hobbyists and clubs have recognized this and have purchased light-measuring devices and many more are considering a purchase. This article will explain the differences between several of the commonly available 'light' meters and will also examine the pros and cons of each.

Many of the tips listed below are applicable to any sort of light meter.

LUX METERS

'Lux' is an internationally accepted measure of light intensity. Lux meters do not 'see' blue and red light very well, and it is these wavelengths that are most responsible for promoting photosynthesis. They are designed to report light intensity to which the human eye is most sensitive (green light). Maximum lux is about 120,000 (in the tropics at noon on a cloudless day (many lux meters will report lux up to 50,000, making them adequate for many reef aquaria, but unsuitable for brightly lighted tanks and outdoor work).

Many use lux meters for measuring light and although these are better than not taking measurements at all, the preferred method is using a quantum meter (although see **'Converting Lux to PAR'** section later in this article). Lux meters are generally less expensive than PAR meters.

QUANTUM 'LIGHT' METERS

Quantum meters or PAR meters (PAR is an acronym for Photosynthetically Active Radiation) are rather specialized light meters. PAR meters are the preferred method of measuring light within any aquarium containing things that photosynthesize whether they are corals, anemones, freshwater plants, etc. This is because the PAR meter can sense and report light ('photons' or 'quanta') that is responsible for promoting photosynthesis. Technically, this is described as those light wavelengths that are between 400 nanometers (nm) and 700nm. PAR, or Photosynthetic Photon Flux Density (PPFD) is reported in units of 'micro-Einsteins per square meter per second' ($\mu E \cdot m^2 \cdot sec$) or 'micro-Mol per square meter per second ($\mu Mol \cdot m^2 \cdot sec$). Either term is acceptable, and they are equivalent to each other (i.e., 1 $\mu E \cdot m^2 \cdot sec$ = $\mu Mol \cdot m^2 \cdot sec$); however, $\mu Mol \cdot m^2 \cdot sec$ seems to have gained wider acceptance over the last few years.

Maximum PAR value (in the tropics at noon on a cloudless day) is 2,000 - 2,200 $\mu Mol \cdot m^2 \cdot sec$).

Quantum meters were once very expensive, with the most inexpensive units selling for ~$1,200. This is no longer the case, with decent meters selling for under $300.

There are a couple of quantum meters I can recommend. A 'laboratory grade' quantum meter (model LI-250A equipped with an underwater cosine-corrected sensor - LI-192) is built by Li-Cor (Lincoln, Nebraska). The meter (weather-proof but not submersible) and underwater sensor are rugged and will stand up to harsh conditions in the field. The meter can be calibrated for 'air' or 'water' readings (due to an optical property called the 'immersion effect'). There are some drawbacks - the meter and sensor combination is relatively expensive (>$1,100). The sensor itself (the body is made of brass) is large and does not lend itself to work in smaller aquaria. Li-Cor also offers a second sensor option for underwater light measurements - the spherical LI-193. Its appearance is similar to that of a light bulb, and this sensor can collect light from all angles. This sensor would be the best choice for those wanting to measure light intensity in micro-algae cultures.

It is truly a world-class instrument and is used by coral researchers around the globe and the best bet for those with exacting needs and/or really large aquaria. The spectral or quantum response is excellent.

Li-Cor also offers a datalogger capable of storing months of information (model LI-1400), but it is difficult to imagine the usefulness of this instrument to the majority of hobbyists. Note that all Li-Cor meters are capable of measuring very high PAR intensity - 20,000 µMol·m²·sec (almost a magnitude greater than the most intense sunlight!).

Perhaps the best alternative is the quantum meter made by Apogee Instruments (Logan, Utah). The sensor is submersible (the meter itself is not!) and comes with a standard cable measuring about 6 feet in length. Custom cord lengths are available at additional cost. The Apogee's price is well below that of the Li-Cor meter, making it attractive to advanced

hobbyists (clubs may want to consider its purchase, thus making it available to many).

The Apogee meter's construction is not as stout as that of the Li-Cor, but its cosine-corrected sensor is small and made of relatively inert anodized aluminum and plastic. The Apogee meter is limited in its measurement range - it reports PAR intensity up to 1,999 µMol·m²·sec, and the sensor's spectral response is not as good as that of the Li-Cor sensor. However, its measurements compare favorably with that of the Li-Cor meter and are accurate enough for the sort of measurements we'll make in aquaria. In short, the Apogee meter will likely be the meter of choice for most. All Apogee meter/sensor combinations retail for less than $300.

HOW TO TAKE MEASUREMENTS

A quality sensor will be 'cosine-corrected', meaning that it can effectively collect light from low angles with good efficiency. However, this does not mean that the sensor should be held in a position other than straight up. A sensor held in the vertical position will help ensure that accurate measurements are made.

HOW TO MAKE A SENSOR HOLDER

Making a holder for your PAR sensor has several advantages. As most hobbyists know, it is best to avoid putting your hands in the aquarium - some corals don't like it, and some corals don't like you! It allows putting the sensor into spots too small for a hand and also allows better visuals on sensor positioning.

A holder for your sensor does not need to be elaborate. Over the years, my holders have evolved and become simpler and easier to transport and use. It is also very inexpensive (<$10) to make (See Figure 2 for a photo of the completed assembly).

Here's the parts list:

- 1 - Length of ½" CPVC pipe (usually sold in lengths of 10 feet)

- 2 - 1" diameter ceramic magnets

- 2 - ½" CPVC 90° elbows (a fitting called a 'wing 90' offers more surface area, and is shown in Figure 2)

- 1 - fine-point Sharpie pen

- SuperGlue (for permanent attachment) or aquarium-safe silicone cement (allows for future removal, if necessary).

Figure 1. A relatively inexpensive PAR meter.

Although a bolt can be used to attach the sensor to a 'leveling plate', it is less expensive and more convenient to

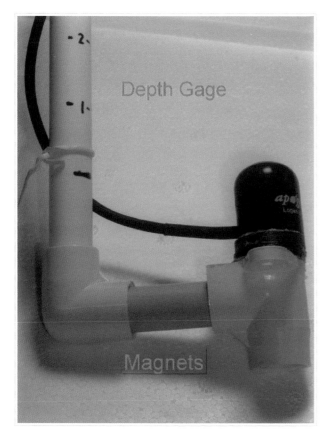

Figure 2. An inexpensive and easily constructed sensor holder.

use magnets as a holdfast to the measuring rod. Use your choice of glue to attach a magnet to the 90° fitting. Also glue a magnet to the bottom of the sensor.

Once assembled, mark the rod in increments of 1 inch from the bottom up with the Sharpie or other indelible pen. This will serve as your depth gage.

Bear in mind that couplings are available to allow unusually long measuring rods to be 'broken down' for easy transport.

EFFECTS OF TEMPERATURE

Temperature will *usually* have an insignificant effect on PAR readings. Sensors are generally calibrated at a given temperature (20 °C, or 68 °F) and temperature below this point will cause a very small (~0.1% per °C) 'low' reading. In the same vein, 'warm' temperatures will cause 'high' readings. Operating temperature of the meter/sensor combination is limited by the sensor's temperature tolerance (usually up to 55°C, or 131°F).

SENSOR CLEANING

Any fouling on the sensor lens could cause inaccurate measurements, so, obviously, the lens should be kept clean. We usually pride ourselves on our water quality management skills, but aquaria without overflows (such as sumps and refugia) may have a nearly invisible oily surface film that can coat and build up on the lens.

Use only a mild detergent and water along with an 'optical' quality paper for cleaning. Vinegar can be used to dissolve 'hard water' deposits. Blot the sensor dry in order to avoid 'fogging' or scratching the lens. Avoid petroleum or other 'strong' solvents and abrasive cleaners - these can damage the sensor's lens and ruin it!

RE-CALIBRATION

PAR meters and their sensors should be routinely re-calibrated. Apogee and Li-Cor recommend recalibration every 2 years. This is done at the factory for a nominal fee.

CONVERTING LUX TO PAR

If you have a lux meter, it is possible to convert lux to PAR. Since spectral quality plays a part in these conversions, each light source (actinic lamp, 6,500K metal halide, etc.) will have a difference factor. The equation is:

$$\text{Lux} \div \text{Constant} = \mu\text{mol·m2·sec}$$

CORAL LIGHT REQUIREMENTS

Although we generally think of corals as originating from brightly lighted natural reefs and naturally assume corals need lots of light, the truth is that most corals require

Lux to PAR Conversion Factors

Light Source	Constant
Sunlight	54
Warm White Fluorescent	76
Cool White Fluorescent	74
URI (now UV) Actinic Fluorescent	18
URI (now UV) Daylight Fluorescent	54
Actinic/Daylight Combination	38
Philips 03 Actinic Fluorescent	40
Panasonic 6,700°K Power Compact	72
Panasonic 7,100°K / 6,700°K Combination	55
Osram Powerstar Metal Halide	57
Ushio 10,000°K Metal Halide	54
Coralife 10,000°K Metal Halide	30
Venture "Daylight" Metal Halide	46
Radium "Blue" Metal Halide	51
Fusion Sulfur Lamp	41
Westron Mercury Vapor Lamp	70
Iwasaki 6,500°K Metal Halide	57

relatively little in order to thrive. For example, the 'Fox' coral (*Nemezophyllia* sp.) does quite well in low light. Thriving specimens have been noted in as little light as 35 µMol·m²·sec! On the other hand, an *Acropora* specimen (commonly called the 'Purple Monster') displayed magnificent coloration in the highest light intensity I have ever measured in an aquarium - almost 900 µMol·m²·sec (later research reveal that this coral photo-saturates at 300-400 µMol·m²·sec. I was wasting a lot of light and money!). Most corals will grow quite well in light intensities of 200-300 µMol·m²·sec.

CONTACT INFORMATION

See these sites for further information:

- www.apogeelighting.com

- www.licor.com

Have questions? Have PAR/lux data you'd like to share? Contact me at RiddleLabs@aol.com, and I'll get a response to you as soon as possible.

IN CLOSING

Hobbyists using a light-measuring device for the first time will probably be surprised at how rapidly the light field can change within an aquarium (especially when using a point-source lamp such as metal halides. Stay cool - this is normal!). And it will become apparent that aquaria are not so bright (when compared to 'outdoor' measurements), and our rooms are actually very dimly lighted!

POST SCRIPT

The Marine Aquarium Conference of North America will be hosted by the Atlanta Reef Club in September 2008. You're missing out if you don't attend! See www.masna.org for details.

FEATURE ARTICLE

CORAL COLORATION AND INCIDENT LIGHT: A PHOTOGRAPHIC ESSAY

By Ken S. Feldman, Sanjay Joshi, Lauren F. Vernese, Elizabeth A. Huber, Kelly M. Maers, Matthew R. Test

Departments of Chemistry and Industrial and Manufacturing Engineering, The Pennsylvania State University, University Park, PA 16802

Published March 2008, Advanced Aquarist's Online Magazine

Keywords: Coloration, Coral, Elizabeth A. Huber, Feature Article, Kelly M. Maers, Ken S. Feldman, Lauren F. Vernese, Matthew R. Test, Sanjay Joshi
Link to original article: http://www.advancedaquarist.com/2008/3/aafeature1

INTRODUCTION

Viewing a reef tank as "kinetic art" has sensitized many aquarists to the complex multifactoral relationships between a host of tank parameters and the color of corals, particularly small polyped scleractinians (SPS's). Nowhere does this issue arouse more debate and more passion than on the topic of light. In no small part, the evolution of aquarium lighting sources has driven the successes experienced by numerous aquarists in sustaining captive acropora, montipora, etc. This evolution has been fueled by the introduction of metal halide light sources characterized by Kelvin ratings up to 20K, and more recently by the availability of high-output fluorescent bulbs (called T5 bulbs) with a range of spectral signatures. This broad palette of lighting options has been embraced by the contemporary reefkeeping community, and spectacular tableaus of colorful SPS's have been achieved under a variety of lighting conditions. The lack of a single unique lighting solution has led to the inevitable comparisons/debate about the relative merits of 10K vs. 14K vs. 20K metal halide bulbs, inter alia, as well as much animated discussion on the related topic of metal halide vs. T5-based lighting solutions.

Discussion and debate have their place, but in the absence of hard data, it is difficult to resolve anything. It should be possible experimentally to test directly the effect of T5 vs. 10K MH vs. 20K MH lighting on a given coral's coloration. In order to gain useful information from this type of experiment, it is important to define the variables involved, identify the constant elements, and arrive at a meaningful measure of experimental output. With these thoughts as background, we set out to probe the following question:

How does the observed color of an SPS coral vary as per the type of lighting used to grow it?

The whole concept of coral coloration impinges on many different areas of science, from the molecular genetics of corals, to the physical chemistry of light absorption by pigment molecules, to optics, visual perception, and finally to camera/computer graphics. Events at each of these levels impacts on the color the viewer perceives when observing the coral or examining a photographic representation of a coral. Corals produce a multitude of colored molecules, mostly but not exclusively proteins, in response to a variety of stimuli. The relationship between stimulus and colored molecule (protein) expression is a matter of speculation at present, and the control/regulatory elements that presumably operate at the genetic level have yet to be elucidated. Hypotheses spanning the gamut from offensive functions (i.e., light gathering antennas) to defensive capabilities (i.e., sunscreens) have been discussed, and there is no decisive evidence at present to discourage any of these lines of thinking. Salih et al. generated much interest by reporting data that they interpreted as being consistent with the sunscreen hypothesis, particularly for GFP (Green Fluorescent Protein) in *Acropora palifera*, *Acropora nobilis*, *Pocillopora damicornis*, and *Goniastrea retiformis* from shallow water at the great Barrier Reef, Australia (Salih, 2000). However, this conclusion was challenged by Mazel, who did not find any support for the idea that GFP modulated in any way the quantity of light reaching the zooxanthellae of *Montastraea cavernosa* and *Montastraea faveolata* (Mazel, 2003a). Schlichter described observations consistent with the antenna hypothesis, where fluorescent proteins appear to aid in converting photosynthetically unusable incident light into wavelengths readily absorbed by the zooxanthellae's photosynthetic reaction centers (Schlichter, 1985). Finally, Fabricius recently has reported that lighter colored corals absorb less infrared radiation, which contributes to coral heating, than darker colored corals (Fabricius, 2006). This observation might be interpreted in terms of enhancing or suppressing thermal bleaching of the coral, depending upon the darkness of the color. Riddle has detailed the UV/VIS (UltraViolet/VISible) characterization of many coral coloration proteins, and his latest article is an excellent source of contemporary thinking on this topic, along with leading references (Riddle, 2007b). In addition to the coloration molecules produced by the coral itself, the symbiotic zooxanthellae, of course, contribute a golden brown color largely as a consequence of reflectance from the pigment peridinin (Hochberg, 2006).

The color of a coral that is perceived by a viewer is a combination of incident light, reflected light and re-emitted light (fluorescence) from the coral under observation. The reflected light does not interact productively with any coral molecules, and so the coral surface acts essentially like a mirror reflecting selective wavelengths of light. Therefore, the wavelengths (colors) contained within the incident light play a dominant role in the color of this reflected light. For example, a bulb shifted toward the blue end of the spectrum (i.e., 20K) lacks a large component of red light, and so any object reflecting 20K bulb light will appear biased toward the blue end of the color spectrum by virtue of this red light deficiency. Re-emitted light (fluorescence emission) does involve a molecular-level interaction between the light particles (photons) and a receptor molecule in the coral. Coral coloration molecules are capable of absorbing light at a specific spectral range of wavelengths, and this absorption has two consequences: (1) it removes from the reflected light those absorbed wavelengths (colors), and (2) it opens the possibility of fluorescence emission. Fluorescence results from a re-emission of light from the coral coloration molecule at a longer wavelength (shifted away from the blue and toward the red end of the color spectrum). The energy drop between the absorbed photons and the emitted photons is a consequence of the loss of excited state energy via molecular vibrations, a process well studied within the discipline of physical chemistry. Thus, a given coral coloration molecule may absorb blue light but emit green light through this fluorescence mechanism. Typical fluorescent efficiencies, as defined by (fluorescent) photons emitted-per-available incident photons, range from 3% - 10% (Mazel, 2003b). Mazel and Fuchs have attempted to quantify the amount of the fluorescent component in the observed light from the strongly fluorescent corals Agaricia sp., Colpophyllia natans, Diploria labyrinthiformis, Montastraea cavernosa, Montastraea faveolata, and Scolymia sp. (Mazel, 2003). Their estimates for the fluorescent component at a 2-meter depth range from 7% - 30% depending upon the precise fluorescence efficiency and the spectral properties of the coral coloration molecule(s). There are other mechanisms by which light might interact with corals to produce wavelength-shifted emitted light, including phosphorescence and diffraction, but the contribution of these processes to coral coloration is not clear at present. Overall, the perceived coral color will depend on a blend of reflected light (incident light absent absorbed wavelengths) and fluorescence emissions, if applicable. A good discussion of light and color can be found in the series of articles in Reefkeeping entitled "Facts of Light" (Joshi, 2006); see also Fenit (Fenit, 2005).

Color rendition by electronic devices is a complicated topic well outside the scope of this article. It is important to recognize, however, that all color rendition schemes involve compromises between the "true" color of an object and the "calculated" color depicted, whether by a camera, computer, or display device. In fact, software processing of an object's color through multiple devices may lead to even greater deviations from true color. Some details of the color processing procedure used with the images in this article, and color correction using the Gretag-MacBeth color checker technique employed herein, are provided below. A good starting point for further reading can be found in: http://www.cambridgeincolour.com/tutorials.htm.

The idea that the wavelength (color) of the light under which a coral has grown can influence some characteristic of the coral is not new. Kinzie and later Schlacher both have probed specific hypotheses is this general area of coral research. Seminal studies by Kinzie assessed coral skeletal growth rates under the influence of blue, red, green, and white growth lights for both Montipora verrucosa and Pocillopora damicornis (Kinzie, 1984). They concluded that these corals grew fastest under blue light, followed closely by white light, then green light, and finally the slowest growth was observed under red light. They followed up this study by measuring photosynthesis rates of Montipora verrucosa under these same lighting conditions (Kinzie, 1987). Once again, the highest photosynthesis rates were achieved under blue light; slightly lower but similar rates were observed for corals grown under both white light and green light, followed distantly by photosynthesis rates under red light. More recently, Schlacher et al. examined growth rates of Acropora solitaryensis under 150W metal halide bulbs rated at 5.5K, 10K, 14K, and 20K color temperatures (Schlacher, 2007). After 3 months of grow-out, the overall growth rates under the different bulbs were quite distinct: 6.2 mg/day at 5.5K, 4.9 mg/day at 10K, 8.5 mg/day at 14K, and 10.9 mg/day at 20K. Thus, the bulbs delivering the highest proportion of blue light (20K and 14K) promoted the highest growth rates. One concern clouds the interpretation of these results; the authors positioned all of the bulbs at the same height above the corals, leading to significant differences in the measured Photosynthetic Photon Flux Density (PPFD) delivered to the coral from each of these lamps. For example, the PPFD of the 20K lamp at the 400-450 nm spectral range of chlorophyll absorption is about 7.5 times greater than the PPFD of the 5.5K lamp at this same spectral range. The significance of these photon quantity differences on growth rate, independent of overall bulb "color", remains to be determined. The relationship between incident light color and consequent coral coloration, the topic of this essay, was considered by Riddle (Riddle, 2003). Using a brown Pocillopora meandrina as a test case, coral coloration was visually assayed after exposure of this SPS to focused light from either blue, red, green, yellow, or ultraviolet LED's over a period of greater than 7 weeks. The coral section irradiated by the blue LED turned from brown to pink, whereas the other colored lights either had no effect, or promoted coral bleaching. This limited investigation led to some intriguing speculation about the connection between growth light and coral color, and it sets the stage for the more extensive studies described below.

EXPERIMENTAL DESIGN

The experiment was designed as follows: Three 10-gallon tanks were set up to hold coral fragments on eggcrate. These tanks were connected in series along with an Eheim canister filter containing live rock. The Eheim filter provides the motive force to circulate water among the three tanks, at a rate of approximately 1 turnover of the 30-gallon system volume every 3 hrs. A Phosban reactor charged with granular activated carbon (GAC) and phosban was installed for water purification. The GAC/phosban was changed every 3 weeks. A Remora skimmer completed the water purification apparatus, and an Ebo Jagger heater and Tunze osmolator held the system temperature and the system water level, respectively, constant. For circulation, each tank was equipped with a Maxijet 1200 feeding a spray bar set just under the waterline. Livestock consisted of nothing more than a few turbo and astrea snails and a peppermint shrimp, per tank. This setup equalized all of the other parameters among the three tanks, such as water quality, water temperature, water flow, salt, trace elements, etc., and isolated the light source as the only variable affecting coral coloration.

Weekly additions of alkalinity (Two Little Fishes solution B) and calcium ($CaCl_2 \cdot 2H_2O$) were employed to maintain the levels of the former at 2.4-2.9 meq/L and the later at 350 - 400 ppm. Magnesium ($MgCl_2 \cdot 6H_2O + MgSO_4 \cdot 7H_2O$) was added occasionally as needed to maintain the Mg level at 1250 - 1300 ppm. A 5-gallon water change was conducted weekly, and the tanks were fed cyclopeeze, oyster eggs and Salifert Amino Acids on a weekly basis as well.

Three approximately equal sized 0.25 - 0.5 inch frags from 6 different montipora and 5 different acropora parent colonies were cut, glued onto Aragacrete frag plugs, and placed on the eggcrate in each tank. By this protocol, each tank had one frag from each unique coral specimen. The frags from each parent colony were placed in the same locations in each of the tanks so the frags from each unique coral should experience the same, or at least very similar, light exposure and water flow. Above one tank was placed a 20K 175W XM single-ended metal halide bulb; a second tank was illuminated with a 10K 175W XM single-ended metal halide bulb, and the third tank was topped with a Tek Light fixture featuring 4 x 24W T5 bulbs (2 x 24W Aquasun VHO's in the exterior positions, 1 JALLI 10000K, and 1 AB actinic blue in the interior positions). The MH bulbs were situated in Spider reflectors, and small muffin fans were used to cool the tanks. No UV shielding was positioned between the bulbs and the tank.

Note that T5 (fluorescent) bulbs do not produce significant light in the UV-A region of the spectrum (Riddle, 2007a). Likewise, the single-ended MH bulbs used in this experiment have adequate shielding in the UV-A region as a consequence of their borosilicate glass housings. In contrast, many double-ended MH bulbs do produce significant quantities of UV-A light, but the effects of this higher energy light on coral coloration are beyond the scope of these experiments. The tanks were separated by opaque white posterboard to prevent cross-contamination of light sources. With this arrangement, the tank temperature fluctuated from 76 °F (lights off) to 80 °F (lights on) over the course of 24 hours; the irradiation

Figure 1. Left-hand view (top) and right-hand view (bottom) of three interconnected tanks for coral frag growout; the left tank is irradiated at 20K, the middle tank at 10K, and the right tank is under T5 lighting. The opaque dividers that separated the tanks were removed for these photographs.

period lasted 8 hours/day. The height of each of the lights was adjusted to provide a constant amount of PAR at the coral level, measured by an Apogee Quantum Meter; the initial height settings of the lights delivered about 140 - 160 mE/m^2 of light intensity, but unsatisfactory coloration in this nutrient poor environment prompted the elevation of these bulbs so that the PAR readings at the corals were about 80 - 100 mE/m^2. These readings were taken at the center of the tanks, directly under the MH or T5 bulbs. Therefore, not every coral received the same amount of light, as the intensity drops off as distance from the center increases. Nevertheless, identical placement of each type of coral in the three tanks ensured, at the very least, that the light intensity for each type of coral was approximately equal between the two MH tanks, with some uncertainty in the amount of intensity variance between the MH tanks and the T5 tank. Note that this approach normalizes the PPFD, in contrast to the Schlacher experiment. The corals were grown under these conditions for 14 months. All bulbs were replaced after 12 months of continuous use. The experimental setup is illustrated in Figure 1.

The corals colored up and grew at appreciable rates under this experimental regimen. Photography was used to provide a visual comparison of the frag coloration from each of the tanks. A Nikon D80 camera equipped with a 105 mm Macro lens was mounted on a tripod for the photography. These pictures were taken in RAW mode through the (cleaned) front glass of the tanks, without flash. Thus, the tank lighting itself provided the only illumination for the photographs. In order to ensure that accurate colors are portrayed, color correction via white balancing was employed in the photograph workup. A Gretag-MacBeth color checker was used to regularize the white balance setting (details are given below). In addition, the computer monitor (Apple MacBook Pro) used to perform these color corrections was color calibrated using the native color calibration software provided. The corals were allowed to grow out over the course of 14 months. At that time, their colors appeared to have stabilized, and there was visible and often substantial new growth in each of the

frags. At that point in time, the coral frags were photographed, and these photographs are presented below.

RESULTS

WHITE BALANCING VIA THE GRETAG-MACBETH COLOR CHECKER

The Gretag-MacBeth color checker illustrated in Fig. 2 is the standard used for white balancing in the photography industry. As an illustration of the methodology, Fig. 2 (left) shows the color checker photographed in sunlight using the automatic white balancing function of the Nikon D80 camera. Fig. 2 (middle) captures the same checker, illuminated by sunlight, taken in RAW mode. Fig. 2 (right) demonstrates how Adobe Photoshop (CS3) can be used to "correct" the color of the 2 (middle) photograph by adjusting the color scheme. Since these photographs were taken under a light source for which the camera's software is optimized, there is little difference between Fig. 2 (left) and Fig. 2 (right). In fact, the color squares of the Gretag-Macbeth color checker have standard hue values accepted by the photography profession, and so the degree of color "accuracy" can be quantified. Both the Gretag-MacBeth color scheme and the color settings used by Adobe Photoshop3 adhere to the sRGB scale. Each color utilized by Photoshop (or displayed in the color checker) is composed of a mixture of red, green, and blue primary colors ranging in intensity from 0 (= black) to 255 (= white). The scale is set up such that if RGB = 0/0/0, the displayed color is black, and if RGB = 255/255/255, the displayed color is white. If all three RGB intensity values are equal, the result is a shade of gray. The official color "red", as an example, is composed of a red intensity of 175, a green intensity of 54, and a blue intensity of 60 (Table 1, line 1, column 2), whereas yellow (not a primary color) is more of a blend: 231/199/31 (Table 1, line 5, column 2). For photographs 2 (left) - 2 (right), values spanning a representative suite of colors are shown in Table 1. Whereas there is some variance between the official hue designations and the processed colors, these differences are rather minor and almost imperceptible to the human eye.

Figure 2. The Gretag-MacBeth color checker white balance correction for photography under sunlight. Left: the camera-auto white balanced file. Middle: the uncorrected RAW file. Right: the corrected colors in the processed picture file.

Unlike photography under sunlight, pictures taken under high-Kelvin tank lighting conditions present significant challenges for most cameras, as the photo processing software is not designed to handle such blue-biased lighting. This problem has been discussed extensively elsewhere (Rothschild, 2005). While white balancing in Photoshop via the color checker may be an imperfect solution, there appears to be no better option for eliminating the biases of color adjustment. Fig. 3 illustrates the outcome of white balancing in the most difficult case, 20K incident light. Similarly, Figs. 4 and 5 present the optimized color corrections realized under the 10K bulb and the T5 bulbs, respectively. A quantitative representation of these corrections is displayed in Table 2. It is evident that the corrected colors differ from the accepted colors by greater margins with the aquarium lighting, especially under the 20K bulbs, than with sunlight as the light source.

One approach to quantifying the differences between the corrected color values and the true values is shown in Fig. 6. In these graphs, the accepted intensity values for all hues (and colors within hues) listed in Table 2 were plotted on the X-axis against the corrected values on the Y-axis. In the ideal case of perfect color correction, the correlation lines between these two sets of data will have a slope of 1.00, and the scatter of the data, as represented by the r^2 value, would be negligible (r^2 approaches 1.00). In practice, these criteria for success are met best by the T5 color correction, and least by the 20K color correction. The 20K color correction in general tends to significantly underestimate the red intensities overall (slope = 0.77), but that underrepresentation is partially compensated by an enhancement of the green channel (slope = 1.23). Simply increasing the red intensity and/or decreasing the green intensity in the color correction process leads to obviously false color images. The difficulty with color correcting the light from the 20K lamps may be due to the fact that these lamps are not true 20K lamps and lie far off the black body curve used to determine the color temperature of the bulbs (Joshi 2006) Nevertheless, these corrections are the best available, and they will be applied to the coral photographs presented below.

ACROPORA PHOTOGRAPHS

Five acropora species were fragged and grown out as described in the Experimental section. The origins of the coral are indicated, and all five corals are given a provisional species identification. This identification should be considered tentative, and typically was provided by the vendor. Correct species identification would be greatly appreciated and

Table 1. Color (hue) comparisons via the Gretag-MacBeth color checker. The data are reported as Red/Green/Blue values.

color	accepted hue	Fig. 2 (left) hue	Fig. 2 (middle) hue	Fig. 2 (right) hue
red	175/54/60	225/74/67	216/99/89	218/100/86
blue	56/61/150	18/71/213	4/74/195	14/77/190
green	70/148/73	109/198/130	133/193/121	136/194/118
purple	94/60/108	110/69/135	104/79/136	107/80/131
yellow	231/199/31	255/230/76	255/236/115	255/236/107
white	243/243/242	255/255/255	252/253/255	253/253/253
medium gray	160/160/160	161/164/171	157/160/167	160/161/163
black	52/52/52	50/51/55	56/57/61	61/63/62

Figure 3. The Gretag-MacBeth color checker white balance correction for photography under 20K MH 175W XM bulbs. Left: the uncorrected RAW file. Right: the corrected colors in the processed picture file.

should be forwarded to the authors. In each case, a photograph of the parent colony in one of the author's aquariums is provided. Four of these five parent colony photos were taken with a Canon PowerShot S500 point-and-shoot camera with automatic white balancing, whereas the fifth (*A. carduus*) was captured with a Nikon D80, again with automatic white balancing. Both growth light and photography light for these parent colonies was provided by 10K 400W XM bulbs.

Figure 4. The Gretag-MacBeth color checker white balance correction for photography under 10K MH 175W XM bulbs. Left: the uncorrected RAW file. Right: the corrected colors in the processed picture file.

Figure 5. The Gretag-MacBeth color checker white balance correction for photography under T5 24W bulbs. Left: the uncorrected RAW file. Right: the corrected colors in the processed picture file.

Table 2. The result of color (hue) correction, via the Gretag-MacBeth color checker, of the 20K, 10K, and T5 bulbs. The data are reported as Red/Green/Blue values.

color	accepted hue	20K hue (Fig. 3)	10K hue (Fig. 4)	T5 hue (Fig. 5)
Red	175/54/60	171/85/94	190/70/79	188/84/59
blue	56/61/150	117/0/237	85/64/180	53/33/157
green	70/148/73	119/190/127	132/180/99	95/168/63
purple	94/60/108	117/5/178	109/75/127	98/56/120
yellow	231/199/31	233/232/106	245/224/110	242/226/43
white	243/243/242	229/238/255	246/246/246	237/237/237
medium gray	160/160/160	180/173/230	187/187/187	178/178/180
black	52/52/52	49/43/79	52/52/52	45/45/45

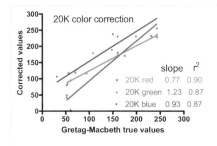
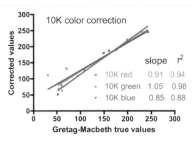
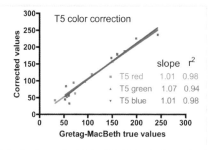

Figure 6. Graphical representation of the fidelity of the Gretag-MacBeth color checker-based corrections for the three different light sources, using the data for the colors listed in Table 2.

1. A. CARDUUS (FIG. 7)

An aquacultured "baby blue bottlebrush" was purchased from Atlantis Aquarium and tentatively identified as *A. carduus* by one of the authors. Under 10K 400W XM lighting, the mother colony remained largely beige in color, with a slight hint of blue when viewed from the top. When viewed under either 10K or T5 lighting, the frags of this coral grown under any of the experimental lights appeared uniformly beige, much like the parent colony. However, when viewed under 20K lighting, the frag grown under 20K irradiation, uniquely, did appear to have a slight greenish tinge, especially near the base growth area. The frags grown under either 10K or T5 lighting did not display this faint color when viewed under 20K light. Thus, this observation is consistent with a scenario wherein 20K growth light actually induces the production of a green coral coloration molecule, but that same pigment is not induced when the coral is grown under either 10K or T5 lighting.

2. ACROPORA INSIGNUS (FIG. 8)

This aquacultured coral was purchased from Pacific East Aquaculture as a small colony. It appeared to be light blue with darker blue corallites when grown under 10K lighting. In the experimental tanks, it never achieved this blue color, but it did take on a greenish cast. All frags under a given photography lighting appeared to be colored identically. When viewed under either T5 or 10K lighting, the green color was barely perceptible. However, when viewed under 20K lighting, all frags, irrespective of the specific growth light, displayed a bright green pigment (GFP??). Thus, this coral appears to be an example of a case where the higher temperature lighting is necessary to bring out the striking green color, but the coral coloration molecule that is responsible for this hue is present under all three growth lights.

3. ACROPORA HOEKSEMAI (FIG. 9)

This aquacultured *Acropora hoeksemai* was purchased from Atlantis Aquarium. It exhibited the typical blue-purple coloration seen in many hoeksemai specimens imported over the past several years, although the parent colony picture below does not do it justice. In the frag propagation tanks, this rich blue-purple color was never duplicated under any of the lighting conditions. In addition, the incident light frequency had no demonstrable effect on the coral's coloration. All three frags photographed under 20K light exhibited a vibrant greenish-yellow tint. Similarly, each frag set under either 10K or T5 lighting appeared identical, and furthermore, there was little difference between the hoeksemai frags' color when viewed under either of these light sources. In these 10K- and T5-illuminated photographs, the coral frags appeared to be a uniform golden-brown with a hint of green tint. Thus, the coral coloration molecules of this species are present/induced under all of the three lighting regimens. However, the viewing light has a profound influence on the perceived color, and 20K lighting clearly provides the most captivating colors.

4. ACROPORA SARMENTOSA (FIG. 10)

This *Acropora sarmentosa* was purchased as a wild colony from Reefer Madness. The parent colony photograph shown below was taken just after purchase, and the colors are somewhat muted from the shipping ordeal. Upon fragging and grow-out in the propagation tanks, the coloration story with this species is similar to that described above for the *A. hoeksemai*. There is no visual evidence that growth light frequency has any influence on the coral's coloration. The frags appeared to be identically colored under a given photography lighting scheme, and it is only the viewing light that matters in any material way. Once again, the 20K lighting scheme provided specimens with the most pronounced and vibrant colors. In this case, the full richness of the green is apparent. As these frags grew out further, the characteristic pink tips of the sarmentosa appeared as well (not shown). The specimens photographed under both 10K and T5 lighting

all appeared identical, with just a sheen of the green color observed under the 20K lighting. Once again, viewing lighting, and not growth lighting, makes the difference.

5. ACROPORA MILLEPORA (FIG. 11)

The aquacultured *Acropora millepora* recruited for this study was purchased from Phishy Business. Its color was not stable in its home tank, and over an approximately 1.5 year period it went through several color changes. It initially arrived as a "bubblegum" pink colony, but that color faded to peach as the coral grew. In addition, the new growth of the encrusting base, but not the growth tips, was green! Eventually, the

Figure 7. Acropora carduus: Parent colony under 10K lighting, 20K (top), 10K (middle), T5 (bottom).

Figure 8. Acropora insignus: parent colony under 10K lighting, 20K (top), 10K (middle), T5 (bottom).

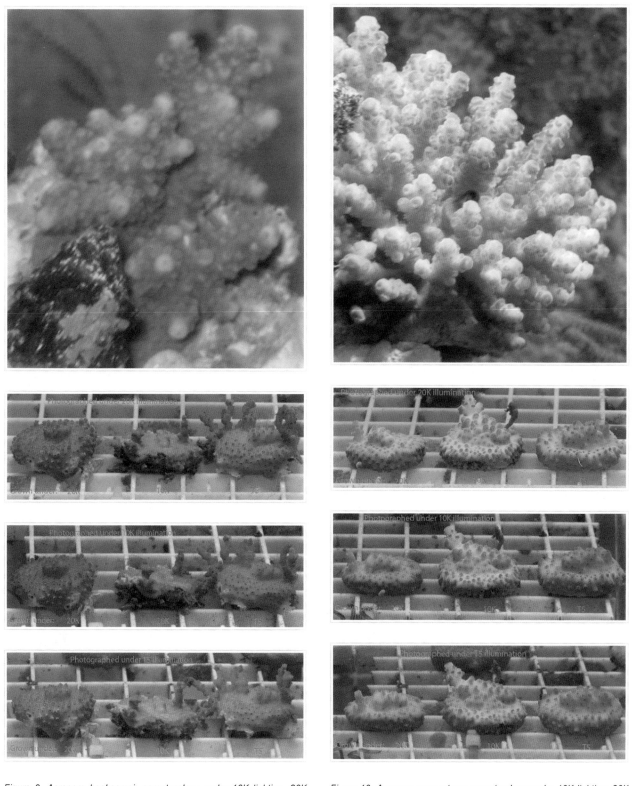

Figure 9. Acropora hoeksemai: parent colony under 10K lighting, 20K (top), 10K (middle), T5 (bottom).

Figure 10. Acropora sarmentosa: parent colony under 10K lighting, 20K (top), 10K (middle), T5 (bottom).

overall peach color morphed into a rust red-brown. The environmental stimuli that drove these changes are unknown; reaction with molecular oxygen ("oxidation") has been cited in pigment color shifts (called "kindling"), and it is possible that slow protein oxidation plays a role in these shifts (Riddle, 2007b). The photograph of the parent colony shown below depicts this coral in its "peach" phase. True to its behavior in its home tank, the frags grown out under the different illumination conditions did shown color sensitivity to the growth light frequency. When viewed under 20K lighting, the frag grown out under 20K illumination had a peach colored body, green growth tips, and a distinct purple cast to the

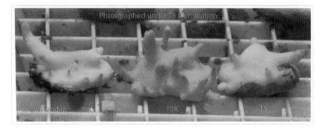

Figure 11. Acropora millepora: parent colony under 10K lighting, 20K (top), 10K (middle), T5 (bottom).

Figure 12. Montipora digitata (orange): 20K (top), 10K (middle), T5 (bottom).

growth edge of its base. In contrast, the 10K-growth/20K-photographed frag expressed the peach body color/green growth rim seen in the parent colony during one of its early phases. The frag grown out under T5 lighting and visualized under 20K lighting was different again: a green body with a purple growth rim. The color variations observed under both 10K and T5 lighting were much less dramatic. Under 10K photographic illumination, all corals appeared as mainly beige-peach, but the one frag grown under 10K lighting had unique and distinct green growth areas at its burgeoning tips and the rim of its base. When viewed under T5 lighting, all frags appeared similarly beige-peach, and the green growth rim of the 10K-grown specimen was barely detectable. As with the other acropora species, viewing this millepora under 20K lighting brings out more dramatic colors. Apart from this obvious conclusion, this coral exhibited the most pronounced variation in color as a function of growth light among all of the coral species examined. The 20K photography results suggest that perhaps three coral coloration molecules are involved: peach, green, and purple. Alternatively, the purple color might be attributable to the superposition of green and peach coloration molecules, and not to a distinct third pigment. The frag grown out under 20K lighting appears to express all three colors in different growth zones. The frag grown out under 10K lighting appears to lack substantial amounts of the purple pigment, or alternatively, it lacks spatial overlap between the peach and green pigments. The frag

grown out under T5 lighting appears to lack substantial areas containing only the peach colored pigment. Thus, these observations provide evidence in support of the hypothesis that different growth lights can induce the production of different coral coloration molecules, and help rationalize the color variations in the parent colony over time.

MONTIPORA PHOTOGRAPHS

Six montipora species were fragged and grown out as described in the Experimental section. The origins of the coral are indicated, and five out of the six specimens are given a provisional species identification. This identification should be considered tentative, and typically was provided by the vendor. Correct species identification would be greatly appreciated and should be forwarded to the authors. In four out of the six examples, a photograph of the parent colony in one of the author's aquariums is provided. These parent colony photos were taken with either a Canon PowerShot S500 point-and-shoot camera with automatic white balancing (orange *M. digitata, M. capricornis, M. sp.?*) or a Nikon D80 also with automatic white balancing (*M. danae*). Both growth light and photography light for the parent colonies was provided by 10K 400W XM bulbs.

Figure 13. Montipora digitata (purple): 20K (top), 10K (middle), T5 (bottom).

Figure 14. Montipora Spongodes (green): 20K (top), 10K (middle), T5 (bottom).

1. *M. DIGITATA*, ORANGE (FIG. 12)

The orange *Montipora digitata* was acquired from a 10-year old colony with multiple generations maintained by one of the authors at the Penn State Aquarium. The parent colony maintained its robust orange color with pinkish growth tips in its home aquarium over the course of many years. In the experimental tanks, however, it never regained this solid orange hue, but rather acquired a much more pink tint to the orange base color throughout. When viewed under 20K lighting, the frags grown under either 20K or T5 lighting appeared identical and largely pink throughout. Under this same lighting, the specimen grown under 10K lighting had the most noticeable orange tint, especially in the polyps. These color relationships are maintained throughout the other two viewing light schemes. Under both T5 and 10K viewing lights, the coral frags grown under both 20K and T5 lighting appeared

the most pink, and were essentially indistinguishable in color. The frag grown under 10K lighting, whether viewed under either 20K or T5 lighting, maintained its decidedly orange cast with pink overtones. Thus, this coral exemplifies a case where growth light does matter - the frag grown under 10K lighting has distinctly more orange pigment than pink pigment, but viewing light does not matter - the color variation noted above is evident under all three viewing lights.

2. *M. DIGITATA*, PURPLE (FIG. 13)

The purple *Montipora digitata* was acquired from the Penn State Aquarium. This coral originally came from Joe Yaiullo at Atlantis Marine World, Long Island. Unlike the orange color

Figure 15. Montipora capricornis: parent colony under 10K lights, 20K (top), 10K (middle), T5 (bottom).

Figure 16. Montipora danae: parent colony under 10K lighting, 20K (top), 10K (middle), T5 (bottom).

morph discussed above, this montipora appears to be colored identically whether grown under 20K, 10K, or T5 lighting. However, there is a distinct difference in apparent coloration as a consequence of the viewing light. Only 20K lighting clearly reveals the purple coloration of this specimen, and this purple color molecule is expressed under all growth lights. With both 10K and T5 photography lighting, this coloration molecule is not dominant in the reflected (visible) light, and the coral adopts the typical brown coloration of zooxanthellae.

3. *M. SPONGODES*, GREEN (FIG. 14)

The green *Montipora spongodes* was acquired from the Penn State Aquarium. The original source of this coral is no longer known. When grown out as a larger colony, it can develop

Figure 17. Montipora sp.: parent colony under 10K lighting, 20K (top), 10K (middle), T5 (bottom).

light purple tips, which are just becoming evident in the pictures below. Like the purple digitata discussed above, there does not appear to be any compelling visual evidence to support the conclusion that incident growth light influences coloration. All corals appear to have the same color under a given photography (viewing) light. However, this species does display dramatic color differences when viewed under the different lighting schemes. When viewed under 20K illumination for any growth lighting, the green color is much more vivid than under either of the other two photography lights. It appears to have a fluorescent quality, and the purple of the growth tips is more pronounced. Under 10K viewing/photography light, the color of this coral, irrespective of its growth lighting, is beginning to shift from the unmistakable green of the 20K photograph to the muddy zooxanthellae-inspired brown frequently encountered by disappointed hobbyists. This trend is extended when viewed under T5 lighting, where the "browning out" of this coral is complete. Thus, these pictures provide strong impetus for use of 20K lighting to enhance the viewing color of this particular montipora species.

4. *M. CAPRICORNIS* (FIG. 15)

The *Montipora capricornis* pictured in Fig. 15 was won at a frag swap raffle with the parent colony acquired from Aqua Marines. It is likely the same coral widely sold as the "Idaho grape monti". The parent colony is quite fast growing and colored lavender throughout with purple/blue polyps. The growth lighting for this coral does appear to have a slight influence on the final coloration. Specifically, the specimen grown under 20K light appears to have a uniquely ruddy, or slightly brownish, cast to it under any photography light. The samples grown out under either the 10K or T5 lights do not share this color characteristic, and they appear to be the conventional lavender color expected for this coral, when viewed under 20K, 10K or T5 lighting. Thus, this montipora species may be another example of a coral whose coloration molecule(s) can be induced selectively by the incident light source.

5. *M. DANAE* (FIG. 16)

This fast-growing montipora was purchased from Atlantis Aquarium under the title of "Superman monti". Common to the montiporas already discussed, this coral's coloration does not seem to be responsive to the frequency of the growth light source. As the pictures in Fig. 16 illustrate, both the lavender base and the red/orange polyps appear identical when photographed (viewed) under any of the light sources. As with the other corals, the 20K photographic illumination causes the colors to "pop" out more than the 10K or T5 examples. Clearly, the same coral coloration molecules are present under any of the lighting regimes examined.

6. *M.* SP., PURPLE (FIG. 17)

This slow growing montipora was the grand prize at a local frag swap raffle. It was obtained from Aqua Marines. In what is now a recurring theme, the growth lighting of this coral does not seem to have any substantial impact on its coloration, with one curious exception. The specimen grown under 10K lighting and photographed under T5 lighting is conspicuously tinted more toward the pinkish purple than the frags grown out under 20K or T5 lighting, which are more bluish purple. The significance of this observation is unclear at present. Once again, the color of this coral under 20K illumination appears to be a richer, more vibrant hue of purple than its color under 10K or T5 lighting.

CONCLUSIONS

It is not possible to draw sweeping generalizations about the relationship between coral growth lighting and coral coloration based upon this limited data set of 11 SPS corals. Nevertheless, two focused conclusions are supported by these data: (1) the colors of these specific corals viewed under 20K lighting appear more vibrant compared to either 10K or T5 lighting. In addition, the coral colors appear quite similar under these latter two lighting schemes. The former observation could be due to the inability of the human eye and/or the color correction procedure to completely eliminate the dominant effect of the blue light in the 20K bulb's spectrum. (2) In some cases, the growth light does induce, uniquely, the production of specific coral coloration molecules. Whereas the first conclusion has been recognized for as long as 20K bulbs have been available, the experiments described herein suggest, for the first time, that the specific coloration molecules that define these vibrant colors are actually present in the coral even if it is grown out under lower Kelvin-rated lighting. Lighting color, of course, is just one of the possible input parameters that influences coral coloration. Water nutrient levels, light intensity water flow, salt and trace element content, oxygen concentration, temperature, pH, etc., may all contribute as well (see Riddle, 2007a for a more thorough discussion). It will be interesting to see if carefully designed experiments that isolate each of these parameters in turn can be conducted with the intent of further elaborating the specific inputs that, when summed together, lead to the stunning coral colors that aquarists find so captivating.

REFERENCES

1. Fabricius, F. 2006. "Effects of Irradiance, Flow and Colony Pigmentation on the Temperature Microenvironment around Corals; Implications for Coral Bleaching." Limnol. Oceanogr., 51, 30-37.

2. Finet, B.; Lesage, F.; Will, N. 2005. "Colors by the Thousands - Light, Colors and Corals, Part 1. Advanced Aquarist; http://www.advancedaquarist.com/2005/12/aafeature2.

3. Hochberg, E. J.; Apprill, A. M.; Atkinson, M. J.; Bidigare, R. R. 2006. "Bio-Optical Modeling of Photosynthetic Pigments in Corals." Coral Reefs, 25, 99-109.

4. Joshi, S. 2006. "Facts of Light. Part IV: Color Temperature" Reefkeeping; http://reefkeeping.com/issues/2006-05/sj/index.php.

5. Kinzie, R. A., III; Jokiel, P. L.; York, R. 1984. "Effects of Light of Altered Spectral Composition on Coral Zoozanthellae Associations and on Zoozanthellae in vitro." Mar. Biol., 78, 239-248.

6. Kinzie, R. A., III; Hunter, T. 1987. "Effect of Light Quality on Photosynthesis of the Reef Coral *Montipora verrucosa*." Mar. Biol., 94, 95-109.

7. Mazel, C. H.; Lesser, M. P.; Gorbunov, M. Y.; Barry, T. M.; Farrell, J. H.; Wyman, K. D.; Falkowski, P. G. 2003a. "Green Fluorescent Proteins in Caribbean Corals." Limnol. Oceanogr., 48, 402-411.

8. Mazel, C. H.; Fuchs, E. 2003b. "Contribution of Fluorescence to the Spectral Signature and Perceived Color of Corals." Limnol. Oceanogr. , 48, 390-401.

9. Riddle, D. R. 2003. "Effect of Narrow Bandwidth Light Sources on Coral Host and Zooxanthellae Pigments." Advanced Aquarist; http://www.advancedaquarist.com/issues/nov2003/feature.htm.

10. Riddle, D. R. 2007a. "Coral Coloration, Part 4: Red Fluorescent Pigments, a Preliminary Report of Effects of Various Environmental Factors and Color Mixing." Advanced Aquarist; http://www.advancedaquarist.com/2007/2/aafeature.

11. Riddle, D. R. 2007b. "Coral Coloration, Part 8: Blue and Green Fluorescence: Environmental Factors Affecting Fluorescent Pigmentation." Advanced Aquarist; http://www.advancedaquarist.com/2007/11/aafeature.

12. Rothschild, G. 2005. "White Balance and Your Aquarium." Reefkeeping; http://reefkeeping.com/issues/2005-03/gr/index.php.

13. Salih, A.; Larkum, A.; Cox, G.; Kühl, M.; Hoegh-Guldberg, O. 2000. Nature, 408, 850-853.

14. Schlacher, T. A.; Stark, J.; Fischer, A. B. P. 2007. "Evaluation of Artificial Light Regimes and Substrate Types for Aquaria Propagation of the Staghorn Coral *Acropora solitaryensis*." Aquaculture, 269, 278-289.

FEATURE ARTICLE

SUPER CORALS - *MONTIPORA UNDATA*

By Dana Riddle

This coral will grow very quickly when conditions are correct. Specimens can double in size in just a few months.

Published March 2008, Advanced Aquarist's Online Magazine

© Pomacanthus Publications, LLC

Keywords: Coloration, Coral, Dana Riddle, Feature Article, Lighting, Pigment, Temperature, Water Circulation, Water Quality
Link to original article: http://www.advancedaquarist.com/2008/3/aafeature2

This month, our discussion of Super Corals continues with a focus on an attractive stony coral *Montipora undata*. To my knowledge, this coral has no common name.

With proper conditions, this *Montipora* species can grow quickly, and its green fluorescence along with reddish-purple tips and white polyps makes it appealing.

Note that observations presented in this report are of only one specimen containing an unknown zooxanthella clade. However, there is still a lot of information available. We'll begin our discussion with the 'types' of zooxanthellae known to infect *M. undata* specimens.

- **Family:** Acroporidae

- **Genus:** *Montipora*

- **Latin Name:** *Montipora undata* (see Basis of Identification below)

- **Geographical Range:** Indian and Pacific Oceans.

- **Known Symbiont Types:** *Symbiodinium* species, Clade C1 and Clade C·.

SYMBIONT TYPES

CLADE C1

Chen et al., (2005) found this clade in Taiwan *M. undata* specimens at depths of 3-5m. Clade C1 is considered a 'generalist' zooxanthellae in that it infects a large number of coral genera hosts in the Pacific as well as the Atlantic, and is distributed over a wide variety of depths. Thus, corals containing this clade could be considered highly adaptive as they can tolerate high light (but are probably best suited for lower light intensities). Evidence seems to indicate that these zooxanthellae photo-saturate at 200 - 400 µmol·m²·sec or less (or 15,000-20,000 lux; see below). Clade C1 (along with

C3, C21, C3d, C1c and C45) is believed to be an ancestral type from which other clades evolved (LaJeunesse, 2004) and has been found in these corals: *Acropora cervicornis* (Baker et al., 1997), *Acropora divaricata, A. humilis, A. hyacinthus, A. longicyathus* (from the GBR; van Oppen et al., 2001), *Acropora palifera* (from Taiwan, Chen et al., 2005), *Acropora sarmentosa* , *A. tenuis* (GBR; Van Oppen et al., 2001), *Astreopora* (GBR, LaJeunesse et al., 2003), *Astreopora myriophthalma* (Taiwan; Chen et al., 2005), Caribbean anemones *Bartholomea* and *Condylactis* spp. (LaJeunesse et al., 2003), Great Barrier Reef 'corallimorpharia' and *Coscinaraea, Coscinaraea wellsi* and *Cycloseris vaughani* from Hawaii (LaJeunesse et al., 2004), *Cyphastrea* (LaJeunesse et. al., 2003), *Cyphastrea chalcidicum* (van Oppen, 2005), Atlantic and Pacific *Discosoma* spp. (LaJeunesse, 2005), *Echinophyllia orpheensis, Echinophyllia lamellosa* (Chen, 2005), Caribbean *Eunicea* (LaJeunesse et. al., 2003), *Euphyllia ancora, Euphyllia glabrescens* (Chen, 2005), *Favia* (LaJeunesse et. al., 2003), *Favia favus* and *Favites abdita* from Taiwan (Chen, 2005), *Fungia* (LaJeunesse et. al., 2003), *Fungia crassa* (van Oppen, 2005), *Galaxea, Goniastrea* (LaJeunesse et. al., 2003), *Goniastrea rectiformis* (Chen, 2005), *Goniopora* (LaJeunesse et. al., 2003), *Goniopora columba, Goniopora lobata* (Chen, 2005), *Herpolitha, Hydnophora* (LaJeunesse et. al., 2003), *Hydnophora excessa* (Chen, 2005), *Icilogorgia, Lebruna, Leptastrea* (LaJeunesse et. al., 2003), *Leptoria phrygia* (Chen, 2005), *Leptoseris incrustans* (LaJeunesse, 2004), *Linuche, Lobophytum, Merulina* (LaJeunesse et. al., 2003), *Merulina ampliata* (Chen, 2005), *Merulina scrabicula* (van Oppen, 2005), *Millepora* sp. ((LaJeunesse et. al., 2003), *Montipora aequituberculata* (Chen, 2005), *Montipora cactus* from Indonesia (van Oppen, 2004), *Montipora cactus, Montipora curta* from Taiwan (Chen, 2005), *Montipora confusa* (van Oppen, 2004), *Montipora digitata, Montipora effluorescens, Montipora hispida, Montipora* sp., *Montipora spongodes, Montipora undata* from Taiwan (Chen, 2005), *Mycedium* (LaJeunesse et. al., 2003), *Mycedium elephantotus* (Chen, 2005), *Pachyseris, Palauastrea,* Caribbean *Palythoa,* Hawaiian *Palythoa* (LaJeunesse et. al., 2003), *Pavona desucata, Pavona frondifera, Pavona varians, Pavona venosa* (Chen, 2005), the 'bubble' coral *Plerogyra* (LaJeunesse et. al., 2003), *Plesiastrea verispora* (Chen, 2005), gorgonians

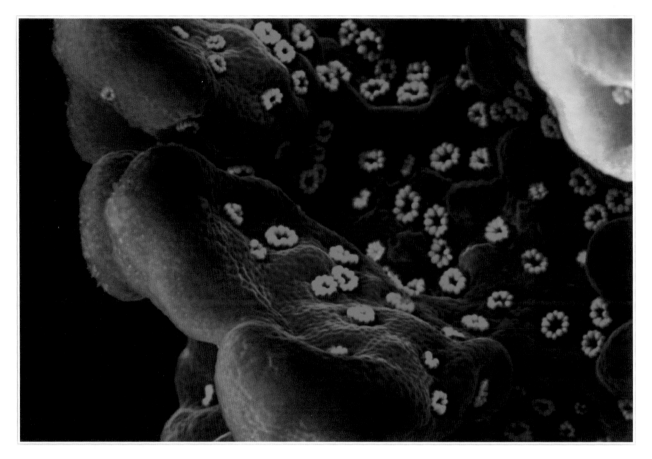

Montipora undata contains at least one fluorescent pigment (green) and a non-fluorescent chromoprotein (purple). Polyps appear white under full spectrum lighting.

Plexaura and *Plumigorgia* (LaJeunesse et. al., 2003), Taiwanese *Pocillopora damicornis* (Chen, 2005), *Polyphyllia, Porites* sp. (LaJeunesse et. al., 2003), shallow-water *Porites cylindrica, Porites lutea, Porites solida* (from Taiwan; Chen, 2006), GBR *Psammocora* (LaJeunesse et. al., 2003), *Pseudosiderastrea tayamai* (Chen, 2005), *Rhodactis, Rumphella, Sarcophyton*, Pacific *Scolymia, Siderastrea, Sinularia* (LaJeunesse et. al., 2003), *Stylocoeniella guentheri* (Chen, 2005), *Stylophora* sp. ((LaJeunesse et. al., 2003), *Stylophora pistillata* (Chen, 2005), a giant clam (*Tridacna* sp.), *Turbinaria* sp. (LaJeunesse et. al., 2003), *Turbinaria mesenteria* (Chen, 2005), and Pacific and Caribbean *Zoanthus* spp. (LaJeunesse et. al., 2003).

CLADE C·

Van Oppen, 2004, reports *M. undata* specimens from Indonesia contain Clade 'C·'. Clade C· is believed to have co-evolved with *Montipora* species, but sometimes found in *Porites attenuata* and *Porites cylindrica*. Other *Montipora* species containing Clade C· include *Montipora aequituberculata, M. altasepta, M. angulata, M. cactus, M. capitata, M.*

crassituberculata, M. danae, M. delicatula, M. digitata, M. gaimardi, M. hispida, M. hoffmeisteri, M. mollis, M. peltiformis, M. spongodes, M. stellata, M. turtlensis, and *M. verrucosa* (van Oppen et al., 2004). This clade is presently known to be distributed from Indonesia southward to the Great Barrier Reef. One has to wonder if this clade has high-fidelity to *Montipora* spp. and is one of those listed in LaJeunesse's more-or-less concurrent paper (namely Clades C17, C26a, C27, C30, C31, C31a, C31b, C32, C58 and C73). Van Oppen's IDs are based on ITS1 sequences (while LaJeunesse's - and many others'- are based on ITS2 DNA fingerprinting).

These works are important to hobbyists if we subscribe to the hypothesis that corals containing the same clade(s) zooxanthellae will have the same adaptive capacities to light intensity. As technology evolves, and more samples are studied, our knowledge will undoubtedly change about coral/symbiont relations. For the moment, this is the best information we have.

M. UNDATA- HOW MUCH LIGHT?

Second only to 'How much is it?' is usually 'How much light does it need?' And, the answer is 'Not much, relatively speaking.' Figure 1 shows the rate of photosynthesis of a single *M. undata* specimen under various light intensities (See 'Methods and Materials' for a description of equipment used to measure photosynthesis).

Perhaps some explanation is needed in order to understand the chart. The curved orange line demonstrates the rate of photosynthesis (rETR, for Electron Transport Rate between Photosystem II and Photosystem I) relative to light intensity (the yellow numbers at the bottom of the chart and labeled as 'PAR' - for Photosynthetically Active Radiation). A quick inspection says maximum photosynthesis occurs at PAR values of about 180-200 μmol·m²·sec (or ~9,000 - 10,000 lux). The chart also has other information - that of 'on-set of photosaturation.' The method described by Kirk (1983) is used to determine on-set of saturation. If the initial rate of photosynthesis (characterized by the left hand side of the orange line in the chart of Figure 1) was to continue in a linear fashion (the green line), its intersection with the maximum rate of photosynthesis (the red line) is the onset of photosaturation (the vertical yellow line intersect with the PAR values at the bottom - in this case, onset of saturation is in the neighborhood of 110 μmol·m²·sec (or ~5,500 lux) with full-blown photosaturation at 180-200 μmol·m²·sec (or ~ 9,000 - 10,000 lux).

Note: The specimen in the introductory photograph is maintained under one of PFO's very early LED prototypes.

PIGMENTS

Some *Montipora undata* specimens contain at least two pigments generated by the coral animal. These include a fluorescent protein with an emission peak at ~490nm (blue-green; See Figure 2) and an unidentified non-fluorescent chromoprotein (that appears reddish-purple under full spectrum lighting. It will appear bluish under high kelvin light sources).

Interestingly, Fluorescent Pigment (FP-490) has been found in only Acroporidae corals, including *Acropora* and *Montipora* species. The corals species containing FP-490 are *Acropora digitifera* (peak excitation at 425nm - violet light; Dove et al., 2001); *Acropora millepora* (excitation at 405nm - violet light; Cox and Salih, 2005); *Acropora aspera* (fluorescent shoulders at 501 and 514nm; excitation at 480nm - blue light; Papina et al., 2002); *Acropora nobilis* (excitation at 462nm - blue light; Karan et al., 2006); *Montipora monasteriata* (broad excitation at 420-450nm; Dove et al., 2001) and *Montipora undata* (this report).

In all cases, excitation wavelengths are in the violet/blue portion of the spectrum. This suggests FP-490 is best viewed under high kelvin lamps (note that UV energy also excites this fluorescent pigment and causes it to 'glow', but is not necessary). However, the purple-red non-fluorescent chromoprotein will appear dark blue. Supplemental warm light will make the purple apparent and, subjectively, more appealing.

I have not been able to identify the non-fluorescent protein's maximum reflectance or absorbance. This pigment is generated by the coral animal (and not zooxanthellae) and is usually seen in high growth areas. It is uncertain if this particular pigment eventually 'kindles' into the fluorescent green pigment (which would explain why the pigment disappears as the growth areas phase from new to old. Much work remains to be done before we understand these pigments' natures and purposes, if any).

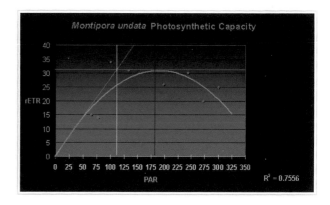

Figure 1. The rate of photosynthesis (relative Electron Transport Rate, or rETR, shown by the orange line) of a Montipora undata. In this case, maximum photosynthesis occurs at a PAR value of ~200 μmol·m²·sec. Increasing light intensity above this point is counter-productive as photoinhibition occurs.

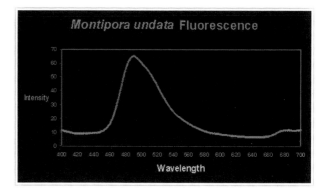

Figure 2. The blue-green fluorescent pigment has an emission peak at ~490nm.

WATER MOTION

This coral species does not seem especially demanding in its water flow requirements - flows measured in an aquarium found water velocity to be 'average' for a 'real' reef - 0.5 ft/sec (See 'Methods and Materials' - below - for water velocity testing protocols).

Although one half foot per second does not seem like excessive velocity (it equates to roughly 1/3 mile per hour), it does take some effort to generate this velocity in aquaria. Fortunately, the 'propeller pumps' now on the market make generating this sort of water flow quite easy.

ALKALINITY AND CALCIUM

Carbonate alkalinity is important for two reasons - it buffers against downward shifts of pH and also provides carbonates necessary for building the corallum or skeleton. Use any of the commercially available buffers to maintain an alkalinity of 175 mg/l (as CaCO3) or ~3.5 meq/l. Calcium concentrations of at least 400 mg/l are recommended although values of up to 450 mg/l have been observed and seem acceptable.

TEMPERATURE

Zooxanthellae clades (a clade is something like a sub-species) found in M. undata are not known to be particularly heat-resistant.To avoid potential overheating of coral specimens, water temperature should not exceed 80° F when using metal halide lamps or other lamps that operate at very high temperatures (mercury vapor lamps, for instance. See Riddle, 2006 for details). This is due to absorption of heat by the coral skeleton, where it can become warmer than ambient water temperature.

COMMENTS

This coral will grow very quickly when conditions are correct. Specimens can double in size in just a few months.

Fragmentation of this coral is easy. It can be accomplished with a Dremel tool with 'cut-off' blades or with a 'wire cutter' pliers (preferably stainless steel).

Mahalo to Steve Ruddy with Coral Reef Ecosystems (www.coralreefecosystem.com) for his invaluable assistance in preparation of this article.

BASIS OF IDENTIFICATION

Veron's Coral ID (2002) software was used for identification with 30 data points entered.

The ocean realm entered was Indo-Pacific. The exact collection point is unknown, so two likely locations were entered:

1. If the coral was collected from the Central Indo-Pacific (including the Philippines, Malaysia, Indonesia and the Solomon Islands), choices are M. undata, M. danae and M. confusa (with the software's 'Best Bet' Option choosing M. undata).

2. If the coral was collected from the oceanic west Pacific (including the Palau, Vanuatu, Fiji, and the Marshall Islands), the software's 'Best Bet' Option chose M. undata).

These are the other data points used for identification (based on microscopic examination of the skeleton and inspection of enlarged photographs of living animals):

- Colonial coral
- Attached to substrate (as opposed to free-living)
- Growth form is encrusting or solid plates (but can include columnar growths)
- Branching is absent (in this case)
- Calice width <1mm
- Corallite centers distinct
- Corallites separate
- Neither axial nor central corallites
- Corallites are widely spaced
- Corallite protrusion immersed
- Tentacles expanded during the day
- Tentacle Length <10mm
- Tissue partially masks skeleton
- Daytime tissue projection <1mm
- Columella absent
- Costae absent
- Unequal septal length
- Radial septa
- 2 cycles septa
- Septa not exsert

- No septal fusion

- Septal height: not exsert

- Septa not petalloid

- Septal margins not smooth

- Paliform structures absent

- Extra-thecal skeleton present

- Extra- thecal surface perforated

- Extra-thecal elaborations present

- Linear elaborations > calice diameter

METHODS AND MATERIALS

Water velocities were measured with a Marsh-McBirney Flo-Mate 2000 electronic digital water velocity meter. This meter operates on Faraday's Law and reports velocity with a resolution of 0.01 foot per second.

Rates of photosynthesis were determined with a Walz 'Teaching PAM' Chlorophyll Fluorometer (Effeltrich, Germany) equipped with a fiber optic cord. A fluorometer is basically a 'photosynthesis meter' and exploits measurements of chlorophyll fluorescence in order to determine rates of photosynthesis (in terms of 'electron transport rate' or ETR between Photosystem II and Photosystem I within zooxanthellae). Corals were maintained in total darkness for at least one hour before initial measurements were made in order to allow Photosystem reaction centers to 'open'. The external actinic light source was a 400-watt Iwasaki 6,500K metal halide lamp that was shielded for ultraviolet radiation by a clear acrylic material. Intensity was adjusted upwards by moving the light source closer to the coral (which was contained in a 3-gallon plastic container). Light intensity (Photosynthetically Active Radiation, or PAR) was measured with an Apogee QMSS quantum meter and a submersible, cosine-corrected sensor. Water motion was provided by a magnetic stirrer and 3" stir bar.

After the dark-adaptation period, minimum chlorophyll fluorescence (Fo) was determined with a weak pulse of light generated by the instrument's internal actinic lamp. Maximum Fluorescence (Fm) was estimated by increasing the intensity of the internal actinic lamp, resulting in a photosynthetically-saturating pulse of light. Once minimum and maximum fluorescence values are established, the instrument can determine the relative Electron Transport Rate (rETR) under different lighting conditions.

The metal halide lamp was then turned on and allowed to 'warm up' until PAR values stabilized (15-20 minutes). Chlorophyll fluorescence values were determined and the light intensity increased. The coral's zooxanthellae were allowed to adjust to the new light intensity for 15 minutes and another chlorophyll fluorescence measurement was made. This procedure was repeated multiple times, with three measurements taken at each light intensity. These results were averaged.

The PAM meter calculated Photosynthetic Yield, which was simply multiplied by the appropriate PAR measurement in order to estimate the rETR. This is a valid method for observing photosynthetic trends. Technically, it is not the preferred method of determining absolute ETR, but it is fine for our purposes.

Fluorescence was determined with an Ocean Optics USB-2000-FL fiber optic spectrometer (Dunedin, Florida) using an 18-watt black light (maximum emission at 365nm) as the excitation source. Light was collected with a cosine-corrected CC-3 lens and a 600 micron fiber optic cable.

The photograph was taken with a Canon Rebel XTi digital camera (10.1 megapixels) equipped with two stacked teleconverters and a 60mm macro lens.

REFERENCES AND SUGGESTED READING

1. Baker, A., R. Rowan and N. Knowlton, 1997. Symbiosis ecology of two Caribbean Acroporid corals. Proc. 8th Int. Coral Reef Symp., Panama. 2:1295-1300.

2. Chen, C., Y-W Yang, N. Wei, W-S Tsai and L-S Fang, 2005. Symbiont diversity in scleractinian corals from tropical reefs and sub-tropical non-reef communities in Taiwan. Coral Reefs, 24(1): 11-22.

3. Cox, G. and A. Salih, 2005. Fluorescent lifetime imaging of symbionts and fluorescent proteins in reef corals. In: *Multiphoton Microscopy in the Biomedical Sciences V*, edited by A. Periasami and Peter So. Proc. SPIE, 5700:162-170.

4. Dove, S., O. Hoegh-Guldberg and S. Ranganathan, 2001. Major color patterns of reef-building corals are due to a family of GFP-like proteins. Coral Reefs 19: 197-204.

5. Karan, M., B. Filippa, J. Mason, S. Dove, O. Houegh-Guldberg and M. Prescott, 2006. Cell visual characterisitic-modifying sequences. US Patent US2006/0107351 A1.

6. Kirk, J.T.O., 1983. *Light and Photosynthesis in Aquatic Ecosystems*. Cambridge University Press, Cambridge. 401 pp.

7. LaJeunesse, T. and R. Trench, 2000. Biogeography of two species of Symbiodinium (Freudenthal) inhabiting

the inter-tidal anemone *Anthopleura elegantissima* (Brandt). Biol. Bull. 199: 126-134.

8. ----------, 2000b. Investigating the biodiversity, ecology and phylogeny of endosymbiotic dinoflagellates in the genus *Symbiodinium* using the ITS region in search of a species level marker. J. Phycol., 37: 866-890.

9. ----------, 2002. Diversity and community structure of symbiotic dinoflagellates from Caribbean coral reefs. Mar. Biol., 141: 387-400.

10. ----------, W. Loh, R. vanWoesik, O. Hoegh-Guldberg, G. Schmidt and W. Fitt, 2003. Low symbionts diversity in southern Great Barrier Reef corals, relative to those in the Caribbean. Limnol. Oceanogr., 48(5):2046-2054.

11. ----------, D. Thornhill, E. Cox, F. Stanton, W. Fitt and G. Schmidt, 2004. High diversity and host specificity observed among symbiotic dinoflagellates in reef coral communities from Hawaii. Coral Reefs, 23:596-603.

12. ----------, R. Bhagooli, M. Hidaka, L. de Vantier, T. Done, G. Schmidt, W. Fitt and O. Hoegh-Guldberg, 2004b. Closely related Symbiodinium species differ in relative dominance in coral reef host communities across environmental latitudinal and Biogeographical gradients. Mar. Ecol. Prog. Ser., 284: 147-161.

13. ----------, 2005. "Species" radiations of symbiotic dinoflagellates in the Atlantic and Indo-Pacific since the Miocene-Pliocene transition. Mol. Biol. Evol. 22(3): 570-581.

14. ----------, G. Lambert, R. Andersen, M. Coffroth, and D. Galbraith, 2005. *Symbiodinium* (Phyrhophyta) genome sizes (DNA content) are smallest among dinoflagellates. J. Phycol., 41: 880-886.

15. ----------, S. Lee, S. Bush and J. Bruno, 2005b. Persistence of non-Caribbean algal symbionts in Indo-Pacific mushroom corals released to Jamaica 35 years ago. Coral Reefs, 24(1): 157-160.

16. ----------, H. Reyes-Bonilla and M. Warner, 2007. Spring 'bleaching' among *Pocillopora* in the Sea of Cortez, Eastern Pacific. Coral Reefs, in press.

17. Papina, M., Y. Sakihama, C. Bena, R. van Woesik and H. Yamasaki, 2002. Separation of highly fluorescent proteins by SDS-PAGE in *Acroporidae* corals. In press, Comp. Biochem. Physiol.

18. Riddle, D., 2006. Temperature and the reef aquarium. Advanced Aquarist Online. http://www.advancedaquarist.com/2006/2/aafeature2/

19. Van Oppen, M., 2004. Mode of zooxanthella transmission does not affect zooxanthella diversity in Acroporid corals. Mar. Biol., 144: 1-7.

20. ----------, F. Palstra, A. Piquet and D. Miller, 2001. Patterns of coral-dinoflagellate associations in *Acropora*: Significance of local availability and physiology of *Symbiodinium* strains and host-symbiont selectivity. Proc. R. Soc. Lond B., 268: 1759-1767.

FEATURED AQUARIUM

GREG TIMMS' 130 GALLON REEF

By Greg Timms

This month Greg shares the evolution of his 130 gallon reef aquarium with us.

Published March 2008, Advanced Aquarist's Online Magazine

© Pomacanthus Publications, LLC

Keywords: Featured Aquarium, Greg Timms, Bulbs, Calcium, Carbon, Chiller, Clams, Coral, Equipment, Gorgonians, RO/DI, Sump, pH
Link to original article: http://www.advancedaquarist.com/2008/3/aquarium

I first would like to thank the Advanced Aquarist's staff for all their hard work in creating a first class online magazine. What a benefit it is for us "regular folk" in this great hobby to have a place like this, that with just a few mouse clicks we can access so much valuable information. When Wade invited me to have my reef featured I felt honored yet a little hesitant. I was a little worried my aquarium may not be quite up to the standard people might expect but then thought it's not always about where you are right now but where and what you are striving to be. I hope that through my photos and remarks you will be able to feel the passion I have for this hobby and get a sense of the enjoyment I receive from it. I have always been fascinated with the ocean and diverse life forms we find there. It truly is another world and I love this hobby that allows us to keep a small part of it in our homes. I am grateful to be given this opportunity to share my little piece of the ocean with you.

HISTORY & TANK PROFILE

I ran freshwater aquariums for years, African cichlids mainly and like many people seldom had less that two tanks going at any given time. When I shut my last one down in the late 1980's due to a leak I decided at that time that when I eventually got back into the hobby I would switch to salt water. In October 2004 that dream became a realization when I had a tank custom built. I thought I would begin my salt water adventure with a FOWLR and maybe add in a few soft corals to sway back and forth in the flow. I had seen this kind of display at some fish stores and thought they looked pretty cool. Within about four months I found I was actually buying coral as often as fish and my tank slowly started to become a reef. By spring 2005 I was up to about 24 fish, an RBTA, several LPS with a few leathers and mushrooms as well as some Montipora caps and digitata. My original lighting was a 72" Power Compact fixture which I thought was pretty bright and assumed it was all I would ever need. However, by the summer 2005 I knew I wanted to upgrade to Metal Halides so I could add in some so called "harder to keep" sps coral such as acropora. In July 2005 I upgraded to a 72" fixture with 3x175 watt & 2x 96 watt PC actinics. In September 2005 I added a sump and Dec 05 upgraded my protein skimmer. I once again figured I was all set. Then in summer 06 I added in an RO/DI unit with an auto top-off going to the sump. I finally switched to R/O because I had a major hair algae outbreak that almost killed my reef. It got so bad that I did a complete tear-down in September 2006 and was rethinking whether or not to even stay in the hobby. I obviously kept going which is a decision I

am pleased I made. It turns out that my skimmer was running at about 1/3 capacity for several months which sent my nitrates through the roof. I fixed the skimmer which worked fine for awhile. Right after the skimmer ordeal my main ballast went in my light fixture so I was again at a crossroads. It helped me realize my reef wasn't where I wanted it to be anyway, so in October 2006 I once again upgraded my lighting. I decided on a 72" fixture that houses five HQI bulbs, two 150 watt 20 K and three 250 watt 10 K, that would allow me to create a better sunrise and sunset effect with a higher intensity and then added in some moon lights for extra effect. I have since added a T5 fixture to supplement the lighting to help give that little extra pizazz I had been looking for. Now I was closer to the intensity I wanted but the water was getting too hot. I decided after loosing many sps colonies from the heat that I needed a chiller. After installing the chiller I still questioned why it had to keep running so often to keep things cool, I mean my light was hot but not that hot. Anyway, I did some checking and discovered I had a faulty heater that was staying on 24/7 and this had likely been my biggest problem all along. That said the chiller is still a definite necessity and really helps keep the water temperature stable.

Around that same time I also changed out the powerheads to Tunze's with a multi-controller. The difference in the flow and random surge has made a huge difference in keeping my reef happy and growing.

In November 2006 I connected what had been my acrylic 40 gallon cichlid aquarium in-line to use as an ornamental Refugium & Softie tank. The refugium is made up of live rock, soft corals, and macro-algae. This tank has an "old school" sump in the rear where I also keep a "cheato chamber" running on a reverse photo period. I have since added in a 40 gallon frag propagation tank. This has increased my water capacity to approximately 250 gallons. This extra volume along with the increased nutrient exportation has made a huge difference in helping to stabilize the system as well as virtually eliminate nuisance algae growth in the display. Adding more volume to the system meant more water draining to the sump in case of a power failure. Since it will only hold the amount of water that drains from the main display I drilled the sump wall and added an emergency overflow going to a 10 gallon tank. Fortunately, I haven't needed it so far but I am sure the day will

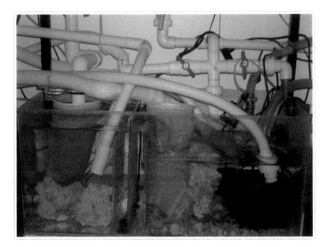

Refugium.

Frag tank.

come and it helps give some peace of mind against flooding. As you can see the last two years, have been a "reefer's roller coaster ride." It seems whenever my reef starts to do well "Murphy's law" kicks in and something else happens. The summer of 2007 was to be no different. I discovered our dishwasher located in the kitchen, on the floor directly above where the tank is, had been leaking and dripping straight into the tank for an undetermined amount of time. The drain hose had sprung a leak and who knows what chemicals ended up in the tank between the soapy dish water and the basement ceiling tiles, etc. Needless to say I took immediate action. I changed and added extra carbon and did seven water changes in eight days of 15% each and managed to save the majority of livestock but the SPS took a big hit. Most of it lived although I did I loose several nice pieces. Unfortunately what did live either bleached or browned out, but for the most part over the last six months it has bounced back quite nicely. There are still a few pieces I am patiently waiting on to color back up but my hopes are high. Bad things seem to happen in waves, so of course while the dishwasher incident was occurring my skimmer had also quit working. I was without a skimmer for most of the summer and in late August 2007, I upgraded to a much bigger unit that could handle the load. I was very fortunate to not have a huge algae bloom and I give Polyp-labs a lot of credit for keeping my nitrates under control as I kept dosing with "reef-resh" during that time. The new skimmer has a 24 inch footprint and is 30" tall so I had to install it away from the main display as there was no room for it. I modified the skimmer to drain into a 5 gallon bucket both as a help for emptying skim mate because it's inconveniently located under the frag tank and as a safe guard against it overflowing. No good sps drama would be complete without having a few "red bug" battles so I of course have had run ins with them and learned the hard way that nothing goes into the system without being given a dip for such pests. I have been lucky so far and never had acropora eating flatworms. Anyway, things have been pretty stable since then so I am keeping my fingers crossed and keep "knocking on wood" that this present trend will continue.

TANK SPECIFICATIONS

- Main Display - 130 gallon ½" glass euro-braced, 72"Wide x 18"Deep x 24" High.

- Refugium - 45 gallon acrylic hex front with built in rear sump (old school), 48" Wide x 18: Deep x 24" High

- Frag Prop tank - 40 gallon euro-braced

- Sump - 30 gallon acrylic

WATER PARAMETERS:

- Temp - 27 C / 79-80 F

- SG - 1.026

- pH - 8.2

- Ammonia - undetectable

- Nitrates - undetectable

- Calcium - 440 ppm

- Alk - 8 DKH

- Mag - 1350 - 1400 ppm

EQUIPMENT

- Return Pumps - Ocean Runner 6500 - Ocean Runner 3500 (return for frag tank)

- Protein Skimmer - Euro-Reef RC500

- Skimmer Pumps - 3x Eheim 1262

- Chiller - Aqua Medic AT5000

- Lighting Fixtures - Aqua Medic "Sexy" Ocean Light (all HQI) - Aqua Medic T5 fixture 72"

- Bulbs - Aqualine 3 x 250 watt 10k & 2x 150 watt 20k - T5's Koralen Zucht 4x 39 watt Fiji Purple

- Moon Lights - 2x 1 watt LED (blue)

- Powerheads - 2x maxi-jet (for additional flow in behind the rock work), Seio 820, Hydor Koralia #4, Tunze Nanostream 6045, Tunze *Turbelle* Stream 1x 6000 & 1x 6100 with Tunze 7095 Multi Controller (with single white LED moon phase light)

- Refugium Lighting - 2x 96 watt Power Compact 2x 96 watt Actinic Power Compact

- Filters - 100 micron pre-filter socks installed in sump beneath tank's overflow and on the skimmer return to improve water clarity and bubble control

- Heater - 200 watt titanium heater with Aqua Medic Temperature Controller

- RO/DI - Coralife 3 stage with pump

- F/W Reservoir - 45 gallon container aerated 24/7 to maintain PH level

- Top-Off Unit - Aqua Medic SP3000 Single Dosing Pump

HUSBANDRY

In January 2007 I started running the Polyp-Labs "Reef-Fresh" program which helps keep the nitrate levels in check using bacterial strains, amino acids and other supplements. It is said to give results similar to Zeovit, basically encouraging a

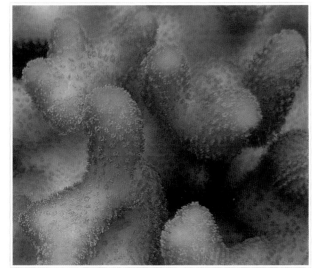

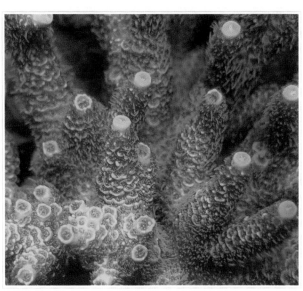

low nutrient environment. I have been pleased with the results over this past year or so.

I use Randy Holmes Farley's 2 part recipe for dosing Calcium & Alkalinity. My reef has a demand which requires almost 500 ML of each on a daily basis to keep the levels stable. Magnesium is added at approximately 500 ML per week as per Randy's recipe. Potasium is also dosed daily while other trace elements such as Iodine & Strontium are dosed biweekly.

ROUTINE MAINTENANCE:

- Skimmer - empty & clean twice a week

- Pre-Filter bags - change twice a week

- Carbon - change out monthly (media bag runs through an Aquaclear filter in the refugium)

- Water Changes - 10-15% monthly

- Prune & frag corals - as needed

LIGHTING SCHEDULE:

MAIN DISPLAY:

- 8:00 AM -1 watt moonlights on 10:30 AM - moonlight off

- 9:00 AM - T5's on 9:30 PM - T5's off

- 10:00AM - 150 watt 20k m/h on 10:30 PM - 150 20k's off

- 12:00 PM - 250 watt 10k m/h on 8:30 PM - 250 10k's off

- 10:45 PM - 1 watt moonlights on 12:00 AM - moonlights off

- white led moon phase light runs automatically via sensor while main lights are out

NOTE: I try to time the photo period in a way in which I can spend more time on the reef while it's active. By starting the lights a little later in the day they are on for a longer time after I get home from work which gives me more time to tinker and enjoy.

REFUGIUM/SOFTIE TANK

- 40 watt light on reverse photo period in the rear sump "Cheato chamber"

- 8:00 AM -actinics on 11:00 PM - actinics off

- 9:00 AM - pc's on 10:00 PM - pc's off

- Frag Tank (250 watt Geisman HQI pendent)

- 9:00 AM - on 9:00 PM - off

FEEDING SCHEDULE:

Feeding is provided on a daily basis, generally twice per day, and food is alternated to give their diet a variety of flakes, pellets, brine(super)shrimp, mysis shrimp, cyclopeze and

"nori" seaweed. I also mix in some "Reef-roids" or similar product, on occasion to provide some extra food for the corals.

LIVESTOCK

FISH & INVERTS

MAIN DISPLAY

- 1-scooter blenny
- 1-yellow tang
- 1-blue tang
- 1-naso tang
- 1-chevron tang
- 1-coral beauty angel
- 1-royal gramma
- 1-bi-colour blenny
- 1-yellow tail damsel

- 1-4 stripe damsel
- 3-green chromis

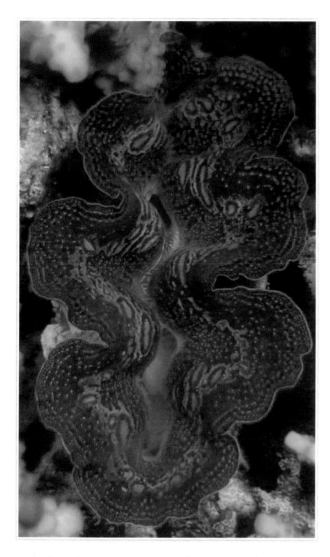

- 2-black & white ocileris clowns
- 1-blue devil damsel
- 2-watchman gobies
- 1-niger trigger
- 1-black brittle star
- 1- *Nardoa novaecaledoniae* star
- 1 - yellow coris wrasse
- Foxface rabbit fish
- 1-Blood Red hawkfish
- 1-longnose hawkfish
- 1-red serpent star
- Hermit crabs
- 2-conches
- Snails (Too hard to put a number on)
- 1-*Entacmaea quadricolor* (Green bubble tip anemone)
- 5-hawaiian feather dusters

REFUGIUM/SOFTIE TANK

- 1-flame angel
- 2-skunk cleaner shrimp
- 1-yellow clown goby

- 1-marine beta
- 1-purple fire fish
- 1-blue striped pipefish
- 2-orchid dottyback
- 1-pencil urchin

FRAG PROP TANK

- 2-banggai cardinals
- 3-fairy wrasses
- 1-potters angel
- 1-sailfin tang
- 1-rabbitfish
- 1-watchman gobie

- 1-fire shrimp
- 1-sea cucumber

CLAMS

- 5-*Tridacna crocea*
- 1-Gigis
- 1-*Tridacna maxima*

LIVE ROCK

Approximately 400 Lbs containing a mixture from: Australia, Fiji, Jakarta, Vanuatu, Caribbean & Belize, Hawaii, Mexico & Tonga.

CORAL

I don't know all the proper names of many of the corals in my collection so I will only list those that I have identified through research and/or a lot of help from others in the hobby who are more knowledgeable than me. Identification can sometimes be tough when trying to compare an aquarium coral with a picture of one in the wild from a book, especially when you enter reticulate evolution into the

equation. With some acropora, I find that I often know what species they aren't but can't always tell exactly which species they are, at least while they're alive. Anyway, I have tried to list the corals by the general taxonomic family first and then by genus and species.

SCLERACTINIAN (STONY) CORALS

SMALL POLYP SCLERACTINIA

ACROPORA

A.Loripes, A.Lovelli, A.Rosaria, A.Nana, A.Verweyi, A.Hoeksemai, A.Microphthalma, A.Humilus, A.Gemifera, A.Caroliniana, A.Jacquelineae, A.Prolifera, A.Loisetteae, A.Prostrata, A.Youngei, A.Austera, A.Tortousa, A.Valida, A.Proximalis, A.Millepora, A.Aspera, A.Kimbeensis, A.Batunai, A.Formosa, A.Tenuis, A.Turaki, A.Lokani, A.Horrida, A.Abrotanoides, A.Robusta, AAbrolhosensis, AStriata, A.Pichoni, A.Efflorescens, A.Plana, A.Pulchra, A.Subulata, A.Aculeus, A.Insignis, A.Maryae, A.Cerealis, A.Echinata, A.Bifurcata, A.Convexa, A.Chesterfieldensis, A.Divaricata, A.Hyacinthus, A.Convexa, etc.

POCILLOPORIDAE

Pocillopora Damicornis, Pocillopora Verrucosa, Stylophora Pistillata, Stylophora Subseriata, Seriatopora Hystrix, Seiatopora Caliendrum, Seriatopora Stellata.

MONTIPORA

M.Digitata, M.Capricornis, M.Danae, M.Verrucosa, M.Capitata, M.Confusa, M.Samarensis, M.Flabellata, M.Tuberculosa, M.Aequituberculata, M.Undata, M.Setosa, etc.

Misc SPS.

Hydnophora Pilosa, HydnophoraRigida, Porites sp., Merulina Scabricula, etc.

Large Polyp Scleractinia

Lobophyllia sp, Symphyllia sp, Caulastrea Furcata, Echinopora sp, Favia Speciosa, Trachyphyllia Geoffroyl, Euphyllia Ancora, Euphyllia Divisa, Turbinaria Peltata, Acanthastrea Lordhowensis, Acanthastrea Echinata, Turbinaria Reniformis, Echinophyllia Aspera, Mycedium Elephantotus, Oulophylia sp, Duncanopsammia Axifuga, etc.

Soft Corals

Corallimorpharians (mushroom corals)

Rhodactis, Actinoddiscus (=Discosoma) Striata, Mutabilis, Cardinalis, etc.

Octocorals

Tubipora Musica, Xenia sp. , Alcyonium, Lobophytum Pauciflorum, Sarcophyton Elegans, Sinularia Notanda, Sinularia Dura, Capnella Imbricata, Heliopora Coerulea, etc.

Gorgonians

Briareum Asbestiumi, Rumphella

Zoanthids (Various species)

Pachyclavularia Violacea (green star polyps)

A Few Comments I've heard:

In Michael Paletta's book "Ultimate Marine Aquariums" he asks his subjects about some of their favorite remarks people make when they see their reefs. I hope he won't mind me

borrowing his idea as I thought it's a good one and I often get a kick out of people's reactions when they see my reef for the first time. Here are just a few first time comments:

- *Oh my gosh, I've never seen anything like this before.*

- *Is that salt water? Is all that stuff alive? Are those plants? They're all corals? Even those? Are they real? How did you get them?*

- *Do you bring these back when you go scuba diving?*

- *I used to have goldfish but it wasn't like this.*

- *I've been diving before and it wasn't nearly as colorful as this.*

- *One reaction I find quite rewarding is when people simply stand there and say wow. (repeatedly)*

- *But being of Christian faith, I think my all time favorite comment was when one individual out of the blue stated "I've always believed in evolution but after seeing this I think there must be a creator."*

ACKNOWLEDGEMENTS

I would once again like to thank Advanced Aquarist's for their interest in featuring my reef and as previously mentioned it's an honor. I also want to thank all the people who have helped to educate me and given their support since I got started. I would also like to thank the suppliers that have put up with my bending their ear trying to learn from their knowledge. There are so many people I have learned from, too many to mention here but I again want to thank all those who have willingly shared their knowledge, time and friendship. Thanks also to Mike Paletta who was very gracious in giving his blessing when I asked to borrow his idea. I especially want to thank my wife Penny for her years of unquestioning support and always giving me plenty of room to run with my dreams.

SUMMARY

My aquarium's look and especially my tastes have continuously evolved. This amazing hobby has taken me up and

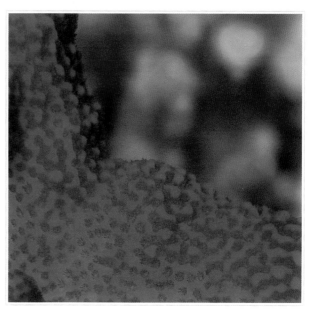

down and back and forth, through euphoric feelings of reward to great depths of frustration. It is said that experience is what you get when you were doing one thing and expected something else. All the "school of hard knocks" experiences along with my desire to learn and improve have brought me to where I am today and I wouldn't trade them for anything else. There are of course many things I would do differently if I had a "do-over" but overcoming challenges and hard lessons are often the best teachers. I still have much to learn and am never satisfied for very long with what I've achieved so more changes to my reef are imminent. But for now anyway, I have what I would call an "SPS dominated Mixed Reef." With my reef continually growing and corals so often crowding each other, I have found that regular pruning is necessary so starting a "frag business" became the next

logical progression of the hobby for me. Having frags available creates an opportunity for me to meet lots of great people in the hobby, make a lot of cool trades and even get a few costs covered now and then. This hobby has had quite a profound effect on me and has even changed the way I scuba dive. I used to mainly look for the big things; dolphins, rays, turtles, sharks, eels, etc which I will always enjoy seeing, but since having my own reef I spend more of my dives looking at coral details and the small things many people miss such as Christmas tree worms, nudibranchs, flatworms, tunicates, etc. I enjoy it more than ever. I hope that my write up and pictures have provided a little something for everyone to enjoy and that my love for the hobby is apparent through my story. I wish you all good luck and happy reefing.

BREEDER'S NET

AMAZING ARTEMIA!

By Suzy Q Applegarth

I have found it possible (actually very easy) to have a continuous culture of brine shrimp.

Published March 2008, Advanced Aquarist's Online Magazine

Keywords: Breeder's Net, Breeding, Suzy Applegarth, aquaculture
Link to original article: http://www.advancedaquarist.com/2008/3/breeder

One of the most interesting landmarks in the State of Utah is the Great Salt Lake. Tourists flock here in the summer, to test the buoyancy effect the high salinity level provides. Those of us who live here always find it interesting to see tourists voyage into the water, and the look on their faces is always amusing! Obviously, it is not what they expected.

The Great Salt Lake is what remains of a huge lake once known as Lake Bonneville. Over the millenniums, the water evaporated, leaving the salts behind and increasing the salinity of the water. As the salinity rose, the species of fish able to adapt to the elevating salt levels plummeted. Eventually, only one remained: Artemia. Not a fish at all, a crustacean. A shrimp, to be precise. Without any predators, this species has thrived.

Now, in 2008, this lake is in the midst of a large metropolitan area. The rain that feeds our lawns runs off into rivers that feed the lake, and the lake is high in nutrients from our lawn fertilizers. This environment, during the warm months, is a predator-less paradise where the artemia gorge on the abundant microalgae, grow rapidly and reproduce live nauplii. Because their diet is so abundant in various microalgae, their colors vary, ranging from dark to light red and green. When the cool weather begins, these shrimp begin producing cysts that are ready to hatch the next spring. The artemia then die, producing a stench smelled for miles. The brine shrimp eggs (or cysts) produced are large and abundant.

HATCHING OUT THE CYSTS

Techniques for hatching out these cysts vary. You can decapsulate the cysts (remove their shell) using a 1:3 part solution of FW and household bleach to remove the shell. Use a covered container to gently toss the eggs in the bleach solution and rinse well when they turn orange. I use a micro sieve to rinse them. You can use a spaghetti strainer lined with a coffee filter. These eggs are great to spot feed your corals, but will not hatch as easily. The shell is what creates their buoyancy.

I use a lot of artemia to feed my fry and my corals, so I do not go to the extra step of decapsulating. My fry are very discriminating about only eating motile food and I have not had an issue with shells. Some feel the extra step of decapsulating is worthwhile, so evaluation of your particular need is important.

I have tried a few commercially available hatcheries and the best I have tried thus far is the inverted 2 liter soda bottle. When cut in half and the top placed into the bottom, a vessel is created that encourages the heavier unhatched cysts to sink into a small area that houses a piece of rigid airline tubing. The rigid tubing is attached to a piece of flexible tubing to bring air from a small pump. Using a gentle flow, the air bubbles then lift the cyst up and into the water column. As the brine shrimp hatch, the empty shells float. After a day, I turn off the pump and wait a few minutes, then siphon the live brine shrimp from the bottom of the vessel, leaving the last inch of shells in the vessel to be rinsed into the sink.

When the cyst is newly hatched, and it has not yet consumed its egg sack, it does carry some nutrition. Some sources I have read say it is a few hours to up to a day. I have found it difficult to tell exactly when the cyst has hatched, thus making it difficult to say when the brine shrimp has lost its value. You can evaluate with a microscope, but that is a tedious step when I want to feed and go on with my life. So, I just enrich them. I look at these tiny napulii as a grocery sack, carrying the real nutrition into my aquatic home.

To enrich really means to gut load. I feed the nauplii the products I am trying to deliver to my tank: phytoplankton paste and concentrates; a fatty acid supplement, Selco; even medications or Betaglucan. Brine shrimp are filter feeders after their second molt so they will consume what ever is in their random path. According to Brine Shrimp Directs website, the fatty acid supplement Selco not only gets consumed, it "sticks" to the napulii. I keep the hatched artemia in a jar with an air line and just enough phyto paste to tint the water green for days. I use a turkey baster to feed a bit to my reef just before the lights go out. If you have a smaller tank, you may want to drain the water to avoid adding excess nutrients to your system.

I have found it possible (actually very easy) to have a continuous culture of brine shrimp. It takes around 2 weeks for a nauplii to grow into an adult. At that point, they produce live nauplii. I use a simple 2 gallon container. I feed just enough phytoplankton concentrate to keep the water tinged green. I place an airline in and a piece of macroalgae for filtration, and keep the culture in a brightly lit area. I harvest a cup a day, filtering the water out into the drain, and then releasing the

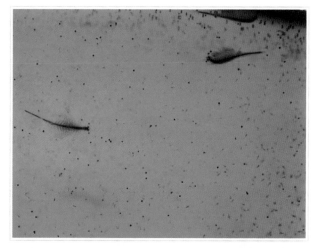

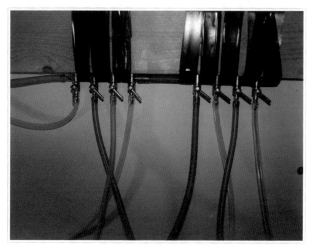

live adults, almost adults and the napulii into my reef. The chase begins and the fish love it!

Tips:

- I use old tank water from my last water change to hatch cysts. Room temp works great. If you fill the bottom of the 2 liter hatchery with hot water, you can hatch the batch quicker if you need BBS fast. Also, having the water weight in the bottom makes the hatchery much more stable.

- If you have multiple hatchers and grow out containers, using different colored tubing from your gang valve will make it easier to visualize which tube is going to which culture vessel. It is helpful when trying to adjust the bubbling to the proper flow. It is a necessary to find the right flow: too much flow will push the cysts out of the water; too little and the cysts sink to the sides of hatchery.

More information about these amazing shrimp can be found at: http://ut.water.usgs.gov/greatsaltlake/index.html

AQUARIUM FISH

LARGE ANGELS IN THE HOME AQUARIUM, PART II

By Jim McDavid

With a little thought, a little planning and a desire to provide the animals in your care with research, there is no reason why you can't keep one of these beauties healthy for 15+ years in your living room!

Published March 2008, Advanced Aquarist's Online Magazine

© Pomacanthus Publications, LLC

Keywords: Angelfish, Aquarium Fish, Fish, Jim McDavid
Link to original article: http://www.advancedaquarist.com/2008/3/fish

Welcome back! Last issue we began discussing the larger marine angelfish and the requirements to keep them successfully in the home aquarium. We talked about space requirements; as well as how to make sure that the variables are on your side when you go to select a specimen at your local store

This time, we'll talk about how to properly introduce your newly acquired angelfish into his new home, how to properly feed it, and some information on a few of the more commonly seen species in the hobby.

WHAT ABOUT FILTRATION?

Marine angels need perfect water conditions for the most part. While a few species are a bit more forgiving in this regard, and one or two are arguably "bullet proof" (I'll deal with these species later), most of them will not suffer neglect or laziness on the part of the keeper with the same aplomb as your average damselfish. Tank size goes a long way toward mitigating water quality fluctuations since the greater volume means that dissolved metabolites are more diluted and have less of an effect on the organisms within the tank.... in theory. This of course only holds true if the aquarist avoids stocking the tank in such a way that the "large" volume of water is negated by too many fish, or fish that are too large - something that is easily done with marine fish, and all too common. It's very easy to bring home a fish from your local store that will overwhelm a 1000-gallon tank as easily as a 100-gallon tank. A 150-gallon tank that provides a nice piece of real-estate for an Orchid Dottyback gets very small, very fast when an 11" annularis angel is placed inside of it! Such a scenario is far too common however. Go as large as you have the space and funds for, and pick your angelfish accordingly!

Further, effective filtration is a must! Angels are very sensitive to poor water quality. The best way to provide appropriate water conditions is a combination of live rock, protein skimming, and water changes. A large refugium with a healthy growth of macro-algaes certainly helps as well. Angels are grazers, and consume a large volume of food on a daily basis. A 10" angel consumes a respectable amount of food, and projects a corresponding amount of waste matter into the tank. Maintenance regimes will vary considerably depending on all factors, including the size of the tank, the number and types of other fish present, how much live rock or other filtration is present in the system, feeding regime, etc. A 300-gallon reef housing a 6" Regal Angelfish along with 20 or so other small fish will be a very low maintenance proposition indeed. On the other hand, that same size tank with a 10" imperator angelfish, along with a few other larger marine fish species and a smaller amount of live rock might require a 20% water change weekly in order to maintain proper water conditions.

Pygoplites diacanthus. Photo by Michael G. Moye.

As far as decor goes, this is slightly dependent on the age of your angel, and to some extent species. You'll find that you will see youngsters or initially shy species such as *P. navarchus* out in the open more often if they know that they have a plethora of hiding spaces close by. This need for numerous caves and overhangs lessens just a bit in some species as the fish matures, but never disappears, and is essential while the angel is growing and becoming accustomed to his new environment. A lack of hiding places will cause the animal stress, something we want to avoid at all costs.

I'M READY TO BRING HIM HOME ALREADY! WHAT ELSE?

Not so fast! We'll discuss stocking order in a minute, but first I have to mention the all-important factor when introducing a new fish, especially an angelfish - **quarantine**. This word seems to be the bane of many inexperienced (or unwise) marine aquarist's existence. It seems that the minor amount of effort and expense, relatively speaking, is just too much for them to be bothered with. That is, until they suffer the consequences of skipping this step - then suddenly the trouble and expense of a quarantine tank seem miniscule in comparison to dealing with a pathogen that has invaded their display system and starts wiping out fish! It never ceases to amaze me how many fish keepers are ignorant of just how important proper quarantine procedure is to the longer-term success of any closed system. The bottom line is this, if you can't afford to set up a small quarantine tank, then you cannot afford to keep a marine fish display tank - it's really that simple. A similar statement can be made if pure laziness, or simply space is the limiting factor. Over the years I've typed more words admonishing lazy or nonexistent quarantine procedures while responding to "help, my fish has ich!" threads on online forums than all the words in both parts of this article combined several times over! Even the most inadequate effort into the basics of marine fish husbandry will yield information on the importance of quarantine, thus anyone not

doing so is either ignoring such wisdom, or had not bothered to investigate at all how to keep these animals alive. Neither scenario puts this author in the most compassionate of moods! If you neglect to quarantine your fish, you will have problems sooner or later - this is never truer than where relatively delicate species are concerned.

Terry Bartelme has written an excellent article on proper quarantine procedure, and the reasons for it, which can be found here. I'll leave you to it, and simply add that quarantine is absolutely necessary not only to ensure that your new acquisition does not succumb to disease, but also to ensure that you do not introduce disease organisms into your display tank.

WHEN DO I ADD MY ANGELFISH TO THE DISPLAY TANK?

This gets tricky folks, and it depends on many factors. I would submit that if the well being of our angel is the primary concern, then most species should be the first fish added to the display tank - with the possible exception of a few dither fish such as Chromis virids. Not only will the presence of these dither fish make the angel more at ease, and speed up acclimation to the display tank, but it's an absolute *must* that the tank be well established and healthy before any species of angel is introduced. The pugnacious nature of some species toward newly introduced fish however, (and sometimes just any other tank mate in general) as well as other mitigating circumstances dictates that adding the angel to your display first is not always the best course of action. A few species are even hardy enough to allow their introduction whenever convenient. At the very least then, young individuals or more delicate species of any age should be added first when possible, or at the very least before any other fish that will compete with it for food or hide spots. *P. navarchus* and *P. diacanthus* are best added first, and the same goes for *P. imperator,. P. asfur* and *P. annularis*. There are also species, which should almost always be added last due to their more pugnacious nature. Chief among these are *H. passer*, and *H. ciliaris* - as well as *P. paru*. Please note that just because an angel is potentially aggressive, does not mean that newly imported specimens are not somewhat fragile, even if behavior is assertive and the fish looks like he has things handled. Often all seems well until a disease outbreak. Take steps such as rearranging the rockwork to break up existing territories, and do not introduce an angel into a tank containing a well-established and aggressive species such as triggerfish or a Dragon Wrasse. There is not always a perfect solution to problems presented with stocking order, and more often than not a compromise has to be made. For instance, I would normally suggest that due to its fragile, temperamental and extremely shy nature, a young Majestic Angel always be added to the display first, or after a few dither fish. Although this means he may cause problems with further additions to the tank later on, we can take steps to mitigate this,

Pomacanthus maculosus

(rearranging the rockwork to break up existing territories for instance) and it's more than worth it to get him established, eating well and healthy.

A big reason for the caution I'm advocating here is something that many aquarists do not realize about these fish, and that is that the moderately hardy to delicate species go through a prolonged period of acclimation - longer than casual observation will make manifest. The most important thing to keep in mind here is that their immune response often does not function at full tilt until months after they are seemingly established in a display tank. There is no hard answer to how long this period is, as it varies greatly from individual to individual and the circumstances involved. What this means is that you may have quarantined your angelfish properly, and he may be swimming around in your display and all may look fine and dandy for weeks. Quite often the reality is that the fish is still in a state of low-level stress, has not fully acclimated to the surroundings, and is moderately susceptible to disease still. At this stage, there are many things that can send the fish into a tailspin. Among these stressors are inadequate shelters, low quality of food or inadequate feedings, temperature or pH fluctuations, nitrogen spikes, and the one we are concerned with here, harassment by a tank mate.

Harassment can be as subtle as twitching or arching the body and tail on the part of the aggressor, or as blatant as out and out chasing. The simple matter of the resident fishes having claimed the best shelters is enough to cause your new angel a modicum of stress, even if no other aggressive interactions are apparent. In any case, this spells bad news for any new addition to a display tank, and doubly so for a juvenile angelfish not yet fully acclimated to it's new home - even a species that will later likely become aggressive itself such as those species noted above. Again, we want to do everything possible to allow the angel to establish itself - competition during feeding is eliminated for a time, and stress will be drastically reduced during this critical period. While juvenile specimens in the 2 to 4 inch range are always best since they acclimate more readily than smaller or larger specimens, it's especially important to heed this with aggressive species such as *H. passer*. Purchase one that is too much larger than this, and you'll cause the same problems with later additions to your tank as we sought to avoid with the angelfish!

WHAT DO THEY EAT?

Providing proper nutrition is arguably THE most important factor in maintaining the prolonged health of your angelfish, and one of the greater challenges. In the wild, the diet of marine angelfish varies from species to species. The diet of one species may be very eclectic, as is the case with *P. semicurculatus* and *P. navarchus*, to decidedly specialized, as is the case with *P. diacanthus* or *H. tricolor*. Often, difficulties with feeding is the downfall that plagues the aquarist who has otherwise managed to procure and acclimate a healthy, vibrant angelfish specimen, only to watch it succumb to illness

brought on by malnutrition. A consistently widely varied diet is the key here, along with vitamin supplements, which can be applied directly to the food, usually by soaking the food items in the vitamins before feeding.

Angels are consummate grazers in the wild, and some of them, most notably those of the genus *Holocanthus*, are obligate spongivores - that is they feed almost exclusively on sponges in their natural habitat. Even most species that are not sponge specialists nevertheless ingest a fair amount of sponge matter, such as *P.paru* and *P.imperator*. This can pose a huge problem for the would-be angel keeper since sponges are not normally found at the local grocery store. Furthermore, even a species with more eclectic feeding habits such as *P.navarchus* can be difficult to get acclimatized to captive fare at times, necessitating a sort of shotgun approach until something is accepted. Once that happens, more foods will be accepted over time.

Fortunately, there are some very high quality angel preparations on the market these days that contain many of the vital dietary components of our Pomacanthid friends, including sponge matter and algae. Aside from sponge matter, which we normally can only feed in small amounts due to practical considerations, macroalgae is also of primary importance. As with sponge matter, the high quality frozen preparations mentioned here provide some of this, but it can also be purchased in dried form from certain stores, as well as grown in a refugium by the aquarist. Other food items that can and should be offered in rotation are high quality flakes such as OSI and Formula 1 and 2 (both flake and frozen versions) frozen preparations such as Prime Reef, VHP, Angel Formula, Pygmy Formula etc, along with mysis shrimp, plankton, silversides, krill and brine shrimp. Anything available at your local fish market should also be fed, such as crab, squid, scallops, octopus, halibut, oysters, clams, shrimp,etc.

WHAT IF HE WON'T EAT?

Assuming we're not talking about a chronically problematic species in this regard, an angel refusing to eat is a common stress reaction, but fortunately a problem that is in many cases only fleeting. For starters, it's always best to ask to see the fish eat in the store before you bring it home. Of course the fish may greedily gobble down brine shrimp in the store, then refuse food again for a time once you have him in his quarantine tank - but at least you know that the problem will right itself in a matter of days. Other times their refusal of food in the store is not necessarily an indication that you should steer clear of the fish, especially with very shy species. At the end of the day this is a judgment call, and the keeper should be aware that some fish that don't eat initially will NEVER eat, or else don't eat enough. This is most often true with very tiny specimens, adult specimens, or certain problematic species such as *H.tricolor* or *P.diacanthus* - two species that frankly should be avoided by most hobbyists anyway.

Getting a newly acquired Pomacanthid to eat that is stubbornly refusing everything offered is truly an exercise in patience and resolve. After all, the clock is ticking! As the interval of time that the fish refuses food increases, so does the danger of malnutrition and further depredation of the immune response. Perseverance and diligence is the key here - this is one of those times when the lazy aquarist is in danger of experiencing a very unpleasant loss, both financially and otherwise.

Simply put, you must offer a large variety of foods, multiple times a day, with perhaps multiple methods of presentation. While brine shrimp are far from a nutritionally suitable staple, they are often useful in jump-starting the feeding response in these fish. All of the foods mentioned above should be offered at this time, and macro-algae should always be available, and can be submersed and secured with a clip. Nori is a good option here. Once feeding commences on a given food item, you're in business! Well, at the very least you're on the way! Other foods should be offered at the same time in rotation along with whatever the accepted food is -often brine shrimp. Slowly but inevitably the list of accepted foods will grow, and you now have the ability to ensure the nutritional health of your angelfish. That wasn't so hard, was it?

ARE THEY REEF COMPATIBLE?

Ahh, the eternal question! For the most part, the safe answer is "no" with regard to most species. As with most things in life however, nothing is all the time. Certain species are sometimes workable with most or some sessile invertebrates, at least for a time if not permanently. The key is acquiring the fish while young so that you can condition it to captive food offerings, and hopefully mitigate its natural grazing habits. The shortage of aquarists who've kept angels of various species in reefs for a period of 5 or 10 years is notable however, so regardless of what you do, you'll be firmly ensconced in the experimental crowd. Indeed, many of the opinions out there with regard to keeping large angels in reefs are the result of a lack of empirical data on the subject.

Even among those few species that are sometimes an option, there are individuals among them who will prove me wrong! Again, nothing is all the time, and behavior is highly variable within the group -keep that in mind as you read the rest of this section. You may attempt a species that some aquarists have had good luck with, only to find that it attacks every invertebrate in your tank! Also, some species of inverts are almost always picked on to some extent by even "reef safe" angels, including some soft corals, (especially open brain types and zooathids) some large polyped stoney corals, and tridacnid clam mantles. By far the safest type of reef to attempt an angel in is an SPS (small polyped stony coral) reef. These corals are not generally on the menu for Pomacanthids, although *anything* is fair game for an exploratory nip now and then. This brings me to my next point, which is that the aquarist must discern between a random

exploratory nip, (which is very common, and normally harmless to most inverts), and more determined efforts to make coral or clam a meal. Most recently I myself had an Emperor Angel in an SPS dominated reef that also housed 3 tridacnid clams. The imperator would give the mantel on one tridacnid clam or another a good tag every few days. This wasn't enough to damage the clams or keep them closed as is often the case with angels that have decided the clam would make a proper meal. This fish did however decimate my zooanthid population, but left all other invertebrates in the tank alone. This fish did fine for over a year until the tank had to be taken down due to a move.

If in fact your angel behaves like a model citizen in your reef, this does not mean that someday , for no apparent reason, he won't decide to make a meal of one of your favorite invertebrates.

Species that can be attempted in the reef in probable order of safety include, but may not be limited to *P. diacanthus P. imperator*, *P. navarchus*, *P. maculosus* and *P. annularis*. Also, *P. asfur* can usually be maintained with SPS corals (Michael 1999), and angels of the genus *Chaetodontoplus can also be attempted, again with the caveat that some LPS and soft corals will be in danger (Schiemer, 2003)*. Indeed, more often than not you'll be faced sooner or later with making the decision of whether you'd rather sacrifice certain corals, or your angelfish. Depending on the sessile invertebrates present, you'll almost certainly lose a few to your angel. Zooanthids and open brain corals seem to be among the most inviting to these fish. The good news is that small-polyped stony corals (SPS corals) are almost always ignored by the above-mentioned species.

The various species of the genus Holocanthus must absolutely be avoided - this is not the genus to attempt if you're bitten buy a bug to try something different! While I have not included angels of the genus Genicanthus in this article, they are most appropriate for larger reefs.

WHAT CAN I KEEP WITH MY ANGEL?

This question is dependent on a lot of factors, including tank size and the species of angel. In general, aspiring to keep an "angel tank" is a bad idea -keeping more than one individual, regardless of species, is usually a recipe for disaster. Pomacanthids are initially delicate, yet growing into territorial, often quite pugnacious fish with capacious space demands. The average aquarist is well advised to keep one per tank. Remember the immense size of their territory in the wild! This author has kept 5 species together at once in a 200 gallon, but these were mostly juveniles, and the setup was not permanent. Certain species can sometimes be paired, but this is not an avenue for the average aquarist to pursue. However (nothing is all the time remember!) in a very large tank, say 250 gallons plus, 3 or so species can coexist if introduced properly as juveniles, if they are if disparate size and color, and allowed to grow up together. Even with 250-gallons, a larger tank will likely be necessary at some point. If attempting to mix angels, certain species should nevertheless be avoided at all cost due to their aggressive nature; among these are *H. ciliaris, H. passer, P. paru*

As far as other species are concerned, there are hundreds to choose from. Overly bellicose species such as Clown Triggers should be avoided, and while growing up they should be the dominant fish in the tank. Remember that while angels can be aggressive,

they can also succumb to stress rather quickly if they themselves are the targets of bullying.

WHICH SPECIES DO I GET?

Good question! There are a lot of variables to consider, including just about everything mentioned above, both in this article and Part 1. How large is your tank? Will you be in a position to upgrade in a few years? Are you looking to keep your angel in a reef? How experienced are you? Do you go on long vacations and leave your tank in less than experienced hands? These are things you want to consider before choosing a species, as not all of them will be appropriate for your circumstance, indeed none of them may be. So be honest with yourself before bringing one of these beauties home.

POMACANTHUS IMPERATOR

Large, garish and, intelligent the Emperor Angel fish reaches 15" plus in the wild. They begin life garbed in juvenile colors that are nothing short of stunning. A dark blue background, with white circles and crescents (see photo in part I of this article) it's always been a heartbreak to me that they change at all. While their brilliant yellow, blue and black adult coloration is the height of brilliance, almost too extraordinary to be real - the juvenile stage is by far the height of beauty as far as this aquarist is concerned.

If net caught and treated well during it's trip to your local store, and then quarantined and acclimated properly, they are fairly hardy fish in captivity. Specimens from the Indian Ocean, Red Sea or Australia are the most suitable due to cyanide use in other regions discussed in part I. If kept properly, growth in this species can be quite rapid, (although any individual attaining a size close to that of the maximum adult size in the wild is rare) and a full color change can be witnessed within 3 years. If kept in quarters that are too small, and/or the diet is less than adequate, the color change can be incomplete, or else rather dull and disappointing.

One of the more eclectic eaters in the wild, *P. imperator* will accept, and should be fed a wide variety of foods, including spirulina algae, high quality angel formulations containing sponge matter, pygmy angel formulations (good for all large angels) as well as any seafood at the local grocer.

Pomacanthus navarchus

Plan ahead when adding to a reef tank, as it will eat some soft corals, and some individuals will pick at clam mantles. Adding this fish to a reef when it's between 2 and 3 inches, and feeding it well will help mitigate potential problems in this area. The species will usually leave SPS corals alone. Needs at least a 250 gallon tank for long-term well being.

POMACANTHUS NAVARCHUS

Often called the Majestic Angel, this species is truly deserving of the name. Its delicate, jaw-dropping beauty often leads to an impulse purchase by uninformed keepers. Not one of the more appropriate species for captivity, this is one of the most delicate Pomacanthids, and should only be attempted by veteran aquarists who have experience keeping other angel species. They are extraordinarily shy when first introduced, which exacerbates a prolonged period of acclimation. Feeding during this period is often problematic despite the fact that their diet in the wild is diverse.

To aid their acclimatization to captivity, they should always be the first fish added to the tank (aside from a few dither fish mentioned in part 1). Not for the lazy keeper, or one who considers quarantine tanks a non-essential item! All warnings applying quarantine, acclimation and introduction in the previous installment of this article should be heeded in full with this species. Rarely growing larger than 8" in captivity, they can be kept in slightly smaller quarters as long tankmates are chosen wisely. Once acclimated, and if kept in a spacious tank of at least 180 gallons, this fish can be long-lived in captivity.

POMACANTHUS MACULOSUS

The Map Angel - now here is a species that is most appropriate for captivity, with a few caveats thrown in for good measure of course. Availability of this species is spotty at best, but captive juveniles can be found online from time to time. These fish are very hardy, (I would rank only *H. passer* and *H.clarionensis* slightly higher here) but they still need a modicum of care and patience to adapt in good time to their new home. Quarantine procedures should of course be observed as always, and a varied diet should be offered which includes sponge matter.

With a maximum size of 11 inches, this fish needs at least a 200-gallon tank to thrive and live a proper lifespan in captivity. Of course, larger is always better!

POMACANTHUS PARU

The French Angelfish is big, boisterous, very hardy, and one of the fastest, if not THE fastest growing angelfish in captivity. Growing from a small, fluttering, black and yellow juvenile to an active, somewhat more subdued adult. Feeding heavily on sponges in the wild, they adapt readily to a wide variety of captive fare - variety being the operative word as ever. Make sure to offer sponge matter in their diet, and as ever frequent feedings of a variety of quality foods is key. The tiny quarter sized individuals that are sometimes available do poorly, as do larger wild-caught individuals. Specimens in the 2" to 4" range are usually hardy, and accept a wide range of foods. This species is suitable only for very large tanks in the 250-gallon plus range, and is one of the rare species that should be added last to a tank.

HOLACANTHUS PASSER

Of the angelfish species that are commonly available to the hobbyist, the Passer or King Angelfish is without doubt the hardiest angel one can keep in an aquarium. It's close sibling, *H. clarionensis*, the Clarion Angel may be it's equal in this regard, but they are not available to aquarists on this side of the ocean for less than the equivalent of a steep mortgage payment! How hardy is the Passer Angelfish? Well they are one of the few species that this author can call hardy without adding the "for an angelfish" qualifier in front of it. Once acclimated, which doesn't take long, you'd almost have to hang it on a clothesline to kill it! They are not particularly fast growers, and can be kept in a 135 gallon tank for some time before larger quarters are needed - at least 250 gallons given their large sizes and VERY aggressive nature. Indeed, as with the Queen Angel, keeping other fish with H. passer is often a problem, and unlike some angels, it should be the last fish added to any tank.

The hardiness of this species should not be taken as license to forgo great care while acclimating it to captivity. Juveniles of at least 2" are the best prospect, but be warned that full transition to adult coloration can take upwards of 3 years or longer.

HOLOCANTHUS CILIARIS

The ever-popular Queen Angel. While my own observations indicate that they are not *quite* as bulletproof as the passer or clarion angels of the same genus, other authors rank them right up there. At the very least, the Queen is not far off the mark as long as care is taken with the initial purchase and care once it arrives home. Individuals smaller than 2", and larger than 5 or 6" should be avoided (good advise for the family as a whole) since feeding and acclimation become serious issues outside of this size range. This is a large species, and every bit as aggressive as the passer angel, something not to be taken lightly with a fish that reaches 18" in length!

Adults feed primarily on sponges, but if acquired when young, they can be acclimated to accept the offerings

Pomacanthus paru

Holacanthus passer, juvenile.

discussed above. With any species, variety and quality of food offerings is key, and this is never truer than with this species. Laziness on the part of the keeper that manifests in feeding a single, convenient food item will result in declining health and eventual disease and death for this and most species.

PYGOPLITES DIACANTHUS

The Regal Angelfish, and deserving of this name it is! Unfortunately it's also one of the most problematic species with regard to acclimation, disease resistance and feeding. With a highly specialized diet of tunicates and sponges, duplicating this exclusive diet is impossible, and acclimating this fish to other fare is often impossible. Only for the experienced angel keeper, this species for the most part should be left in the ocean. On the upside, it's smaller size means that it can live long term in smaller quarters than most of it's other Pomacanthid congeners, however I wouldn't be quite as liberal in this area as some authors. Given the clear and obvious need to mitigate stress with this species even more than usual, 135 gallons is probably a reasonable minimum tank size for long term keeping of this species, again refer to part one for my reasoning in this regard. A good article on this species written by the late Gregory Schimer can be found at http://www.advancedaquarist.com/issues/aug2002/Fish.htm. This should cover all you need to know regarding this species. (I would respectfully recommend a slightly larger tank than is stated in his article for reasons spelled out in Part I)

HOLACANTHUS TRICOLOR

The Rock Beauty is the only member of the genus Holocanthus that is almost always an exceedingly poor candidate for captive life. Another sponge eater, they usually do not adapt to captive offerings, nor to the confines of the aquarium. Another fish that is frankly best left in the ocean. While on rare occasions an individual will do well for a time, this author has never seen one over a year old in captivity.

THE GENUS CHAETODONTOPLUS

Not generally as well known or popular amongst hobbyists, this genus holds a few gems that do well in captivity, and some will possibly even do well in SPS dominated reef tanks, (with no first hand experience keeping this genus in a reef, I'll leave the reader to experiment). Smaller in size than representatives from either the genus Pomacanthus or Holacanthus, they can make due with smaller quarters, in the 75 gallon range, with the exception of the Scribbled Angel (*Chaetodontoplus duboulayi*) which reaches almost 10" (8" realistically in captivity) and thus requires a tank at least in the 125 gallon range.

So there you have it! Arguably the most beautiful and elegant fish on the reef, the unparalleled interest that the Pomacanthids enjoy amongst marine hobbyists certainly reflects the validity of such a proclamation. There is nothing more spectacular than a healthy angel swimming the length of a large home aquarium. However, the wide range of size, behavior, hardiness and feeding habits, along with the attention and care required to keep them healthy in captivity dictates that their purchase not be taken lightly or made in haste. A conscientious approach to husbandry, and sense of responsibility to the animals in your charge are key ingredients with these fish, as well as all marine fish species.

With a little thought, a little planning and a desire to provide the animals in your care with research, there is no reason why you can't keep one of these beauties healthy for 15+ years in your living room!

FEATURE ARTICLE

EMERGENCY PROTOCOLS FOR HOME AQUARIUMS

By Jay Hemdal

While this article cannot solve every aquarium emergency, it hopefully gives some ideas that can be implemented with little cost which may pay big dividends in saving the lives of aquarium animals.

Published April 2008, Advanced Aquarist's Online Magazine
© Pomacanthus Publications, LLC

Keywords: Equipment, Feature Article, Jay Hemdal, Emergency
Link to original article: http://www.advancedaquarist.com/2008/4/aafeature1

Many people speak of the importance of being prepared for any "unforeseen situations" with their aquariums. This is actually better stated as preparing for "unwelcome situations" - as all of these situations can be planned for because you should be aware they could happen. Truly unforeseen situations only occur to unprepared people that lack an overall knowledge of aquariums. For instance, it might be unforeseen by a beginning aquarist that a heater that sticks in the on position will raise the water temperature and possibly kill their fish. For an experienced aquarist, the potential for this problem is known, and it then becomes an unwelcome situation if it occurs. With the complexity of aquariums growing, (especially reef tanks) the issue of properly handling emergencies becomes of paramount importance. You should compare aquarium emergency pre-planning to having insurance, but unlike home and auto insurance, nobody is going to mandate aquarium preparedness for you.

All aquarists should be reasonably prepared to preserve the lives of the organisms in their care should some disaster strike. The two points at the heart of this issue is the personal responsibility for the animals in the aquarist's care, and the animal's replacement cost should anything happen to them. To be perfectly frank, aquarists do need to perform a cost-benefit analysis on the potential emergency protocols that they intend to implement. Having no plan is of course the least expensive option - but obviously offers no protection at all. On the other hand, having complete equipment redundancy with automatic back-up power supplies could cost many times more than the animals themselves. Each aquarist needs to determine the risk level that they feel comfortable with. Remember though that you are dealing with the lives of animals that you are solely responsible for, so the effort given towards emergency planning needs to be done with that in mind, not just the replacement cost of the animals.

Just how widespread is the issue of aquarium emergencies? Obviously, we all know the potential is there to lose animals due to emergencies, but how common of a problem is it? In one online poll, 38 percent of a group of marine aquarists reported having lost animals due to a power failure. This is significant in that many more aquarists had experienced problems, but were able to manage the issue without loss of animals. It seems then that it is safe to assume that if you stay active in the aquarium hobby long enough, you will experience an emergency with your aquarium at some point.

TYPES OF EMERGENCIES

Power outages are perhaps the most commonly experienced aquarium emergency. Most marine aquariums develop low dissolved oxygen problems within a few hours of the power going out. During the winter, loss of power may also cause problems with low water temperatures. There are a variety

A natural gas genset used by a public aquarium for 25 years.

of resources discussed later that mitigate the problems caused by power disruptions.

Fires can be devastating to aquariums. Obviously, aquariums will be damaged if exposed directly to the heat or flames from a fire, but even a small kitchen fire can kill aquarium inhabitants due to exposure to smoke. Assuming there is no immediate threat to humans, emergency procedures to prevent smoke damage include temporarily isolating the aquarium by turning off filters and air pumps and sealing the entire aquarium in plastic sheeting. Smoke can further be excluded by then setting up a large air pump or blower outside the smoke-filled area to blow fresh air into the "isolation tent" made of plastic sheeting.

Equipment failure is also a common causes of aquarium emergencies. A stuck float switch or check valve can disable an aquarium's life support system in a matter of seconds. A seized circulating pump may cut off all water flow to an aquarium. Heaters that stick on or off will cause disruptions in the aquarium's water temperature. Catastrophic water loss through a plumbing failure or a tank leak can be devastating to the animals as well as causing water damage to the home. With very large glass aquariums, especially homemade ones, the question is usually not "will the tank leak?" but "when will it leak?"

Any natural disaster that affects a person's home will have an impact on their aquariums. One story goes that Indo-Pacific lionfish having found a new home in the Atlantic Ocean could have possibly arisen from lionfish swept from their aquariums in Miami out into Biscayne Bay by hurricane Andrew.

There is one category of emergency that doesn't quite fit with the topic of this article - when a human health emergency is caused by an aquarium animal. These are cases where the aquarium itself is in no jeopardy, but the aquarist has been injured by one of their animals. Know the relative health risks of all of your aquarium animals and avoid any species that can cause serious human health problems, especially in homes with children.

The life support criteria that must be managed during an emergency include dissolved gasses (primarily oxygen), light (for corals), temperature, and in long-term emergencies, nitrogenous wastes. There are a variety of methods available to help an aquarist maintain life support systems. Some are

AVERTING THE MOST COMMON DISASTER OF ALL!

The most important device to reduce animal loss in an aquarium is a quarantine tank and a comprehensive system to quarantine all new arrivals. It truly is a disaster to introduce a new specimen into your aquarium and bring in a disease at the same time.

just temporary or partial fixes, and the cost can vary greatly between methods. A lesson in pre-planning can be taken from public aquariums that certainly have a need for emergency life support systems for their valuable aquatic exhibits. The Association of Zoos and Aquariums, a member organization that accredits many of these facilities has standards for their members that addresses this issue. First, all AZA members must have written emergency protocols, and then use them to conduct periodic drills. AZA member institutions must also have warning systems such as fire alarms and emergency lighting in place to alert for a failure in any of their aquatic life support systems. In addition, the AZA requires that "emergency backup systems must be available" for the life support systems. Many public aquariums use large auxiliary generators with automatic transfer switches to serve this purpose. What does all this mean for home aquarists? Simply put, anything that is such a high priority with professional aquarists must be considered important for serious home aquarists as well.

POSSIBLE SOLUTIONS

UNINTERRUPTIBLE POWER SUPPLY (UPS)

Commonly used to maintain computer operations during short term power disruptions, a UPS system's greatest attribute is that it automatically switches on when the power goes out. Remember that by design, a UPS unit only needs to power a computer long enough for the user to save their work and shut the computer down. For that reason, the battery bank in a UPS may not have much capacity. Except for the smallest aquariums, a UPS device should really only be relied upon to run a small pump or to maintain power to any computer controls on the aquarium that might lose their memory during a power outage.

POWER INVERTER

Having a power inverter can be very helpful in some instances. These devices convert 12 volt direct current to 115 volt alternating current that can then be used to power aquarium equipment. Like generators, these devices have power ratings for peak and continuous usage, so be sure that your expected total wattage will be less than 80% of the converter's continuous rating.

A 150 watt inverter may cost $20 to $30 and can run basic life support for small to medium aquariums. For $10 you should be able to find a 40 watt inverter that can power a small air pump and maybe even a small circulating pump. It is often recommended not use an inverter rated higher than 300 watts if it plugs into a cigarette lighter socket as it may cause the vehicle's fuse to blow. Inverters with a capacity of greater than 1000 watts may require high output alternator and banked batteries (as might be found in a recreational vehicle). Some electronic devices will only work with inverters that produce what is termed "true sine wave" electricity, so check with the manufacturer for the specific needs of your equipment.

GENERATORS

The primary emergency electrical system for most homes and businesses is an electrical generator that runs on fuel (gasoline, diesel or natural gas). These devices range in size from tiny 600 watt portable units to whole-building generators with automatic transfer switches. When sizing a generator for your needs remember that pumps and chillers all require a peak starting power greater than their rated wattage while running. Advice from an electrician should be sought when planning a power generation system using large generators.

SCUBA TANK

Enterprising aquarists who are also divers may want to rig a device that will aerate their aquariums from a SCUBA cylinder. Using the first stage from an old regulator, the LP hose

An automatic generator transfer switch at a public aquarium.

can be attached to a needle valve that can handle the rated pressure of around 150 psi. From the needle valve, a standard aquarium airline runs into the tank ending with an airstone. Simply cracking open the SCUBA tank valve will aerate the aquarium for at least two hours. Periodically closing the valve can extend the life of the air in the cylinder ten-fold. Anyone with access to a medical or welding oxygen cylinder can rig a similar, but much more effective aeration system.

EMERGENCY COOLING METHODS

Adding ice to an aquarium is one possible solution to high water temperatures resulting from a chiller failure. In marine aquariums the ice must be isolated from the seawater either by a plastic bag, or by freezing water beforehand in two-liter plastic soda bottles. The most important question is, "How much ice will be needed?" The best way to answer this question is to run a quantitative test before you experience an actual failure of the life support system. Prepare a series of ice blocks or frozen two liter bottles of water. Then, disconnect the chiller or turn off the air conditioning and add measured amounts of ice to the aquarium and record the results. As long as some ice remains, do not add more. As the ice melts fully in each container, remove it and replace it with another frozen one. Monitor the water temperature during this process, adding more ice if the temperature rises and removing some if the temperature drops too far. Run this test for 4 to 6 hours and then calculate the amount of ice it took to maintain a stable temperature and divide by the numbers of hours. This number will be the amount of ice you will need to keep the aquarium at a proper operating temperature for the period of the expected equipment failure or power outage. To put this in perspective, in one actual test 4 pounds of ice was found to hold a 30 gallon aquarium at its set temperature (25 degrees below ambient) for three hours. It took 8 pounds of ice to hold a 120 gallon aquarium 25 degrees below ambient for three hours. A 500-gallon concrete tank was held at 15 degrees below ambient for 2 hours with 22 pounds of ice (Hemdal 2006).

EMERGENCY PROCEDURE SAFETY

Aquarists are cautioned that some emergency protocols can create a risk to health and property. Remember that these situations often mix electricity, internal combustion engines and water - all during potential disaster conditions such as storms and floods. The best way to avoid problems is to fully understand the operation of every piece of safety equipment before you need to use them. Always follow the manufacturer's instructions and never use a device outside its operational parameters.

Another method of emergency cooling that works especially well if the temperature does not need to be lowered too much is to use cool tap water running through 50 to 100 feet of vinyl tubing immersed in the aquarium or its sump, with the hose output running to a drain. Turning the tap water flow rate up or down will serve as a rough way to adjust the aquarium's water temperature - a type of cooling coil.

MAINTAINING HYDRATION

In cases where the aquarium has leaked or the plumbing has failed, the animals may be exposed to the air and will soon die if not rescued. For fish and macro-invertebrates, the solution will be to move them to a container housing enough seawater to keep them alive until the situation can be resolved. This may be something as simple as temporarily moving these animals to the aquarium's sump.

What about an aquarium filled with corals and live rock? One often overlooked answer to this problem lies in a roll of paper towels. Corals can survive for varying lengths of time out of water if kept from drying out completely. In fact, some live corals are routinely shipped "damp" wrapped in plastic sheeting or even damp newspaper. Soaking paper towels in seawater and then draping the towels over corals and live rock will keep them alive for anywhere from four to perhaps as long as 36 hours. Covering the top of the aquarium with plastic sheeting and/or ladling fresh seawater on the paper covered corals can extend the time they can survive out of water.

CHEMICAL ADDITIVES

There are cases where basic life support systems can be maintained, but some water quality parameters begin to fail anyway. For example, in a long-term power outage, fish life may be saved by some device, but the corals begin to die due to lack of light or some other factor. In these cases, nitrogenous wastes (ammonia) must be managed. There are a few ammonia neutralizing chemicals on the market, and should be a part of every aquarists "medicine chest". Some aquarists have experimented with using hydrogen peroxide as a supplemental source of oxygen, but as this compound is so reactive, it is difficult, if not impossible to dose correctly during an emergency.

WHEN TO INITIATE EMERGENCY PROCEDURES

Its common practice for aquarists to start up an emergency life support system immediately after the emergency begins. The power goes out, and the natural reaction is to start up the battery back-up system or the generator right away. There are a few cases though where it is best to wait. For example, batteries have a finite amount of energy available to run the life support system. Once that reserve is exhausted, they stop. Think of an aquarium that is operating normally

and has a dissolved oxygen saturation level of 8 ppm. The power goes out and the dissolved oxygen level hold steady for a time and then begins to drop. If you start the battery back-up right away, some of its energy will be wasted holding the dissolved oxygen at, or slightly above the saturation level. On the other hand, the animals can survive oxygen concentrations down to some point below that of saturation. It you wait to start the battery back-up until the dissolved oxygen levels drop a bit, then more of its energy will go to maintaining an acceptable dissolved oxygen level. How long to wait is a matter of good estimating. Without a dissolved oxygen test kit, it may be a bit of a guess, although you can

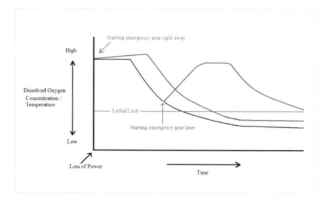

A graph showing when to initiate emergency procedures.

THE AFTERMATH: ADDED INSURANCE

When the emergency is over, regardless of the success you've had in saving the animals, there may be the additional step of contacting your insurance company to file a claim:

1. Always speak with your agent beforehand so that you know what is covered and what isn't (live animals are rarely covered, and you may need a special rider to cover water damage from an aquarium).

2. Prepare an inventory of your aquarium equipment, both as a list and in pictures or video. Receipts are also helpful. Needless to say, don't store these records in the same area where the inventoried items are!

3. Document the loss in the same manner, especially if you took steps to reduce the claim (making repairs to broken windows, renting a generator etc.)

4. Contact your insurance company as soon as possible following the loss.

certainly observe the fish's respiration rates, and don't begin emergency aeration until a slight rise in their breathing rate is noted. Another application of this idea is when using ice or other finite water cooling method. Delaying the use of ice until needed will extend the length of time that the aquarium's water temperature is kept within a range that can be survived by the animals. The associated graph attempts to show this pictorially. Animal loss occurs when any of the lines crosses the red threshold. Notice that by initiating the emergency procedures only when absolutely necessary, the animals can be kept alive a bit longer.

WHEN TO ABANDON RESCUE ATTEMPTS

There are going to be some unfixable situations, where nothing you can do will help your animals. Examples include; the house holding the aquarium sustains structural damage, the power remains out too long or the floodwaters rise to the tank level. In these cases, it may be best to give up trying to maintain life support systems and determine if there is any way to move animals to a safer place. Paramount to all this is you must discontinue any attempts at emergency aid for your aquarium if there is any risk to human safety. An example of this would be staying with your aquarium during a wildfire, or not evacuating your home after damage from an earthquake. While this may seem like obvious common sense, in the heat of the moment people sometimes make poor decisions.

The reaction of the staff of the Aquarium of the Americas in the wake of hurricane Katrina is a good example of proper handling of aquariums after a massive natural disaster that could not prevent animal loss. According to published reports, the Aquarium of the Americas lost many of their 10,000 specimens when their emergency generators failed due to flooding. Aquarium staff that remained behind managed to save certain high value or air breathing animals by moving them out of the facility to safety. In most opinions, there was nothing else that could have been done in this case - emergency generators are typically designed to keep animals alive for the short term, not during months of rebuilding following a disaster of this magnitude.

CONCLUSION

Aquarists should have a written protocol for household members to use to take care of the aquarium in their absence. It does no good to build redundant systems, have power back-ups at the ready and then be out of town when an emergency arises.

Preparing for aquarium emergencies is a bit like listening to a sales pitch for life insurance; it is probably a good idea, but nobody really enjoys the process. While this article cannot solve every aquarium emergency, it hopefully gives some ideas that can be implemented with little cost which may pay big dividends in saving the lives of aquarium animals.

REFERENCES

1. Hemdal, J.F. 2006. **Advanced Marine Aquarium Techniques.** 352pp. TFH publications, Neptune City, New Jersey

BREEDER'S NET

REARING THE GOLDEN DAMSELFISH, *AMBLY-GLYPHIDODON AUREUS*, A PROMISING CANDIDATE FOR AQUACULTURE

By Todd Gardner

Four separate spawns were collected, eggs were hatched, and larvae were reared with a success rate approaching 100%, using rotifers as a first food. These preliminary successes in rearing A. aureus suggest that members of this genus may be good candidates for commercial aquaculture.

Published April 2008, Advanced Aquarist's Online Magazine

Keywords: Breeder's Net, Breeding, Todd Gardner, aquaculture, captive breeding, Damselfish
Link to original article: http://www.advancedaquarist.com/2008/4/breeder

D amselfishes (Pomacentridae) present a quandary for people involved in marine ornamental aquaculture. They are hardy, aggressive feeders that come in an impressive variety of brilliant colors and they are extremely popular in the marine aquarium hobby. However, despite the popularity of the entire family, only two genera of 28, *Amphiprion* and *Premnas*, have been cultured commercially. Attempts to rear species within other genera, including *Pomacentrus*, *Abudefduf*, *Chrysiptera* and *Dascyllus*, have met with little or no success to date. The reason for this is likely that their small size at hatching prevents them from accepting rotifers as a first food. I have been able to verify this hypothesis through my own experience while attempting to rear *Chrysiptera paracema*, *Dascyllus trimaculatus*, and *Pomacentrus leucostictus*. *Dascyllus albisella* and *D. aruanus* have been reared in the laboratory (Danilowicz and Brown, 1992), but not without the use of wild plankton. Although damselfishes account for almost half of the 20-24 million individual marine ornamental fishes traded annually (Wabnitz et al. 2003), their relatively low price fails to provide an economic incentive for aquaculturists and researchers to work toward overcoming the bottlenecks preventing their commercial production.

In the investigation described herein, eggs from a pair of *Amblyglyphidodon aureus* were collected from the living coral reef exhibit at Atlantis Marine World, a public aquarium in Riverhead, NY. Four separate spawns were collected, eggs were hatched, and larvae were reared with a success rate approaching 100%, using rotifers as a first food. These preliminary successes in rearing *A. aureus* suggest that members of this genus may be good candidates for commercial aquaculture.

METHODS

In May 2006, six *A. aureus* were received as a donation from a hobbyist and placed in the 20,000-gallon coral reef tank at Atlantis Marine World. This was our first experience with damselfishes of this genus and our observations of their behavior in quarantine led to our decision to place them in the reef tank. Like *Chromis* spp. and in contrast to many other Pomacentrids, *Amblyglyphidodon* spp. are pelagic and gregarious, swimming out in the open in loose assemblages rather than aggressively defending a territory on the bottom. These characteristics make them much more suitable for a large community tank than many of their solitary relatives.

In August 2006, while working on a piece of plumbing in the tank, an egg mass was discovered on a pipe near the surface. Observation later revealed one of the *A. aureus* defending it. We had no way of knowing how long the spawn had been

there, but after two additional days, the eyes appeared to be well developed and we decided to remove the pipe so we could attempt to hatch the eggs.

The pipe was placed in a 29-gallon aquarium with natural seawater and the eggs were agitated with gentle aeration. Most of the eggs hatched on the second night after moving the pipe. Larvae were approximately 5mm upon hatching. Rotifers (*Brachionus rotundiformis*) were added and maintained at a density of 10/ml. Although the larvae were large and appeared to be eating rotifers immediately, my previous lack of success rearing other damselfish species prevented me from being overly confident and I decided to incorporate cultured copepods (*Acartia hudsonica*) into the daily feeding regime in addition to rotifers. The alga, *Isochrysis galbana* was maintained at an approximate density of $2x10^5$ cells/ml for the first 10 days, after which time the tank was connected to the system. The rearing system consists of seven 29-gallon aquaria, a bio-filter and 40-watt UV sterilizer. Beginning on day 11, HUFA-enriched *Artemia* was introduced to the larval diet and became the exclusive food after a 3-day overlap with rotifers and copepods. Dry foods were introduced at day 20, however *Artemia* remained the primary food through day 50.

Around day 15, the larvae began to change in shape and behavior. They became more compressed, laterally and the body became noticeably deeper. The caudal fin also became slightly forked and small melanophores (pigment cells) began to appear. Larvae began associating with the bottom or some structure in the tank such as airlines and plumbing. Another distinct metamorphosis occurred around day 30 when the body shape deepened further and a sudden, drastic increase in melanophores resulted in the fish taking on a

bright yellow color, virtually overnight. No mortalities were observed during the larval stage except for the 5 individuals sacrificed, weekly for photographing and measuring. The average growth rate of larvae for the first 30 days was approximately 0.17mm/day.

Larval A. aureus immediately after hatching. Photo by Todd Gardner

Larval A. aureus at day 12 post hatching. Note deepening body, differentiation of fins and the first appearance of pigment. Photo by Todd Gardner

1 ½ inch PVC pipe with eggs from the first spawn. Eggs hatch in the evening under gentle aeration 5-6 days post spawn. Photo by Todd Gardner

Larval A. aureus at day 15 post hatching. The fins are almost fully developed. Photo by Todd Gardner

Unfortunately, I must mention one negative habit of this mostly-reef-safe species. Although it is relatively peaceful for a Pomacentrid and does not have an appetite for desirable reef invertebrates, spawning pairs occasionally strip the tissue off part of an Acropora branch and use it as a nest site. This is not a problem in our 20,000-gallon reef tank, where an army of coral-eating fishes is no match for the growth of our scleractinians, however it's easy to understand how a hobbyist with a small reef tank might not tolerate this behavior. I never asked the donor, but I can't help but wonder if that has something to do with why we received the donation in the first place. The good news is, once a pair has decided on a nesting site, they usually stick with it. The pair that is responsible for the spawn shown in **photo #10** has been using this site for more than six months without further damage to the coral. They may even help to protect the coral colony on which they spawn by keeping algae off the exposed skeleton, eating parasites, and chasing away coral grazers.

Three subsequent spawns have been removed, hatched, and reared since the original trial, all without the use of copepods, and all with survivorship approaching 100%. The ease with which A. aureus has been reared in these preliminary trials suggests that it may be a suitable species for aquaculture. We shipped part of the first brood to our friend, Bill Addison, owner of C-quest marine ornamental fish farm in Puerto Rico, so hopefully, captive-bred golden damselfish will soon be available in your local fish store.

A. aureus at day 32. For me, the greatest reward for all my tedious labor in aquaculture is the sight of a tank filled with newly metamorphosed post-larvae. Photo by Todd Gardner

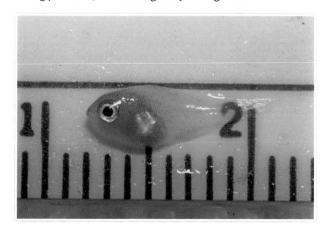

In this 15-day-old larva, pigment cells can be seen over much of the body. Photo by Chris Paparo

By day 30, post hatching, A. aureus has taken on the characteristic damselfish body shape. Photo by Todd Gardner

At day 60, these golden damsels could be considered market-size. Perhaps they will add a splash of color to our 80,000-gallon snorkel tank this summer. Photo by Todd Gardner

A golden damselfish watches over her nest on a gorgonian skeleton. Photo by Joe Yaiullo

Their tendency to build nests on coral skeletons may make Amblyglyph-idodon species a questionable choice for some reef keepers. Photo by Joe Yaiullo

LITERATURE CITED

1. Danilowicz, Bret S. and Brown, Christopher L. 1992. Rearing methods for two damselfish species: *Dascyllus albisella* and *D. aruanus*. Aquaculture 106: 141-149.

2. Wabnitz, C., Taylor, M., Green, E., and Razak, T. 2003. From ocean to aquarium: The global trade in marine ornamental species. UNEP World Conservation Monitoring Centre. 65 pp.

AQUARIUM FISH

CONSPICILLATUS ANGEL

By Pavaphon Supanantananont

This is not the an easy member of the genus because they are sensitive. Because of it price and rarity, make sure that the fish started to feed before you get it.

Published April 2008, Advanced Aquarist's Online Magazine

Keywords: Angelfish, Aquarium Fish, Fish, Pavaphon Supanantananont
Link to original article: http://www.advancedaquarist.com/2008/4/fish

I think that every aquarist would like to have a fish of their dreams, the one that they just want to see once in a lifetime. For me, I also have one too! And that is the fish that I would like to discuss here. It is the Holy Grail for all Angelfish lovers, the Conspicuous Angelfish (*Chaetodontoplus conspicillatus*)

Conspicillatus Angel belongs to the family Pomacanthidae like all other angelfishes. It is one of the rare members of the genus *Chaetodontoplus*, which makes it infrequently seen or available to aquarists. It is a sought after around the world due to its spectacular markings and rarity. The fish has a gray body on the upper part which turns a darker color until it becomes black on the lower part. In some individuals, the different between these two colors may become less obvious. The easiest way to distinguish this species is to look at a bright blue ring-like line surrounding the eyes on the yellow face, which makes it as obvious and attractive as it name: conspicuous.

Like other members of the family, the juvenile of the conspicuous has another color pattern that doesn't look exactly the same as the adult. The juvenile of this species looks similar to the adult but lacks the blue line around the eye and yellow patch on the middle of the pectoral fin. Also, the ventral fin is black instead of white and there's some color missing on the other parts of the body.

This 'angelfish is found south of the great barrier reef toward the islands of the South Pacific like New Caledonia and Lord Howe. In Lord Howe, the fish have been observed in lagoons and at a lesser depths. But Lord Howe is a protected area so that all wildlife cannot be taken out of the wild. Normally, this fish will be found near coral reefs and lagoons or the protected area near harbors at depth between 2-60 meters. Adults will be found at a greater depth, while the juvenile is more common in shallow water. This is a large angelfish species that can grow up to about 10 inches in length.

There was a report of a hybrid between the Conspicuous (*C. conspillatus*) with the Meredith's Angelfish (*C. meredithi*) in the wild. On rare occasions, this hybrid will be caught and sent to Japan where it commands a high price tag. Several pictures of this cross-breeding have been taken and published in many Japanese fish magazines and books.

The first time that I had a chance to see this fish was when I spend my holiday in Hong Kong, at a fish market. The one that I saw was about 10 inches. At first I saw the fish swimming in the main show tank. I was very excited to walk around the tank to get a better look at it. This full grown *Conspicillatus* angel is housed with many 'big size' angels such as Halfmoon Angelfish (*Pomacanthus maculosus*), French Angelfish (*P. paru*), Emperor Angelfish (*P. imperator*), Blue-ring Angelfish (*P. annularis*), King Angelfish (*Holacanthus passer*) and many more. The fish seems to be healthy in appearance, but a crowed tank like this may cause stress in the fish and its health in the long term. After watching for awhile, I asked the owner for permission to take a photo. He was kind enough to let me do so. He told me that the fish was not for sale, and that it was with him for awhile and was eating well.

The Conspicuous Angel is considered a very rare fish from the Thailand fish trade. It has been shipped from Hong Kong on a few occasions long ago and never appeared again. However, this fish is occasionally offered for sale in the U.S. and Japan.

My elder friend, Archen Supasri, who is a rare fish collector, suddenly was able to get one for his tank right after he saw it. The fish that Archen got was about 5 inches. I told him that it might be too big and be too finicky to get to start eating. The one that we selected was the smallest one in this shipment and it was in great condition with no sign of disease. It was amazing to see the reaction of people when it appeared at the front of the holding tank. On that day, I decided to follow Archen to his house when he introduced the fish to his tank.

Archen's tank is 7-ft reef tank that housed mainly *Pseudanthias spp.* together with several wrasses and some angelfish like the Japanese Pygmy Angelfish (*Centropyge interruptus*),

Joculator Angelfish (*C. joculator*), Flame Angelfish (*C. loriculus*) and a Goldflake Angelfish (*Apolemichthys xanthopunctatus*). When first introduced, the conspicuous quickly swam into a rock crevice for protection. We were happy to see that it was not getting bullied by other angelfish which we were concerned about; maybe because it was larger than any of the other angelfish in the tank.

For the first three days, the fish seems not to show any interest in food. It swam peacefully around the tank, but would dash to the crevice when someone approached. The active school of smaller *Pseudanthias* made a perfect type of fish for it to feel more comfortable. It became one of our topics every time when we talked on telephone for almost a week. However, on the fifth day, it started to show interest in dry clam and the pellets which was floating in front of it. Archen cried out loud with happiness on the phone while he was having the conversation with me after he saw it eat pellets for the first time.

After that we both were busy and did not communicate with each other for about two weeks. Then one early morning, I received a phone call telling me with great joy that the Conspicuous Angel became tame and he could feed it from his hand. I was glad to hear the news and immediately rushed to his house.

On weekends, I usually went to visit him to look at the fish. His tank is gorgeous and wonderful for me as it always is.

gets started might help when it stops eating the food we normally offer.

Larger specimens usually refuse to eat and gradually vanish in a home aquarium. The best size to get them eating is the small juvenile around 3-5 inches. If you are lucky enough to acquire one that starts to eat, do not disturb it and let it fully acclimate to the tank so that it doesn't get stressed and stops eating. Newly introduced fish are prone to Ich and fin rot, but it will get better in a tank with good water quality.

These fish will do well in a big tank with plenty of crevices for them to hide when threatened. Good water quality is required like for other members of the genus Chaetodontoplus. This is not the an easy member of the genus because they are sensitive. Because of it price and rarity, make sure that the fish started to feed before you get it.

Archen kept mainly soft corals such as *Sinularia*, *Sacrophyton*, and *Lobophyton spp.*, along with some *Acropora* and *Turbustrea spp*. He was lucky that his *Conspicillatus* did not attack any corals and clams. By the way, many people have reported that this is not a totally reef safe angelfish, especially with zoanthids and brain corals. And some would even nip at the polyps of *Acroporas* or some LPS.

By now, the fish has been kept for about two years. The only problem that we have encountered was cloudy eyes, which was the result of poor water quality mainly from a nitrate problem. But its eyes turned back to normal after water changes. This symptom could be preventing by maintaining better water quality. But for others, the main problem is how to get the fish to eat. At the beginning, the *Conspicillatus* is considered a difficult fish to start eating. But once it starts to eat, it will gradually accept a wide variety of food, from vegetable to meat. It can be feed with pellets and flake or chopped seafood and also ghost shrimp; make sure that it also gets green stuff such as cabbage or Nori as a supplement. Even when it starts eating, many suddenly stop eating. We don't know the exact reason, but switching food once it

References:

1. Allen, G., R. Steene & M. Allen, 1998. - *A Guide to Angelfishes & Butterflyfishes*. Odyssey, USA. 250pp.

2. Debelius, H., H. Tanaka & R. Kuiter, 2003. - *Angelfishes, a comprehensive guide to Pomacanthidae*. TMC-Publishing, UK. 208pp.

3. Michael, S., 2004. - *Angelfishes & Butterflyfishes Plus Ten More Aquarium Fish Families With Expert Captive Care Advice For The Marine Aquarist*. TFH, USA. 344pp.

4. Steene, C., 1978. - Butterfly and Angelfishes of the World Volume 1 Australia. Wiley-Interscience Publ. New York, 144 pp.

5. The Marine Tropical fish catalog 1998. Seibido book. 159 pp. (In Japanese)

LATERAL LINES

WATER FLOW PART II: COMMON DEVICES

By Adam Blundell M.S.

This is a review of some of the more common water flow devices used in the hobby.

Published April 2008, Advanced Aquarist's Online Magazine

Keywords: Adam Blundell M.S., Flow, Lateral Lines, Water Circulation
Link to original article: http://www.advancedaquarist.com/2008/4/lines

Last month I discussed the differing types of water flow. The idea there was to get people thinking about what type of flow they want in their aquarium. This month I'm going to present some very basic information. This is a review of some of the more common water flow devices used in the hobby.

POWERHEADS

Powerheads are submersible water pumps. They have an intake and an output. These have been a staple in the hobby for two decades. There are several manufactures but nearly all powerheads look and work the same. They have a housing with two openings (water to come in and water to go out) and they have a spinning impeller. This impeller is a rotating wheel with many blades, and is driven by a magnet. The magnet spins on a ceramic rod spinning the impeller to push out water.

Shown here a standard powerhead. Water is drawn through the opening in the bottom and pushed out the side outlet.

STREAM PUMPS

After many, many years of the same old thing with powerheads a revolutionary idea came through. Instead of an intake and an output the new series of pumps has a very broad output and the water is drawn in from all sides (a ring

These two pumps may look very similar. One is a stream pump, and the other is a powerhead with a modified casing to create a stream pump.

pattern around the pump) and the flow produced is a wide almost laminar pattern. I describe this is a cylinder of water moving along with the pump in the middle drawing from behind and pushing forward.

Once this type of engineering came into the hobby it spread like wild-fire. The total amount of water pushed around is vastly greater than typical powerheads and the electrical usage is not increased. These pumps are far superior in terms of efficiency.

Two main types of stream pumps are now available. One is a conversion from a standard powerhead where a modification kit is used to replace part of the powerhead. The second is a manufactured stream pump which is designed with a propeller types of blade and not the standard impeller.

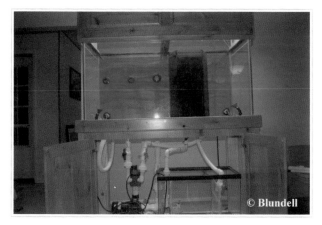

Aquarium Enthusiast "Sukie" shows off her closed loop return system. This system uses four bulkheads where water will re-enter the aquarium. Looking below the aquarium you can see where the water will come out of an external pump, split into four pipes, and go through those pipes back to the tank.

Hang on filters are incredibly popular in the freshwater hobby. For some reason they haven't made a big impact in the saltwater hobby, but that is quickly changing as they are being used more and more in very successful small reef tanks.

EXTERNAL PUMPS

I just like that term because I'm not sure how else to say it. These pumps are not submersible and must be kept out of the water. For these pumps to work they need plumbing. That is they have a pipe that takes water into their intake and another pipe that takes the water out of their output. These pumps can push a lot of water. On average they produce 10 times the water flow and with a considerable amount of head pressure. These pumps are often used as tank return pumps to push water against gravity back up to the display tank.

In recent years the "closed loop" system as become very popular. It should be noted in my opinion the closed loop is about to face extinction. I think a few years from now we'll all be

Shown here are a SCWD which uses gears to push water left, then right, then left, then right and so forth. The water moving through the unit pushes the gears.

The Ocean Motion shown here is being used to divert the return water from an external pump to alternating outlets.

This powerhead has a rotating device on the end which continually spins at a slow speed directing water around in a circle.

The actuated ball valve (Hayward Valve) electronically turns a ball valve to direct water in different directions.

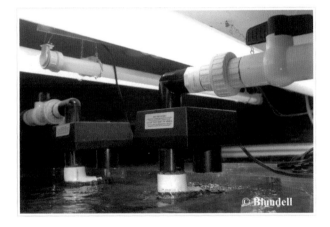

A SeaSwirl is a very common item. This device rotates back and forth at about a 90 degree angle spraying water in a sweeping motion.

looking back on the days' of the closed loop. The idea here is that the water from the display tank runs down a pipe to the pump, then back up another pipe and into the tank. Because gravity is pulling the water down to the pump, it offsets the force needed to pump the water back up to the tank. It produces almost o head loss and the pump can operate at nearly full force. There is more to it than that, but I don't see reason to cover it. Feel free to email me for more details.

HANG ON FILTERS

These filters are super popular in the freshwater hobby. However, they are rarely seen in the marine hobby. That may

be changing as more and more hobbyists venture into the world of nano tanks. These items are great for producing water flow (especially along the surface) for small aquaria.

WATER DIRECTION CHANGING DEVICES

There are four different water direction-changing devices that I frequently see. They are a spinning outlet of some type (usually put on a powerhead), a gear driven item that changes the direction of the water, a valve that opens and closes different outlets, and a powered swiveling outlet. The common manufacture/brands of these items are shown here.

CONCLUSION

While many devices exist for water flow, there are some new revolutionary products on the market and on the horizon. Upcoming articles will introduce these items to the readers. Before exploring these items it is a good idea to learn the basics... and hopefully we just covered that.

AUTHOR INFORMATION

Adam Blundell M.S. works in Marine Ecology, and in Pathology for the University of Utah. He is also Director of The Aquatic & Terrestrial Research Team, a group which utilizes research projects to bring together hobbyists and scientists. His vision is to see this type of collaboration lead to further advancements in aquarium husbandry. While not in the lab Adam provides services for of one of the Nation's largest hobbyist clubs, the Wasatch Marine Aquarium Society (www.utahreefs.com). Adam has earned a BS in Marine Biology and an MS in the Natural Resource and Health fields. Adam can be contacted at adamblundell@hotmail.com.

MEDIA REVIEW

CORAL ID: "AN ELECTRONIC KEY TO THE ZOOX-ANTHELLATE SCLERACTINIAN CORALS OF THE WORLD" AND "CORALS OF THE WORLD"

By Dana Riddle

Dana reviews John Veron's books and CD.

Published April 2008, Advanced Aquarist's Online Magazine

© Pomacanthus Publications, LLC

Keywords: Book, CD, Coral, Dana Riddle, Media Review
Link to original article: http://www.advancedaquarist.com/2008/4/review

Serious reefkeepers will instantly recognize the name of John Veron. He is generally regarded as the world's leading authority on scleractinian corals, and his work has been presented not only in a number of monographs and research articles but in his 1986 *Corals of the Indo-Pacific and Australia*. When this book was released, many serious aquarists acquired it, and few ever dreamed that this classic could be surpassed. But it has been - by John Veron himself, in his 3-volume set *Corals of the World* (with Mary Stafford-Smith as the science editor). As the title implies, corals from the Atlantic and Pacific Oceans are included in these volumes, as well as many newly-described coral species.

Although *Corals of the World* was published in 2000 and *Coral ID: An Electronic Key to the Zooxanthellate Scleractinian Corals of the World* was released in 2002, I suspect quite a few aquarists have entered the hobby in the meantime and might not be aware these valuable volumes. There are many hobbyists who have since advanced to the stage where they can appreciate these works, as well.

If you don't have one or both of these works, you should. Here's why.

CORALS OF THE WORLD

These magnificent volumes contain a wealth of information, with over 2,500 photos and 800 distribution maps (at the family, genus and species level). Eighteen coral families are here (divided into 66 genera and then hundreds of species). Almost all species have either close-up photographs of the each coral's 'skeleton', or (even better) technical pencil drawings that show the corallum structure as few photos ever

could. There is also a short section on non-scleractinian corals (including genera such as *Millepora*, *Tubipora* and others).

Almost all photographs are 'fresh' and are not repeats from *Corals of Australia and the Indo-Pacific*.

VOLUME ONE

Aside from the obligatory Acknowledgements and Introduction, this volume includes an overview of types of coral reefs and discusses the important concept of zonation. This is followed by a chapter on geological history (where you'll learn of 7 mass extinctions of coral reefs over the millennia). Eleven pages are devoted to coral structure which is important for coral identification. The excellent pencil drawings by Geoff Kelley are exceptional scientific renderings. There is a short section on corals in captivity, where Dr. Veron recognizes the importance aquaria can play in public outreach and education, their value as research tools and, lastly, as a way

for developing island nations to protect and manage this sustainable resource while creating modest income.

Volume One then gets down to brass tacks and examines Family Acroporidae, which includes genera *Acropora*, *Astreopora* and *Montipora*. There are a number of newly described species in the 268 discussed. Species are organized by 'groups' (38 for *Acropora*; 4 for *Astreopora* and 12 *Montipora* groupings).

VOLUME TWO

Volume Two in continues in the vein of its predecessor and examines 12 families (56 genera), including:

FAMILY ASTROCOENIIDAE

- *Stylocoenella*
- *Stephanocoenia*
- *Palauastrea*
- *Madracis*

FAMILY POCILLOPORIDAE (INCLUDING NEWLY DESCRIBED SPECIES)

- *Pocillopora*
- *Seriatopora*
- *Stylophora*

FAMILY EUPHYLLIDAE

- *Euphyllia*
- *Catalaphyllia*
- *Nemenzophyllia*
- *Plerogyra*
- *Physogyra*

FAMILY OCULINIDAE

- *Oculina*
- *Simplastrea*
- *Schizoculina*
- *Galaxea*

FAMILY MEANDRINIDAE

- *Meandrina*

- *Ctenella*
- *Dichocoenia*
- *Dendrogyra*
- *Gyrosmilia*
- *Montigyra*
- *Eusmilia*

FAMILY SIDERASTREIDAE

- *Pseudosiderastrea*
- *Horastrea*
- *Anomastraea*
- *Siderastrea*
- *Psammocora*
- *Coscinarea*

FAMILY AGARICIIDAE

- *Agaricia* (3 groups)
- *Pavona* (2 groups)
- *Leptoseris*
- *Coeloseris*
- *Pachyseris*

FAMILY FUNGIIDAE

- *Cycloseris*
- *Diaseris*
- *Cantharellus*
- *Heliofungia*
- *Fungia* (4 groups)
- *Ctenactis*
- *Herpolitha*
- *Polyphyllia*
- *Sandalolitha*
- *Halomitra*

- *Zoopilus*

- *Lithophyllon*

- *Podabacia*

FAMILY RHIZANGIIDAE

- *Astrangia*

FAMILY PECTINIIDAE

- *Echinophyllia*

- *Echinomorpha*

- *Oxypora*

- *Mycedium*

- *Pectinia*

FAMILY MERULINIDAE

- *Hydnophora*

- *Paraclavarina*

- *Merulina*

- *Boninastrea*

- *Scapophyllia*

FAMILY DENDROPHYLLIIDAE

- *Turbinaria*

- *Duncanopsammia*

- *Balanophyllia*

- *Heteropsammia*

FAMILY CARYOPHYLLIIDAE

- *Heterocyathus*

VOLUME THREE

The third volume of this set concludes the work with a look at 4 coral families, plus a highly illustrated synopsis of coral biogeography (including a fascinating look at reproduction), evolution, and a chapter entitled *'What are Species'* (which examines plasticity of coral growth forms in response to environmental and geographical influences). This volume concludes with an important key to coral identification as well as a listing of common coral names. These corals species are examined in detail:

FAMILY MUSSIDAE

- *Blastomussa*

- *Micromussa*

- *Acanthastrea* (2 groups)

- *Mussismilia*

- *Isophyllia*

- *Lobophyllia*

- *Symphyllia*

- *Mussa*

- *Scolymia*

- *Mycetophyllia*

- *Australomussa*

- *Indophyllia*

- *Cynarina*

FAMILY FAVIIDAE

- *Cladocora*

- *Caulastrea*

- *Erythrastrea*

- *Manicina*

- *Favia*

- *Barabottia*

- *Favites* (4 groups)

- *Goniastrea* (3 groups)

- *Platygyra* (2 groups)

- *Australogyra*

- *Oulophyllia*

- *Leptoria*

- *Diploria*

- *Colpophyllia*

- *Montastrea* (3 groups)

- *Plesiastrea*

- *Oulastrea*

- *Diploastrea*

- *Leptastrea*

- *Parasimplastrea*

- *Cyphastrea*

- *Solenastrea*

- *Echinopora*

- *Moseleya*

FAMILY TRACHYPHYLLIIDAE

- *Trachyphyllia*

FAMILY PORITIDAE

- *Porites* (6 groups)

- *Stylaraea*

- *Poritipora*

- *Goniopora* (5 groups)

- *Alveopora*

NON-SCLERACTINIAN CORALS

- *Millepora*

- *Tubipora* and others

Astute hobbyists will have noted that much of this book - coral species, photographs and distribution maps - is available on the internet. See, for instance:

http://www2.aims.gov.au/coralresearch/html/301-400/Species%20pages/342.htm

It should be noted that the internet version does not include all photographs. Those that are included are of reduced size and even when enlarged (and especially when printed) do not reflect the book's quality. Even with the best print quality, the wonderful skeletal drawings are just a little 'fuzzy' when compared to those in the book. Also, there are problems with the scale bars on the internet site (the scale bars in the book are of the correct size).

CORAL ID: AN ELECTRONIC KEY TO THE ZOOXANTHELLATE SCLERACTINIAN CORALS OF THE WORLD

This ambitious endeavor has all corals listed in *Corals of the World*. While chapters are omitted about types of reefs, biogeography, etc., this compact disc contains keys to coral identification, which makes a difficult job relatively easy. The format is well thought-out, and it literally walks the user through the process. While its use can be made easier by understanding the terminology involved in coral ID, it is not mandatory as the keys have line drawings to use as a reference. Don't know what flabello-meandroid means? Not a problem, all one has to do is match the coral to line drawings (see this month's feature article entitled 'Coral Identification Primer for Aquarists').

The CD includes 794 taxa, and with patience, almost any stony coral can be identified through answering up to 45 questions. The identification process is not always lengthy and some corals can be identified after answering just a few questions.

IN CLOSING

Only occasionally does a book transcend the distinctions of multiple disciplines and interests. *Corals of the World* manages to excel as a coffee table book with its amazing photography, yet, for those willing to delve deeper, it becomes a useful resource for the casual snorkeler or experienced diver, an indispensable tool for researchers and taxonomists, plus an inspiration for reef aquaria hobbyists. And it does so at a price that makes it a true value.

I have only one constructive criticism of *Corals of the World*. The undying myth that zooxanthellae are responsible for brilliant coral coloration is continued in this book. In all fairness, we know much more about the subject today than was known when these books were in preparation and now realize certain proteins within coral tissues are responsible for many of corals' brilliant colors.

Coral ID: An Electronic Key to the Zooxanthellate Scleractinian Corals of the World is a worthwhile addition to the library of any serious hobbyist. It offers powerful resources for the coral student and is an excellent research tool for anyone interested in underwater worlds.

Here's a bit of a surprise. I, along with a small group of hobbyists, had the pleasure of having dinner with Dr. Veron at one of San Francisco's sideway cafés a number of years ago. It was a beautiful evening and the food (as would be expected) was excellent, but Dr. Veron regaling us with his stories made for a memorable evening. Of course, there were tales of students trying to trick him by presenting a Caribbean coral skeleton that they claimed was found on the Great Barrier Reef, or his daughter's fascination with the underwater world. But we were astonished to hear that corals are not his true passion (astronomy, and especially star-gazing in the outback, is his hobby). One would never know this judging by the superb quality of his works on stony corals. They are unsurpassed and deserve to be on the bookshelf of every reef hobbyist.

HOW TO ORDER

There are a couple of ways to get these books. The set can be directly ordered from the Australian Institute of Marine Science (www.aims.gov.au/pages/bookshop.html) - shipping of the books from Australian is expensive and slow (unless you opt to pay a premium for expedited shipping). Of course, the standard internet booksellers have the books, but check with one of Advanced Aquarist's advertisers - Marine Depot (www.marinedepot.com) - they have an outstanding price on this 3-volume set. Other online retailers might offer it as well.

To my knowledge the Coral ID CD is available only through the AIMS bookshop. It has been my experience in dealing with AIMS that their shipping is quick, and delivery times are of modest duration. Postage (at least for smaller books and CDs) is reasonable.

FEATURE ARTICLE

WEST ATLANTIC STONY CORALS, PART 3: LARGE POLYP AND FIRE CORALS

By Jake Adams

Jake continues his West Atlantic Stony Coral series with Meandrinids, Mussids, Oculiniids, Caryophillidae, Hydrocorals, and others.

Published May 2008, Advanced Aquarist's Online Magazine

© Pomacanthus Publications, LLC

Keywords: Atlantic, Coral, Feature Article, Jake Adams
Link to original article: http://www.advancedaquarist.com/2008/5/aafeature1

Part 3 will discuss Meandrinids, Mussids, Oculiniids, Caryophillidae, Hydrocorals, and others corals.

MEANDRINIDS

Dendrogyra cylindricus is arguably one of the most majestic Carribean corals after *Acropora palmata*. The colonies form very tall, tightly packed upright pillars which may reach six to eight feet in height and almost as wide at the base. The corallites are meandering, long and continuous and they bare fuzzy golden brown polyps which are extended throughout the day. The species doesn't occur in any great abundance but it is very recognizable and hard to confuse with any other species.

Dichocoenia stokesi is the species of Meandrinids with the smallest corallites. At first glance it closely resembles Faviid species but it is differentiated by the strongly exert corallites with two cycles of prominent septa. *Dichocoenia* colonies are massive, encrusting or plating in colors of dark to light brown or golden yellow. Colonies are most commonly found at intermediate depths, rarely in shallow water where it tends to be very pale in color. *D. stokesi* is the only recognized species with two general forms. The nominal 'stokesi' form has uniform, small round or oval corallites with only one mouth. The secondary 'stellaris' form has more strongly exert, elongated corallites which sometimes have more than one mouth per polyp.

Meandrina is a group of stony coral with an uncertain taxonomy. The genus contains at least one true species with four recognized forms, one of which was formerly considered a separate genus altogether. The yellow to brown surface is characterized by deep valleys and strong ridges made up of long, thin, plate-like septa. *Meandrina* colonies are usually between one to three feet across and they occur

from shallow to deep reef environments, being most common at intermediate depths. *M. meandrites* occurs as plating, encrusting or submassive colonies. The 'danai' form occurs in deeper water as a smallish, stalked colony. The 'brasiliensis' form is also stalked and it can be found attached or free living

Tall upright columns of Dendrogyra cylindricus have long polyps which give the surface a fuzzy appearance.

in calm sandy substrates where it doesn't reach more than a few inches across. *Meandrina 'brasiliensis'* colonies have an elongated appearance with a long central groove surrounded by a convoluted outer edge. *Meandrina 'memorialis'* departs from the typical *Meandrina* shape by growing into columns which somewhat resemble *Dendrogyra*. *M. 'memorialis'* has tightly spaced, strongly meandering corallites and this form was previously classified as the single species in the genus *Goreaugyra*.

MUSSIDS

Isophyllia sinuosa is a large polyped Mussid with loosely meandering corallites which bare large fleshy polyps. *I. sinuosa* prefers a diversity of shallow environments such as fore reefs where it might be exposed to strong surge or back-reefs where it might experience reduced flow and high

sedimentation. The color of the flat or slightly domed colonies is variable between grey, brown, olive or green with pinkish or red streaks and lighter colored polyp interiors. *Isophyllia 'multiflora'* is a growth form with discontinuous corallites and closed polyp valleys. Small colonies of *Mycetophyllia* may be confused with *I. sinuosa* but the latter has a much thicker skeleton and more noticeable polyp tissue. This species somewhat resembles the Pacific Mussid *Symphyllia*.

Isophyllastrea rigida is an unassuming coral which forms small hemispherical or stump shaped colonies. The closely spaced corallites have only a thin margin between them and the polyps are rounded to polygonal in outline. The color is usually a muted brown, grey or green with a pale white or grey polyp valley. *I. rigida* is found in shallow water where it might be common but not abundant. Juvenile colonies have smaller corallites which makes them resemble *Favia fragum* except

Dendrogyra cylindricus with polyps extended on the left column and the polyps retracted on the right column.

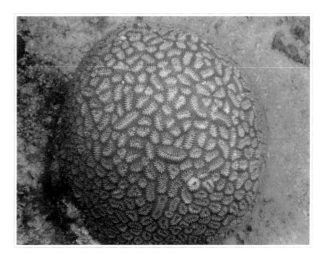

This specimen of D. stokesi with larger, somewhat elongated corallites exhibits some characteristics of the 'stokesi' form.

Dichocoeania stokesi can be very pale when it occurs in shallow water.

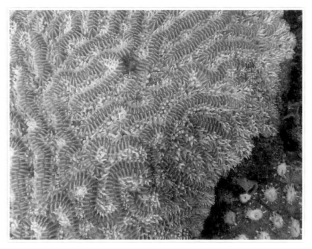

Meandrina meandrites rarely has extended polyps during the day.

for the visibly pale polyp interiors. *I. rigida* very closely resembles the Pacific Mussid *Acanthastrea lordhowensis*.

Mycetophyllia is one the most unique coral genera to be found in the wider Caribbean. Some species of *Mycetophyllia* may resemble the unrelated Pacific *Echinophyllia* except the former has much larger features and structure overall. The species within this genus have a generally flattened colony shape which may encrust the substrate or they may grow plates where the reef structure falls out. The species are mostly identified by the characteristics of the prominent ridges which border long rows of conspicuous corallites. Like many Atlantic Mussids, *Mycetophyllia* tends to be more abundant in intermediate to deep reef environments.

Mycetophyllia aliciae has few large ridges which are sparse towards the interior of the colony and mostly absent in the center. The valleys are widely spaced with two to three polyps between the discontinuous ridges. The perimeter is conspicuous and puffy with folds irregularly growing inwards. The corallites of *M. aliciae* are large for the genus and they are adorned with bright white nodules which contrast with the darker brown or grey polyp valleys. The ridges sometimes exhibit colorful nodules which make them stand out from the rest of the colony.

Mycetophyllia ferox is one of the more easily recognized species in the genus. The small, closely spaced ridges contain a single file of brightly colored mouths within a narrow polyp valley. *M. ferox* colonies display a bewildering assortment of colors with bluish purple ridges, teal to green valleys and

This shallow water *Meandrina meandrites* colony exhibits a submassive growth form.

The small stalked or free living *Meandrina 'brasiliensis'* is often found in shallow or deep sandy habitats.

This stalked individual of *Meandrina meandrites* is known as the 'danai' form.

The close up of this *Meandrina meandrites* skeleton clearly shows the thin, plate-like septa typical of the genus.

orange, pink or red bumps surrounding the polyp mouths. The growth form of *M. ferox* is mostly plating with an overall thinner skeleton and smaller features than other species in the *Mycetophyllia* genus.

Mycetophyllia lamarckiana is somewhat intermediate in features between *M. aliciae* and *M. ferox*. Colonies are encrusting of plating with moderately spaced, meandering ridges which can be continuous or broken into independent ridges and nodules. The darkly colored valleys are contrasted by lighter colored ridges. *M. lamarckiana* is not common but it is most abundant in water that is shallower than other species in the genus.

Scolymia is a recognizable genus to many reef aquarium keepers as the Pacific species are very popular. There are at least

two species of *Scolymia* in the west Atlantic Ocean, both of which are as colorfully adorned as their Pacific counterparts. The polyp of the larger *Scolymia lacera* reaches up to ten inches in diameter when fully extended although they are more typically about six to eight inches across when fully grown. The species can occur in calmer shallow water habitats but it is much more common at intermediate depths, often attached to vertical reef faces. The colors of *S. lacera* can be a muted grey, green and red but some specimens exhibit a darker base color with brilliant red lines radiating from the polyp mouth. Some coral taxonomists believe *Scolymia lacera* to be the solitary form of the colonial *Mussa angulosa*.

Scolymia cubensis is usually found in deeper and cryptic habitats where it grows as a single, neatly circular polyp up to three inches in diameter. The surface of *S. cubensis* is

This stumpy colony of Meandrina meandrites is an example of the 'memorialis' form.

The green polyps and red-streaked ridges of this Isophyllia sinuosa was a common color combination for the species around Puerto Rico.

This shallow water specimen of Isophyllia sinuosa was found on a back reef with reduced flow, turbid water and a high degree of sedimentation.

Isophyllastrea rigida colonies become increasingly dome-shaped or hemispherical as they grow larger.

smoother in appearance than the larger *S. lacera*. The color of *S. cubensis* is a mostly uniform green, red or brown with very little mottling or patterning and it may or may not fluoresce. Juvenile *Scolymia* polyps cannot be reliably identified without careful examination of the skeletal features.

Mussa angulosa is a relatively uncommon coral on West Atlantic reefs but it is very easily recognized. Colonies are composed of large fleshy polyps which have a rough textured surface. The polyps are circular with a single mouth or uneven in outline with multiple polyps. The overall colony shape is flat or hemispherical and they are usually found at intermediate depths. Colors are usually a muted grey or brown with hints of green and red but they can also be colorfully pink or red. *Mussa angulosa* closely resembles some of the large polyped species of *Lobophyllia* from the Pacific Ocean.

OCULINIIDS

Oculina is a group of stony corals occurring in seas throughout the world. The family Oculiniidae also includes the more familiar *Galaxea* corals which are regularly available to aquarists. *Oculina* species are mostly non-photosynthetic with certain species being *facultative heterotrophs* meaning that they may or may not occur with zooxanthellae and they may experience seasonal fluctuations of zooxanthellae densities. Many species of *Oculina* are commonly found associated with deed sea reef formations and at least two species are commonly encountered in shallow water environments of the West Atlantic.

Oculina robusta is an unusual coral which prefers turbid shallow water environments. *O. robusta* is only found in Tampa

The inset features a juvenile colony at about half the scale of the larger image.

Mycetophyllia aliciae has few and widely spaced ridges and lightly colored, contrasting bumps around the polyp mouths.

Mycetophyllia comes in a veritable rainbow of colors..

Mycetophyllia ferox often has very conspicuously colored bumps surrounding each polyp mouth.

Bay and the western coast of Florida and as a result it is commonly imported on the live rock which is cultured in the area. The species grows very sturdy, tapering branches from an even wider base. The large corallites have protruding rims and they are tightly spaced towards the branch tips and widely spaced towards the base. The color is a uniform dark brown with a surface that appears almost shaggy when the polyps are fully extended.

Unlike *O. robusta, O. diffusa* has a much more widespread distribution throughout the Caribbean. *Oculina diffusa* has much thinner branches which are very closely spaced giving the colony a thicket-like appearance. *O. diffusa* occurs in shallow lagoon and calm reef environments and it is frequently found growing among seagrass or on shipwrecks. The species can be deep brown when it is exposed to sunlight or it can be ghostly white if it is shaded or growing in a cave or overhang.

Oculina diffusa colonies do not grow very large because the old skeleton is often dead and covered by encrusting organisms which accelerate the bioerosion of the delicate branching structure.

CARYOPHILLIDAE

The coral family Caryophyllidae is represented in the West Atlantic Ocean by many small solitary and colonial species, only one true reef-building species and perhaps the first documented case of an introduced stony coral species. *Cladocora arbuscula* is a small branching, photosynthetic species. The brown to golden brown colonies of *C. arbuscula* can grow in tight clusters or as loose tangles. *Phyllangia American* grows usually as a single medium sized polyp. *P. Americana* is non-photosynthetic, with clear tentacles and a hint of reddish marking around the mouth. *Tubastrea coccinea* is familiar to

This specimen of *M. ferox* was photographed at intermediate depth without the use of flash

This strikingly colored *Scolymia lacera* is nearly ten inches across.

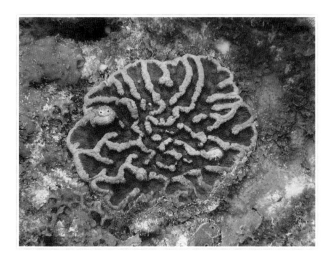

Mycetophyllia lamarckiana often has contrasting polyp ridges and valleys.

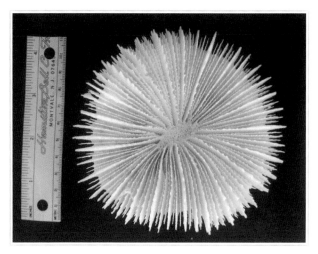

Scolymia lacera is the only solitary coral polyp in the Caribbean that grows over 4"/10cm in diameter.

most reef keepers as sun coral. This coral is normally found in the Pacific Ocean but beginning in the 1940s, this coral started being sighted on Dutch Caribbean reefs. Sun coral is believed to have been introduced by hitching a ride on the bottoms of shipping boats from the Pacific and it has since spread from the Lesser Antilles to the Texas Flower Garden Banks.

Eusmilia fastigiata is the only Caryophyllid in the West Atlantic Ocean which is an important reef-building coral. *E. fastigiata* colonies form hemispherical mounds of stalked polyps which appear to originate from a central point. The greenish or brown polyps are retracted during the day, revealing prominent septa on the circular to oval corallites. This species is most common in shallow to intermediate reefs which are somewhat protected from strong water movement.

HYDROCORALS

Although Hydrocorals are not true corals, no review of Atlantic corals would be complete without at least describing this important group of reef building animals. As the name implies, fire coral has a potent sting that feels like a burning sensation to human skin. The major group of Hydrocorals is fire coral in the genus *Millepora*. Fire coral has a very dense skeleton covered by brown to golden tissue which is pale at the growing edge or tip. The two most common species are *M. alcicornis* and *M. complanata*. *Millepora alcicornis* is a thin branching species which is found in shallow to intermediate water. The branching pattern tends to remain in a single plane but *M. alcicornis* also aggressively encrusts the substrate. *M. alcicornis* is often seen encrusting gorgonian skeletons, sometimes so faithfully that every little vignette of

Scolymia cubensis is very difficult to identify without close examination.

Mussa angulosa has the largest polyps of any colonial coral in the western Atlantic.

Scolymia cubensis remains quite small as compared to other Scolymia species.

Oculina robusta has a thick, tree-like growth form. The conspicuous polyps are retracted in this photograph.

a sea fan remains visible. *Millepora complanata* grows as a succession of short, sharp blades. *M. complanata* is a very sturdy species which is common in very shallow reefs where it is exposed to strong wave action.

ADDENDUM

Solenastrea is a genus which was mistakenly omitted from the overview of West Atlantic Faviids in the previous article. The genus includes two species and it is characterized by intermediate sized polyps which are extended throughout the day, giving the surface a fuzzy appearance. *S. bournoni* is common in a wide range of habitats. The colonies are massive to hemispherical, with a golden brown and somewhat irregular surface. The corallite rims are irregularly spaced and noticeably exert from the surface. *S. hyades* also grows in a wide range of environments but it is particularly abundant in shallow turbid environments which are subject to a high degree of sedimentation. This species grows colonies which are hemispherical and columnar in shape with conspicuous bulges and finger-like projections eventually developing on the top side of colonies. The polyps are dark and widely spaced with pale to white tissue in between them, giving colonies a spotted appearance when the polyps are retracted.

REFERENCE

1. Humann, Paul and Ned DeLoach. 2002. Reef Coral Identification. New World Publications Inc. Jacksonville, Florida.

2. Wood, Elizabeth. 1983. Corals of the World. T.F.H.

Oculina diffusa is commonly found growing in calm back reefs amongst seagrass blades.

Top left, Cladocora arbuscula, Photo by Ernesto Weil. Top right, Astrangia solitaria, not a Caryophyllid. Bottom left, Phyllangia americana. Bottom right, the familiar sun coral, Tubastrea coccinea.

Oculina diffusa has a thin, delicate branching pattern.

Eusmilia fastigiata is the only important reef-building Caryophyllid.

Millepora alcicornis tends to branch in a single plane.

Millepora complanata forms very dense aggregations especially in shallow water where it is exposed to strong surge.

It is much less common for Millepora alcicornis to branch on its own than to encrust an exisitng structure such as the remains of this sea fan skeleton.

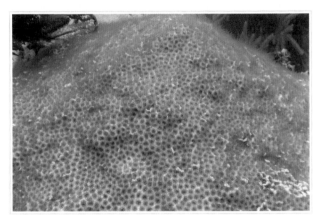

Solenastrea bournoni forms golden brown hemispherical mounds which exhibit an uneven surface.

Millepora complanata is recognized by its fused, blade like growth form.

The light colored tissue and dark colored polyps of Solenastrea hyades give the surface a spotted appearance, especially when the polyps are retracted like in this specimen.

FEATURE ARTICLE

TOP DOWN PHOTOGRAPHING TECHNIQUES AND EQUIPMENT FOR CORALS IN A REEF AQUARIUM

By Sanjay Joshi

This article will explore some of the cheaper options that will allow an aquarist to take stunning top down pictures of corals in the home aquarium with both simple point and shoot cameras and the more expensive SLR cameras.

Published May 2008, Advanced Aquarist's Online Magazine

Keywords: Camera, Feature Article, Photography, Sanjay Joshi
Link to original article: http://www.advancedaquarist.com/2008/5/aafeature2

E very reef aquarist has observed that corals in the aquarium look the most colorful and vivid when viewed looking down into the tank from the top of the aquarium. Often this view is obscured by the rippling surface of the water and reflections of the light from the water surface, making it difficult to view from the top. The only recourse was to turn off the water flow and wait for the surface to get still. Taking pictures from this top view was quite a challenge as even small ripples would distort the surface enough to ruin a perfectly good picture. The alternative was to invest in underwater cameras that allow submerging the entire camera into the aquarium, or encasing the camera in expensive underwater housings. While these are well suited for diving applications, it is quite expensive to purchase an underwater camera or a housing just to be able to take pictures of corals in an aquarium.

This article will explore some of the cheaper options that will allow an aquarist to take stunning top down pictures of corals in the home aquarium with both simple point and shoot cameras and the more expensive SLR cameras. The common denominator in these options is to provide the ability to shoot pictures from below the water surface, thereby eliminating the effects at the air water interface that lead to picture distortion.

USING A SURFACE VIEWING BOX

To enhance the top down viewing experience and allow for taking pictures from this view surface viewing boxes can be designed to eliminate this effect of the water rippling and surface motion. This in its most simple incarnation is a clear flat bottomed sheet of acrylic or glass with side walls. By immersing the viewing box into the water without getting water into the box once can get a clear view without being affected by the surface effects. This is essentially the same concept used by glass bottom viewing boats. Figure 1 shows a commercially available surface viewing box (available through Dr. Foster and Smith). As you can see, the view within the box is clear while the effects of the water surface are visible outside the box.

Using a camera, one can now take pictures of the view of the corals within the box. A major drawback of this technique is that it often requires the use of two hands - one to hold the box in place to prevent it from drifting away and another to handle the camera. A small point and shoot is easier to handle using one hand as compared to a heavier and bulkier SLR. Although this can be made to work, it is not the most convenient method.

CAMERA MOUNTED VIEW BOX

The same concept can be further extended to enable capturing some of the incredible top down views by building simple view boxes for the camera. The key is to attach the box to

the camera so as to keep the lens dry when the viewing area is submerged, and to create a large enough viewing area so the walls do not show up in the field of view.

There are several creative variations of this basic concept that can be used, depending on the type of budget, sophistication and elegance required. All these rely on the basic idea of keeping the camera and lens dry while allowing partial submerging to break the air water interface.

BOX

BOX - this is typically a rectangular box constructed with acrylic, with clear or darkened side walls similar to a surface viewing box. One side is made longer with a screw in it to allow it to be attached to the camera via the tripod mount hole. The box can be made small enough to allow the lens to fit comfortably, or larger to allow the use of your hand for manual focusing. Figure 1 a and 1b shows a typical camera box. This one is made by Marc Levenson. In this design, the long side of the box is bent into a U shape to allow the box and camera to be stabilized against the edge of the tank. This also allows some degree of safety in preventing the box from accidentally getting submerged and filling up with water.

TUBE

TUBE - Another simple variant is to use a cylindrical tube instead of a box. This makes for much simpler construction. The tube is sized to be slightly larger than the lens diameter. Nylon screws are used to hold the tube on the camera lens instead of mounting it to the camera's tripod mount. Figure 2 shows an example of a picture tube given to me by a Boston Reefers club member - Gustavo Pagnozzi. This is currently being used by me on my Nikon D70 SLR camera to take the pictures shown in Figure 5.

Both designs work equally well, and are easy to construct and use. Mounting the tube on the lens allows for manual focusing if the tube is mounted on the camera's focusing ring. However, this approach will not work well with the point and

Figure 1. Top Down Camera Box - pictures curtsy of Marc Levenson

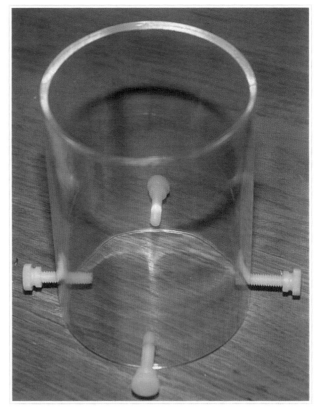

Figure 2. Picture tube built by Gustavo Pagnozzi

shoot camera's where the lens diameter is rather small and the lens retracts into the camera when turned off.

Before using, it is very important to pretest the devices for water proofing, and make sure that the seams are sealed well enough to avoid leaks. Make sure the bottom surface is clean and scratch free. Additionally since these are open be very careful to ensure that you do not submerge the box deep enough to have water go into the box and damage the camera and/or lens.

Figure 3. A cheap version of the top down box designed by Micheal Bollinger

Figure 4. EwaMarine soft water proof bag in use by Jake Adams for taking Top down pics in the Penn State Aquarium. Photo by Gresham Hendee.

3) Cheap 'Ghetto' Version of the Top Down Box

GHETTO - Figure 3 shows a cheap version of the top down box made with Tupperware and plexiglass, designed by Michael Bollinger. Details on construction can be found in this thread on reefs.org (http://reefs.org/phpBB2/viewtopic.php?t=105955). Functionally its servers the same function, allowing the user to submerge the viewing box and keeping the camera and lens dry.

Taking Pictures

Once you have the box (or its variants) mounted on the camera, the following techniques can be used to take the pictures. Keeping the bottom pane submerged use the auto-focus capability of the lens to focus on the corals and take the pictures. To get more close up pictures use a macro lens. Make sure that you keep the inside of the box free of water at all times, else you may make the lens wet and damage it with the salt water. Also make sure the camera is held securely in your hand while taking the pictures. Use the camera strap to further ensure that the camera will not accidentally fall into the aquarium. Stand on a firm stable surface and do not lean too far over the tank so as to fall off balance. Often the lighting system may get in the way. Depending on how the lights are mounted you may be able to move it higher. Usually with the aquarium lights on, you will have enough light to take pictures without any additional lighting. Turn the waterflow off if you want to make sure that the polyps are still and moving polyps are causing blurriness due to slower shutter speeds and/or hand shake. If additional lighting is desired, you can use an external flash.

Other Techniques

There are several relatively cheap plastic water proof soft camera bags that can be used with point and shoot cameras and also with SLR. These bags are made by several companies, such as DiCAPac (www.dicapac.com) and Ewa-Marine (www.ewa-marine.com). Additional advantage of these bags is that they allow the complete camera to be submerged and allow for more flexibility of shooting in an aquarium, with less concern of flooding the photo box. The also provide clear optical quality material windows to take pictures through the bag. These soft bags are designed for underwater photography. When used in an aquarium they are a lot easier to use with camera's that support live view (pretty much all point and shoot camera). With most of the current generation of digital SLRs live view is not an option and view through the viewfinder is not an option when the camera is submerged. In this case, the only option is to rely of auto focusing and some guess as to what the camera is seeing. Figure 4 shows a camera in use underwater in a soft Ewa-marine bag.

Figure 5. Top Down pictures taken using the Picture tube:

FEATURE ARTICLE

HOME FUMIGATION - DO I REALLY HAVE TO REMOVE MY AQUARIUM?

By Dana Riddle

Dana's limited experiences suggest you and your aquarium will make it through just fine.

Published May 2008, Advanced Aquarist's Online Magazine

Keywords: Aiptasia, Dana Riddle, Feature Article, Water Quality, Fumigation
Link to original article: http://www.advancedaquarist.com/2008/5/aafeature3

Fumigation is a means to control pests by enclosing a structure within a 'tent', injecting a gaseous pesticide and allowing the poison time to infiltrate nooks and crannies, thus killing targeted vermin. In Hawaii, using the pesticide Vikane™ (Dow AgroScience's trade name for sulfuryl fluoride - F_2O_2S) is most often used to eliminate drywood termites. It is also used on the mainland to control other drywood termite species. Fortunately, drywood termites do not occur in all states and are restricted to warmer climates. But they can be a real problem in coastal North and South Carolina, south Georgia, Florida, south Alabama, coastal Mississippi, Louisiana, Texas, New Mexico, Arizona and southern California.

Licensed pest control specialists generally recommend removal of aquaria from the structure but *might* allow an aquarium to remain inside during treatment (using, of course, aeration from an air pump situated well away from and outside the building). They are doing what they are trained to do - recommend to the customer the best options for their pets. In fact, little is known about the effects of this pesticide on many animals. Indeed, Kollman (date unknown) states that effects of Vikane on fish, wildlife and other non-target organisms are not known.

Hawaii is a land of eternal summer where killing frosts don't occur (unless you're living on the peaks of the Big Island's Mauna Loa, Mauna Kea or Maui's Haleakala). Hence, invertebrates such as corals thrive, but less desirable inverts such as termites and wood-boring beetles also enjoy the sub-tropical climate, and these pests aren't particular - they live in humble, ramshackle coffee shacks all the way up to multi-million dollar homes. While my home is decidedly somewhere-in-between, several termite colonies were quite content to dine on its wooden frame. Professional help was needed.

My fears were confirmed when the inspector recommended I remove 4 aquaria from the house. This would be a major project! I considered leaving the tanks in the house and simply supplying 'clean' air from outside, but rejected this notion. Instead, at almost the last minute, I decided to conduct a few experiments to determine the effects of the pesticide on a few selected invertebrates. Although this may sound cruel, I knew that moving the animals to an outside home and back again also involved risks to the health and lives of the captive animals. Perhaps something could be learned from this ordeal.

The evening before the scheduled fumigation, I removed a few invertebrates from aquaria and randomly placed them in ten Mason jars containing 750 ml of aquarium water (see Figure 2). Five jars would be left uncovered and aerated from an air pump within the house. This would be the worst case scenario, where nothing was done to prevent the pesticide from making contact with the water and its inhabitants. Another five jars would be covered with two pieces cut from nylon polymer bags (NyloFume™, Dow AgroSiences) which are impermeable to Vikane. These were supplied by the exterminator to bag food, medicine and other goods from exposure. Aeration to these five containers was supplied by an air pump situated well away from the tented house.

Since the air conditioner would have to be turned off during fumigation, I had concerns about the temperature of the jars'

Figure 1. "Tenting" a house for drywood termites. The tent contains the toxic gas within the structure.

contents getting too high. I monitored air temperature and water temperature in one of the covered jars with a datalogger (WatchDog™ model 425, Spectrum Technologies) as well as light intensity (using a Spectrum PAR sensor modified for 60 Hz light). pH and temperature were monitored in an uncovered jar with a separate datalogger (Hach HQ40d™ multimeter). Fluoride (as F⁻) was measured using the SPADNS method and a Hach DR890 colorimeter (chloride concentrations exceeding 7,000 mg/l and sulfate exceeding 200 mg/l will cause high results, and distillation is recommended. This was not done, however it is assumed that there was no difference in the aliquots since they were originally from the same source. Hence the measurements should be valid for comparative purposes).

RESULTS

None of the inhabitants of the covered jars suffered any apparent harm during fumigation. Results were different for some of the invertebrates exposed to the gas. Woven Topsnails (*Trochus intextus*) seemed particularly susceptible to the effects of fumigation and succumbed within 24 hours. Vikane was also deadly to Spiny Brittle Stars (*Ophiocoma erinaceus*), Ten-lined Sea Urchins (*Eucidaris metularia*), and Rock-boring Sea Urchins (*Echinometra mathaei*), but the effects were not immediate and the animals perished over the course of several days. Rock Anemones (*Aiptasia pulchella*) and an unidentified zoanthid (*Protopalythoa* sp.), were 'burned' during the fumigation event but survived (see Figures 3 and 4) and recovered in about 1 week. A green alga (*Ulva*) and unidentified red algae also survived exposure with no apparent harm or loss of photopigments.

DISCUSSION

When examining the possible effects of sulfuryl fluoride on invertebrates, we must consider that another agent is also used during fumigation - chloropicrin. This is a warning agent (a 'tear gas') released in trace amounts into the structure to drive out people or animals the inspector might have missed (there's a scary thought).

Sulfuryl fluoride is soluble in water (solubility = 750 ppm), and in alkaline water (including seawater) it undergoes rapid hydrolysis and forms fluorosulfuric acid ($HSO_3 F$) and fluoride. Hence we would expect to see a drop in pH when Vikane dissolved into the water - and this was noted in the open jar monitored for pH. See Figure 5.

Additionally, we would expect to see an increase in fluoride in the 'exposed' water. This, too, was noted - several days after fumigation, elevated fluoride was found in the water of the jars exposed to the fumigation gases. Natural seawater is used and the covered jars contained ~1 mg/l fluoride while the 'exposed' jars contained an average of 2.2 mg/l fluoride.

Air temperature and hence water temperatures stayed within an acceptable range during the experiment. See Figure 6.

Photosynthetically active radiation stayed at low values during the 12 hour photoperiod. Inadvertently, PAR records indicated exact times the tent was placed on and removed

Figure 2. The experiment's set up. Air temperature, water temperatures, photosynthetically active radiation (PAR) and pH were monitored.

Figure 3. One of the Aiptasia anemones before fumigation with sulfuryl fluoride.

from the structure (the jars were situated near a window; data not shown).

Dissolved oxygen was not measured in the jars but aeration was probably sufficient. Further, decaying matter exerts an oxygen demand and none of the containers with mortalities generated any signs of anoxic or anaerobic activity (judged visually and by smell).

The results from this brief experiment suggest that temperature and pH modulations were not severe enough to cause distress or death in the affected animals. However, swings in these parameters correlated exactly with the release of the pesticide and its warning agent. Further, elevated fluoride

levels found in the 'open' containers several days after exposure suggest sulfuryl fluoride did contribute to the demise of the marine invertebrates.

On a happier note, the specimens in the covered and aerated containers suffered no mortalities. This suggests that covering an aquarium with NyloFume™ bags and providing aeration from a source outside of the affected structure is sufficient to prevent contact with either the warning agent or pesticide.

Based on this evidence, I'll elect to keep the aquaria inside the house and exercise all due precautions next time fumigation is needed. I lost a captive-bred Flame Angel due to stresses of moving him about (and not due to any effects of the pesticide). In retrospect, I should have simply covered the tanks and maintained good aeration and water circulation. If you find yourself in the same situation, where sulfuryl fluoride is the fumigant, perhaps you should consider this too.

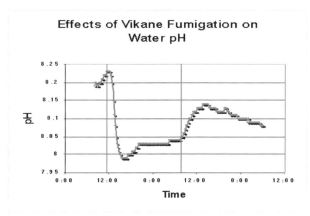

Figure 5. Water pH fell sharply when chlorocipin and sulfuryl fluoride were released into the structure. The green line marks the beginning of fumigation, and the red line is when the 'tent' was removed and structure ventilation began.

Figure 4. The typical appearance of Aiptasia anemones after exposure to sulfuryl fluoride and chlorocipin. They appear to be 'burned'.

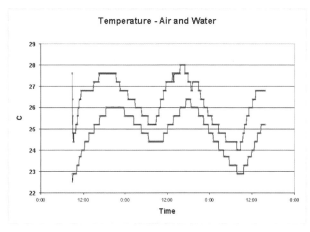

Figure 6: Temperature - Air and Water.

Discuss this with a licensed professional and reach an understanding first. My limited experiences suggest you and your aquarium will make it through just fine.

REFERENCES

1. American Public Health Association, 1998. *Standard Methods for the Examination of Water and Wastewater.* Washington, DC.

2. Environmental Protection Agency, 2008. Structural fumigation using sulfuryl fluoride: DowElanco's Vikane gas fumigant. http://www.epa.gov/ozone/mbr/case-studies/volume2/sulffury2.html

3. Hach Company, 1997. *DR2010 Spectrometer Handbook.* Loveland, Co.

4. Kollman, W., date unknown. Environmental fate of sulfuryl fluoride. Environmental Monitoring Branch, Sacramento, Ca.

FEATURED AQUARIUM

15 GALLON FRESHWATER PLANTED TANK

By Charles J. DeVito

Even in this day and age of exorbitantly colored, ridiculously expensive, inordinately rare corals with over-the-top names like Reverse Radioactive Green Monkey Nipple zooanthids, there's still not much that compares to a school of neons swimming amongst a lush aquatic meadow.

Published May 2008, Advanced Aquarist's Online Magazine

© Pomacanthus Publications, LLC

Keywords: Charles J. DeVito, Equipment, Featured Aquarium, Fish, Freshwater
Link to original article: http://www.advancedaquarist.com/2008/5/aquarium

I stopped keeping freshwater tanks and started keeping saltwater aquariums back in the mid-'80s and set up my first reef tank in 1996. As much as I loved the reef hobby, by the summer of 2007 I decided my conscience simply wouldn't allow me to continue with it. It left me with a dilemma, though, as I loved keeping aquariums and had been doing so for nearly my entire life. In the end I decided to return to the freshwater tanks I'd left behind long ago, and to explore a segment of that hobby that was only in it's infancy way back then, the freshwater planted aquarium.

After a few months of research and gathering parts and supplies, on 10/4/2007 I started up a 15 gallon freshwater planted aquarium. In the months since then I've been amazed at how much I'm enjoying this tank. There's hardly any maintenance involved, and I'm continually surprised by just how easy it is to be successful with it. More than that, I'm genuinely excited by the possibilities of what you can do with this sort of tank, and that's an excitement I haven't felt about reef aquariums

for a long time now. These tanks are about as far from the fruitstand style of most reef aquascapes as you can get.

Best of all, I get to enjoy my hobby without needing to justify it to anyone, least of all myself.

EQUIPMENT

- 15 gallon All-Glass aquarium (24"x12"x12")

- 4 x 24w T-5 lights (6700K)

- Eheim 2213 canister filter

- Hydor in-line heater

- Aqua Design Amano System 72 pressurized CO_2 and solenoid

- Aqua Design Amano bubble counter, diffuser and drop checker

- Aqua Design Amano substrates (Tourmaline, 2 liters of Power Sand, 12 liters of Amazonia soil, 3 liters of Amazonia powder)

I chose a 15 gallon tank for this set up because I felt it offered me a large enough volume to create an attractive aquascape, while at the same time being small enough still that maintenance would be very quick and simple to perform.

The ADA System 72 pressurized CO_2 is designed for use on small tanks. Rather than use a large, refillable CO_2 canister, it instead employs small, disposable 72 ounce cans of CO_2. While not as economical in the long run as a traditional 5 lb canister, these disposable cans are tiny, easy to hide from view and very convenient. I maintain around 30 ppm of CO_2 in my tank, and at that rate one of the disposable cans lasts me just a little bit longer than two months. CO_2 is dispersed via a pollen-glass diffuser, and the concentration of CO_2 in the water is monitored visually with a aid of a drop checker (a nifty little device which displays at a glance if you've got too little, too much, or just enough).

Very little equipment intrudes into the tank itself. The intake and return from the canister filter are positioned in the back left corner, effectively hidden by the plants. The diffuser is partially obscured by the hairgrass at the rear of the tank, and only the drop checker sits out in plain view.

DESIGN PHILOSOPHY

After seeing photos of tanks that featured a "lawn" of *hemianthus callichtroides*, I knew that was what I wanted to do. Although I was intrigued by the Iwagumi ("stone garden") approach currently popular in aquascaping circles, I opted instead to try to recreate the feel of a small meadow at the edge of a forest. As the tank I'm using is only a 15 gallon, one

of the biggest challenges was giving it the illusion of being much larger than it actually is. The open, negative space in the layout helps with that goal, as does the fact that all of the plant species used have tiny, delicate, fine foliage.

TANK SET-UP AND EVOLUTION

I began with 10 pots of *hemianthus callichtroides "cuba"* (more commonly known as HC), 8 pots of hairgrass (*eleocharis acicularis*), 12 *blyxa japonica* and several bunches of *ludwigia repens*. On day one, things looked rather sparse. I had expected the 10 pots of HC to cover more volume than they actually did, and was a bit worried at first because the plant has a reputation for taking some time to get going when introduced to a new tank. The hairgrass looked pretty bad initially as well. Fortunately, just three weeks later both

CO2 can.

Drop Checker

had shown significant growth and had spread a great deal. By the six week mark, the HC lawn had completely filled in.

Also at the six week mark I made my first changes to the aquascape, removing the *ludwigia repens* and replacing it with some java fern and *anubias nana var. "petite"*, both tied down to a stump of driftwood placed where the ludwigia had been. I found I wasn't happy with the finished result, however, and a few weeks later I removed those new additions and replaced them with several bunches of *myriophyllum pinnata* and a dozen or so stems of needleleaf ludwigia (*ludwigia arcuata*).

FISH

- Threadfin rainbowfish (*iriatherina werneri*)

- Spotted Blue-eyes (*pseudomogil gertrudae*)

- Golden Lyretail Killifish (*aphyosemion australe*)

- Otocinclus catfish (*otocinclus affinis*)

- False Siamese Algae Eater (*epalzeorhyncus* sp.)

Diffuser

MAINTENANCE

Surprisingly little is required. My daily routine is just feeding the fish and adding fertilizers. Once a week or so I trim the plants. That mostly consists of topping the stem plants and,

Threadfin rainbowfish (*iriatherina werneri*)

Spotted Blue-eyes (*pseudomogil gertrudae*)

Golden Lyretail Killifish (*aphyosemion australe*)

every now and then, mowing the HC "lawn". Every few weeks I perform a 5 gallon water change, and once every few months I give the canister filter a cleaning.

THINGS I'D DO DIFFERENTLY

This tank has been a learning experience, and as such it's taught me a few things the hard way. Chief amongst them is that mixing HC and hairgrass, while very attractive and effective, is a royal pain. The hairgrass spreads by runners that are often as much as an inch below the substrate, which means hairgrass runners are continuously spreading below the HC lawn. Stems of the hairgrass poke through the HC and require regular removal. If I were to try to use both species in the same tank in the future, I'd use thin sheets of acrylic as dividers in the soil. That way I could keep the hairgrass "caged" and keep it's runners out of everything else.

Otocinclus catfish (otocinclus affinis)

ACKNOWLEDGEMENTS

I'd like to thank Robert Hudson of AquaBotanic, the source of nearly all the plants I've used, as well as Jeff Senske of Aquarium Design Group from whom most of the hardware and supplies were purchased. Both these gentlemen and their companies were very helpful as I got this project started.

I also owe a large "thank you" to Roy Deki of the Arizona Aquatic Plant Enthusiasts. Photos of his planted tanks provided me with the inspiration to begin my own, and the *ludwigia arcuata* stems currently in my tank were sent to me as cuttings from his.

CLOSING COMMENTS

I'd like to encourage the reefing community to give these tanks a try. If you're beginning to feel burnt out on reef keeping, planted tanks offer a beautiful alternative that doesn't involve nearly the amount of work and expense of a reef. If you're having qualms about the morality of the marine ornamentals industry and the health of the world's reefs, the planted tank hobby is the perfect substitute. They also don't require reef-tank levels of patience; even the slowest growing of aquatic plants grows more quickly than the fastest growing of corals. They're appealing; I'll tell you honestly that non-aquarists seem to enjoy a planted aquarium more than they ever enjoyed my reef. They're warm and inviting; a planted tank looks much more natural in any décor than a reef tank does. Where reef tanks can appear alien and eerily blue, the planted tank radiates warmth in shades of green and red and yellow.

Besides, even in this day and age of exorbitantly colored, ridiculously expensive, inordinately rare corals with over-the-top names like Reverse Radioactive Green Monkey Nipple zooanthids, there's still not much that compares to a school of neons swimming amongst a lush aquatic meadow.

PRODUCT REVIEW

ECOTECH MARINE VORTECH PART 1:
BASIC INTRODUCTION

By Adam Blundell M.S.

For a hobbyist who truly wants to create water motion, change the flow, or create a very dynamic system, then this pump is the real deal. The VorTech pump is awesome.

Published May 2008, Advanced Aquarist's Online Magazine

© Pomacanthus Publications, LLC

Keywords: Adam Blundell M.S., Flow, Product Review, Water Circulation
Link to original article: http://www.advancedaquarist.com/2008/5/review

Authors Note - *Between the time of writing this article and the publication date, I discovered that a friend of mine was also working with this product. Jake Adams and I are now working together to co-author a piece showing some of advanced VorTech capabilities.*

INTRODUCTION

Buy this pump! I decided to start this article off with that sentence just to make sure every reader saw it. I've tried out many products and I've seen all the developments and designs used for water motion. The capabilities of the VorTech (mostly derived from the software based computer system) are really second to none.

BACKGROUND

My interest in the VorTech pump stemmed from my constant battle with finding my ideal water flow. I'll admit that I frequently change my opinion on just what is the best flow, but

© Blundell

I've always been leery of laminar flow found in gyre systems. My take is to mix it up and keep it going. In recent months my friend and fellow author Jake Adams has produced some compelling arguments for laminar flow, and I'll address those ideas next month. However I still like some back and forth sloshing in my tank. When it comes to changing up the flow in your tank, nothing beats the VorTech.

VORTECH BASICS

The EcoTech Marine VorTech pump is a propeller style pump. Propeller pumps have made a huge splash in the hobby. Over the last couple years we've seen numerous modification kits and even propeller designed pumps take of the market. The VorTech, however, features a couple unique features.

Magnetic Induction - one of the highly promoted aspects of the VorTech is the induction driven pump. This means that the pump sits on the outside of the tank and magnetically drives the propeller on the inside of the tank. This helps to reduce the amount of heat entering the system as the pump is not in the water. It also removes the pump from the visible area in the tank (some people really don't like seeing large pumps and wire in their tank).

Multiple Controls - the VorTech also possesses many modes of operation. The VorTech has 4 main modes of water flow. They are:

1. Constant Speed

2. Lagoon Random (quickly changing speeds either up or down)

3. Reef Crest Random (slowly changing speeds either up or down)

VorTech mounted to the side of a sample aquarium.

Shown here by using VorTech pumps the aquarist can create a wave effect. Look at the rise and drop of the water level as wave alternates.

4. Pulse Mode (the pump speeds up and slows down at a rate chosen by the user)

These four modes are absolutely fabulous for someone who likes to change up their water flow.

Expanding Abilities - the VorTech pump also has many change-up modes when expanded to more than one pump. Having two VorTech pumps (something highly recommended by this author) allows the user to create an enormous variation in their water flow design. Two pumps could both be set to a Lagoon Random mode and you would have two pumps independently altering their current output. The same holds true for Reef Crest Random and two different Pulse Speed settings. But wait, there's more...

Having two VorTech pumps with wireless sync modes allows for extra variation. Two pumps can be used on a tank and the two pumps can "talk to each other." You can set one pump to a Lagoon Random mode and then "tell" the other pump to simulate what the first pump is doing (speed up when the other pump speeds up and slow down when the other pump slows down). Consequently you can also "tell" the second pump to do the opposite of the first pump (speed up when the other slows down and slow down when the other pump speeds up).

This variation is just one feature that separates the VorTech from other pumps.

VorTech Directions

I decided to list a few important items that I (and others) have found out regarding the usage of the VorTech.

Rise and fall of the water level.

1. EcoTech Marine is awesome. That pretty much sums up their company, their customer service, their care about the effectiveness of their products, and their desire to make something work well.

2. Read the instructions. The VorTech pump (MP40w) includes an instruction book that is well worth reading. In addition to a thorough explanation of how the pump works, it also covers the needed maintenance and warranty information.

3. Keep away from idiots. I was going to say keep away from children, but I've actually seen far more adults

The VorTech propeller was specifically designed to produce a high volume low flow current.

VorTech parts that come with the unit.

with the impulse to pull the pump off the tank and say "what's this?" It is wise to securely attach the pump to the outside of the tank to prevent it from falling to the floor. In fact it is such a good idea that it is described and mentioned 3 times in the instruction manual.

4. Keep your dry-side dry. Don't ever let your wet-side touch the dry-side, and more importantly don't let the dry-side get wet. It is called the dry-side for a reason; keep it out of the water stupid.

5. Keep the wet-side wet. It is explicitly stated in the instruction to not run the pump with the wet-side out of water. It is possible to heat up and melt the wet-side. I tested this by running my pump out of water for several minutes as I recorded the rpm speed of the propeller at low and high speeds (more on this next month). Yep, I can verify that you shouldn't do that.

CONCLUSION

I've spent a lot of time over the last few months playing with this pump. Some things scare me (like someone dropping the dry-side 6 feet to the floor, or someone getting the dry-side wet), but without a doubt this is a super product. If someone is looking to move water in a tank they should look at any one of the much cheaper pumps out there. But for a hobbyist who truly wants to create water motion, change the flow, or create a very dynamic system, then this pump is the real deal. The VorTech pump is awesome. Again that is the best way to sum this up. I'll be showing examples of the water flow produced and the differing modes in an upcoming article. Also, a write up of wave characteristics is on the way.

AUTHOR INFORMATION

Adam Blundell M.S. works in Marine Ecology, and in Pathology for the University of Utah. He is also Director of The Aquatic & Terrestrial Research Team, a group which utilizes research projects to bring together hobbyists and scientists. His vision is to see this type of collaboration lead to further advancements in aquarium husbandry. While not in the lab Adam provides services for of one of the Nation's largest hobbyist clubs, the Wasatch Marine Aquarium Society (www.utahreefs.com). Adam has earned a BS in Marine Biology and an MS in the Natural Resource and Health fields. Adam can be contacted at adamblundell@hotmail.com.

FEATURE ARTICLE

Google SketchUp for Aquarium Applications, Part II

By Shane Graber

In this second part, Shane digs a bit deeper into using SketchUp for modeling aquarium projects. You will learn a bit about using scripts to automate tasks as well as to add new functionality to SketchUp while building a kalkwasser reactor.

Published June 2008, Advanced Aquarist's Online Magazine

Keywords: Feature Article, Shane Graber
Link to original article: http://www.advancedaquarist.com/2008/6/aafeature

In the previous installment, I introduced the Google SketchUp software to the reader, went over installation, basic usage, and created a 120 gallon aquarium. In this installment, we will continue building models for our 120 gallon aquarium and will build a simple Deltec kalkwasser stirrer. This kalkwasser stirrer was chosen due to its straight-forward design which should make it relatively easy for the reader to model as they read through this article.

For reference, you can download both the individual parts and the completed model and look it over while you're reading through this article. I've omitted some of the detail in the stirrer in order to keep this article easy to follow along. Scroll and pan around both model files to see it from different angles to get a feel for how things look in the software.

If at any time things don't quite make sense on what's being presented, please refer to the previous article or look around the SketchUp Help Center . They can go into a lot more detail than what I can in this short article.

Scripting

A new topic that we will learn about in this article is the use of scripts and plugins in SketchUp. Scripts and plugins are very powerful and they are used to automate various tasks and add new functionality to the program. There's a lot of useful scripts out there that can be used to create all sorts of different designs. I won't go into detail on how to create your own in this article as there's plenty of tutorials on the web. I will, however, introduce two scripts that I've found to be very useful when working with aquarium modeling. The first is called "Pipe Along Path" and the second one is called "Centerpoint." The "Pipe Along Path" script is an awesome script that allows you draw anything that looks like a pipe or a rod. You essentially draw a line (or series of lines) and then using the script you can either create a cylinder out of it or create a pipe with a specific outer and inner diameter. It can be used for creating plumbing diagrams, modeling skimmers or just about anything that requires a tubular component. You can even set the number of sides that your pipe/tube has when rendered so if you wanted to make rectangular tubing you could do that easily with this script. The "Centerpoint" script is a nice helper script that plots a centerpoint on any surface that's selected -- square, circle, triangle, etc. This is useful when you want to place an object in the exact center of another object. We will use both of these scripts extensively in this article.

Installation

Let's go over getting and installing the two scripts. It's really pretty simple. For the "Pipe Along Path" script, download (right click, SAVE AS) the script from The Ruby Library Depot and save it to the Plugins directory of your Google SketchUp installation. On my system, the path is "C:\Program Files\Google\Google SketchUp 6\Plugins\". Next, let's download the "Centerpoint" script from Smustard and save it to the same location that you saved the "Pipe Along Path" script to on your computer. After you've saved both scripts to that directory, start SketchUp (or re-start it if you already have it running). Now if you navigate to the Plugins dropdown menu, you'll see an entry for "Pipe Along Path" and another one for "Set Center Point." Once that's complete, we're all set to go.

Let's Dig In

Here is a photo of the stirrer that we will be creating in this article:

I chose this kalkwasser stirrer for its relatively straight forward design and ease of modeling. Per Deltec's website, this unit is 6" L x 6" W x 19" H. I've had to do some estimations on the dimensions for certain items (baseplate thickness', tube heights, etc) as they were not readily available from their website but they should be close enough for this article.

Generally, the easiest way to go about creating a model like this is to make each of the components separately and then stack them together later in the process. The one thing that we will not model in this installment is the power cord. Having it in the model would finish it out, but it's really not necessary for what we're working on here, which is to roughly model a piece of aquarium equipment.

Since it's been a while since the first article, please skim over the previous article to get a feel for the interface again and what each of the icons mean and do.

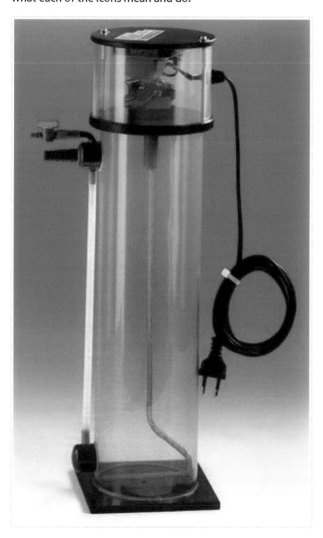

Deltec Kalkwasser Mixer KM500T. Photo courtesy Deltec.

Let's Get Started

The first thing we will do is make our components. I've already measured out what needs to be made in the below components list:

1. Baseplate (1): Square, 6" L x 6" W x 0.25" H

2. Caps (2): Circle, 5.5" diameter (2.25" radius), 0.25" H

3. Motor (1): Box, 2" L x 2" W x 1.5" H

4. Stir Bar Top (1): Cylinder, 2" H, 0.75" diameter

5. Motor Housing (1): Tubing, 2 5/16" H, 5" diameter

6. Kalkwasser Chamber (1): Tubing, 15 5/16" H, 5" diameter

7. Kalk stir rod (1): Tubing, 3" W x 12.5" H, 0.25" diameter

8. Freshwater Input (1): Cylinder (on its side), 1.5" long, 1.5" diameter

9. Kalkwasser Exit Nozzle (1): Cylinder (on its side), 1.5" long, 1.5" diameter

Using what you learned from the previous installment, make components 1, 2, 3, 4, 8 and 9 from the above list in a new SketchUp project window. If you'd rather not make each of the shapes, again the finished individual components can be downloaded instead.

After you've made the components, we're going to add center points to each face. Using your Select arrow tool, select the top of your shape by clicking on it. Now click the Plugins dropdown menu and select "Set Center Point." A center point should now be added to your surface. Now using the Orbit tool, rotate your view so that you're now looking at the bottom of your shape. Again, using your Select arrow tool, select the bottom of your shape and setting a center point on that face as well. So far, so good.

After you've completed each shape, use the "Select" arrow tool to select the shape (mouse click and hold at the upper left of the shape and drag down to the lower right to select the entire shape or triple click on the shape to select all of it), right click on the selected shape and choose the "Make Component" menu item, and then Name it and click the Create button. This binds the shape into a complete unit that is easier to work with later.

When completed with this step, you'll have six shapes created: one baseplate, two caps, one motor, and two ports each with center points on their top and bottom faces. Next, we will get to making some tubing.

MAKING TUBING

Items 4 and 5 will require us to use the "Pipe Along Path" script in order to make the desired components. In order to get started on these two items, we need to move the components that you made in the previous section away from the origin (the point where the red, green, and blue lines intersect). Again using your Select arrow, click and drag across all of the components that were made in the previous step to select all of your shapes near the origin and then use your Move/Copy tool to move them away from the origin.

Now that that space is clear, let's make our Kalkwasser Chamber. Using your Pencil tool, start by clicking at the origin of the three axes in your interface. Drag that up a bit and then type the following into the window:

15 5/16"

This creates a line 15 5/16" tall. Next, select the line with your Select arrow tool and then click on your Plugins dropdown menu and select Pipe Along Path from the menu items (Photo 4). Make sure your units are in "Inches" and that your tube has an outer diameter of 5 inches and an inner diameter of 4.5 inches. Leave the Number of Circle Segments at 24 and click OK. You now have a tube (Photo 5).

Again, either triple-click on the tube or use your Select tool to drag across the entire tube to select it and then make a component out of it. With that done, move it away from the origin so we can make the Motor Housing.

Now, create the Motor Housing the same as you did above. The motor housing is the same inner and outer diameter as the Kalkwasser Chamber except that it is only 2 5/16" tall.

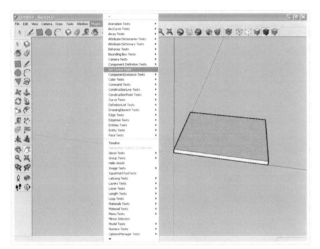

Photo 1: Making a center point on the top surface of a shape.

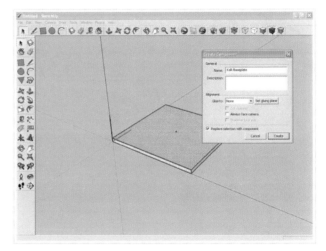

Photo 3: Making a component out of a shape.

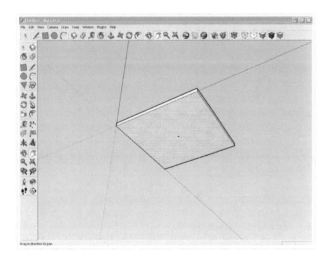

Photo 2: Making a center point on the bottom of a shape.

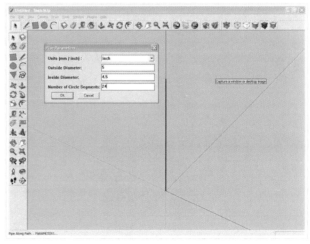

Photo 4: Pipe Along Path dialog box

The stir rod was created in a similar fashion as the above tubes except that its outer diameter is 0.25 inches and its inner diameter is zero inches. A lot of smaller line segments were pieced together to make it. Use your Line tool (pencil) to make line segments that are attached per the dimensions mentioned in the above components list and then triple click on the line with your Select tool to select all of the line segments. Now use your Pipe Along Path plugin to make it 0.25 inches outer diameter and 0 inches inner diameter.

Now your stir bar is created! Make a component out of it and we can proceed to the next step.

PUTTING IT ALL TOGETHER

Now that all of the components have been made, we need to put them all together. The first step in this process is to fill each of the components with color/transparency. To do this, click you Paint Bucket icon on your menu or select the Tools menu followed by Paint Bucket. Fill items 1, 2, 8, and 9 from the above list with either a dark black or a gray color. Items 4 and 7 should be filled with a red color. Item 3 can be filled with a light gray. For items 5 and 6, switch to "Translucent" from the Paint Bucket dropdown box and fill these two items with "Translucent_Glass_Blue." I have done so with the individual components file that you downloaded earlier and you can get it here in case you'd like to see how I've done it.

The next step is to start assembly. The easiest way I've found to assemble everything is to switch into Wire frame mode (View - Face Style - Wire frame menu items) and then begin the moving and stacking process.

Next, switch to your Move/Copy tool (Tools - Move menu items) so that we can begin assembly. The first thing we will

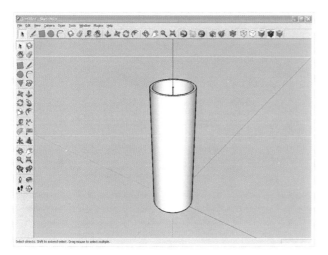

Photo 5: Your finished tube!

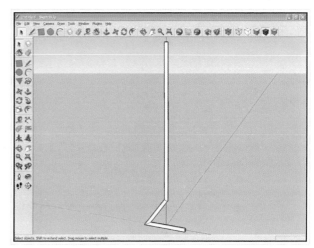

Photo 8: Final Stir Rod.

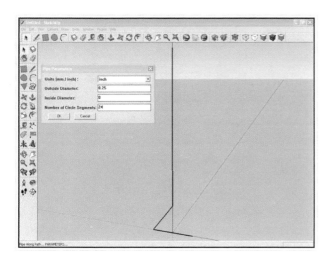

Photo 7: Selected stir rod.

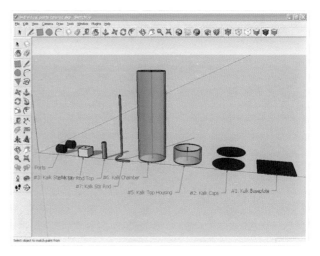

Photo 9: Components after shading.

do is assemble the completed Stir Rod. Grab item 4 (Stir Rod Top) by the bottom centerpoint and drag it up and place its centerpoint on top of item 7's centerpoint (Stir Rod). You may need to switch in and out of Pan and Zoom modes to get in close enough to see the centerpoints and how they line up. When done it should look like Photo 11.

Continue assembly by stacking the components using their centerpoints as a guide until you end up with what the completed model looks like. It may take a while to get the hang of it, but by switching between Pan mode, Orbit mode, and Move/Copy mode, you'll get all the pieces together into one unit. You will end up with something that looks like Photo 12 after you've switched out of wire frame mode.

CONCLUSION

And there you have it, a model of the Deltec KM kalkwasser stirrer. If you have time to play, you can go into much greater detail than I have been able to in this article. You could add the extension cord as well as make the infeed/output ports more realistic or whatever your heart desires.

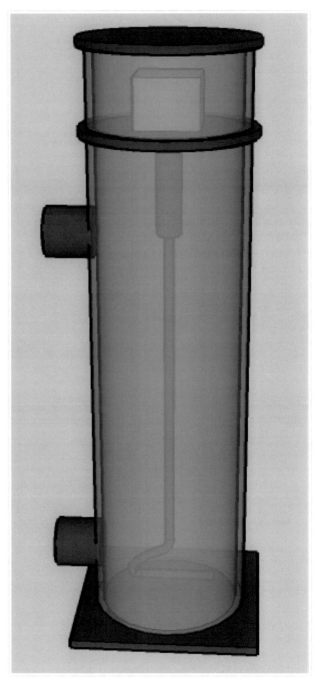

Photo 12: The completed unit!

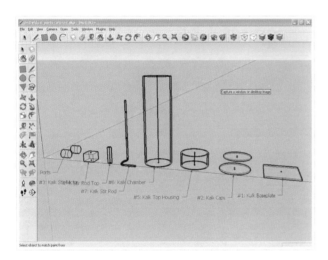

Photo 10: Wire frame mode.

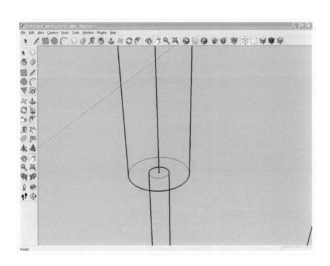

Photo 11: Items 4 and 7 centered on their centerpoints.

Again, I'd like to challenge any and all of the aquarium manufacturers to provide SketchUp models of their equipment for hobbyists like us to use when mocking up our "dream systems." We could quickly switch in and out various pieces of equipment and see what works and doesn't work for our specific needs. I'd also like to challenge the other hobbyists to create SketchUp models and share them with others so they can also benefit. Again, reefs.org has a repository setup for it or else share it on Google's repository. The big thing is to get them out there for people to use.

FURTHER READING

If you'd like to dig deeper into SketchUp, there's an excellent book available from Amazon.com on the subject:

Google SketchUp for Dummies
Chopra, Aidan, Wiley Publishing, Hoboken, NJ, 2007
ISBN: 978-0-470-13744-4
$25 (list price)
$16.50 (street price)
Website: Click here

A review of the book can also be found at PC World's blog for those wanting to read some additional information on the book before purchasing it: http://blogs.pcworld.com/communityvoices/archives/2007/11/book_review_goo.html

ACKNOWLEDGEMENTS

I'd like to thank Adam Blundell for encouraging me at this past MACNA XIX to continue with this series.

AQUARIUM FISH

FISH POLITICS

By Mark E. Evans

We can expect a newly introduced fish to "follow" the general "specifications" and behavioral characteristics of the species to which it belongs. But what the possible behaviors are going to be under all circumstances is the million-dollar question.

Published June 2008, Advanced Aquarist's Online Magazine

© Pomacanthus Publications, LLC

Keywords: Aquarium Fish, Mark E. Evans
Link to original article: http://www.advancedaquarist.com/2008/6/fish

Imagine you're a male seahorse clinging to a strand of algae, swaying rhythmically in the current. Zooplankton drifts by and you snap it up in your narrow mouth. There are several female seahorses nearby for you to court. Also, there are a few males, who are the competition. But the males are mostly peripheral to your territory and of little or no concern. Overall you are content. Everything you require either drifts to you or is in short swimming distance from you. Your world is small but complete. Until one day, to your consternation, you are collected by a marine biologist and set up in a laboratory tank, far away. Your world is suddenly much smaller and very different. Your tank mates now include a single female and several males, all from your species. The males set about bullying you, because you are the now in direct competition for the female's attention.

You continue your existence as a male seahorse inside a lab tank, which is a drastic change of environment from your wild "stomping grounds." Your new captive environment elicits behavioral changes in you and your tank mates, the other seahorses. Yet you are all still the same animals, from the same species. And neither you nor your fellow seahorses have been genetically altered in any way. It's just that the new environmental conditions require different behavioral responses. Although you still have access to a "hitching post," food, and a female, your territory is cramped and too close for comfort to the other males who are competing for the same resources. Your whole world is now in miniature and the neighbors are encroaching upon your "yard," or you are encroaching upon theirs. Either way the cramped living conditions lead to some conflict. Whether it is mortal combat is determined by the degree of environmental change and how genetically prone you are to defending your space. It is the combination and the interaction of the two factors, environment and genetics, which makes you, the seahorse, who you are.

You may be a member of unique species of seahorse, with genes in common with your conspecifics, but within your species you are a unique individual with your own DNA, similar overall, but dissimilar. (In a given species individuals possess enough of a genetic difference to create a range of characteristics and behaviors. For example, in the extremes one individual fish from a population may be the most aggressive while another is the least aggressive, with the rest of the population falling somewhere in between on the scale.) But it's not only you who are unique, so is the environment in which you live, the aquarium. Not just physically but

genetically. All your other seahorse tank mates are genetically unique. So, no other aquarium environment exactly matches yours.

A captive seahorse's perspective helps us to better appreciate the uniqueness of aquarium setups. Each aquarium is a unique environment, housing genetically unique individuals, arranged in a unique configuration, at least to a certain degree. Biological traits or behavioral characteristics often follow a bell curve, from the least to the most. In a population, the difference between individuals is subtle, continuing along a grade; for example, from the most aggressive to the least aggressive. The grade may manifest itself by beginning with 'indifference' followed by 'mild chasing' then 'blatant aggression', and ending with 'outright killing'. (Researchers have determined that in some species of schooling fish the position of individual fish in the school is influenced by fear levels, the most fearful keeping to the inside the school.) The average behavior for a species determines the shape of the curve. (See Different Bell Curve Diagrams: Different species, more aggressive, less aggressive, different shaped curves). But although we might confidently generalize a single species' behavior, we are dealing with uncertainty when species are combined. Published compatibility charts are built on experimentation and experience, but in reality they are only guidelines. Our own observations are key. Several points we should keep in mind when attempting to minimize fish aggression include - size, sex ratio, color, shape, food, territory, and population density. For simplicity's sake, I will sort them into two basic categories: territory and food. The categories sometimes overlap, and they are both altered by the factor of time.

Consider the allocation of space in the average reef aquarium, and the possible areas where conflict can occur between fish. Reef walls create nooks, crannies, caves, passageways, crevices, and perches. In addition, a deep sand bed below the rock offer space for burrowing fish species. But territoriality is relative. One fish may defend a small cave, while another may lay claim to the entire tank's swimming space. But we must remember that it is the layout of the space together with the genetic proclivities of the fish that determine whether or not conflict is inevitable. Each individual fish is a unique genetic package. And as aquarists we assume a degree of uncertainty when we introduce a new inhabitant to our aquarium.

However, we can expect a newly introduced fish to "follow" the general "specifications" and behavioral characteristics of the species to which it belongs. But what the possible behaviors are going to be under all circumstances is the million-dollar question. The previous story of the captive seahorse reminds us of that. The fact is that captive and wild behavior can differ greatly. The limits of an aquarium environment and the potential interactions with tank-mates can alter how a fish "should" behave. The number of environmental variables involved combined with the flexibility of chemical responses (genetically determined) allows for deviation in fish behavior. We can expect common aggressive reactions between two fish species to occur, like a Purple Dottyback reacting negatively to a fish of a similar size and color. But what effect does the presence of a third fish species have to the mix? Will it nullify or amplify the conflict, or will it simply have no effect at all? Will a juvenile species be more aggressive and territorial when it matures or will it relax its guard? The famous paleontologist George Gaylord Simpson wrote "... [T]he development of the individual is affected not only by the inherited growth determinants but also by the conditions under which growth occurs." (Simpson).

So, no one can answer these questions with certainty? In an aquarium the interactions between multiple species is as complex as a wild ecosystem. Finally, we must realize that animals change their ecosystem simply by being present and living in it. My very first marine tank, which I got when I was twelve, contained two Blue Yellow-Tail Damsels, both of which expended time and effort excavating the sandy bottom with their tails, to the point of creating a cave under a large rock. I repeatedly pushed the sand back, but they always rebuilt. Thus the two Damsels not only affected their world, but mine as well. I hated seeing the bare patch of tank

bottom showing, and my aggression was slightly stirred by their behavior.

Consider the ubiquitous Yellow Tang (Zebrasoma flavescens). As an herbivorous schooling species it patrols an aquarium searching for algae. (Herbivores generally must eat meals more often than carnivores because plant material is harder to digest than animal flesh. Consequently, herbivorous species like the Yellow Tang possess longer intestinal tracts than carnivores, and they exhibit greater territorial behavior to protect their food resources.) Therefore, a conspecific, if present, is the most immediate threat. Two individuals of the same species, which are of a similar size and "disposition," are likely to intimidate one another until a hierarchy is established. Competition for the same resources leads to conflict both in the wild and in the aquarium.

Because space is inherently limited in an aquarium, territorial conflict is a common problem. Fish like gobies, blennies, clownfish roam, but center activities around a prime location such as a pit or a cave, defending a small circumference of territory. Conversely, a fish like a puffer that requires greater space may claim the entire tank as its territory, attacking meeker fish or chasing them into hiding. I remember seeing aerial news footage of a shark swimming through a school of small fish. The small fish kept their distance equally on all sides of the shark, creating an almost perfect oval around the shark, like an invisible shield. Fish require their space, and they will create it if necessary by altering their surroundings, through modification of the physical environment or by intimidating or killing their tank-mates. As aquarists we have to utilize an aquarium's space as conservatively as possible, simulating the wild reef while balance our esthetic desires with the requirements of the fish.

Simple Steps For Avoiding Deadly Conflict Between Fish:

1. Keep a watch on fish with similar swimming levels, similar shapes, or colorations. Conflict may erupt if they are of the same species and a hierarchy is under development Different species may need to established a sense of their own territories.

2. Conflicts over food may be reduced by feeding smaller portions more often, or in the case of algae eaters, by creating more than one feeding "station", for the algae to grow or to be clipped to. Similarly, changing the area of the tank where live foods are released or injected may reduce fights over which fish eats first.

3. If a fish is biting or serious injuring a tank-mate, try feeding it more often, or providing it with fresh meaty foods.

4. Shift the physical environment of the aquarium. Relocate rocks or plants to disrupt territorial claims. If a new fish is to be introduced, changing the décor around breaks up previously held territory, giving the new inhabitant an equal opportunity to establish a claim.

5. Try feeding at random times, and at different locations within the aquarium, if you are hanging food from clips or inserting food at specific locations.

6. Change the duration of the lighting. "Lights Out" may force bullies to clam down. And nocturnal fish require their time too.

REFERENCES

1. Barlow, George W. (2000) "The Cichlid Fishes: Natures Grand Experiment In Evolution". Perseus Publishing

2. Bone, Q. and Marshall, N. B. (1982) "Biology Of Fishes". Blackie & Son Limited, London.

3. Coates, David (1980) " Anti-Predator Defense via Interspecific Communication In Humbug Damselfish, Dascyllus aruanus". Zetiag

4. Mahoney, Bruce. (1981) "An examination of Interspecific Territoriality in the Dusky Damselfish, Eupomacentrus dorsopunicans". Bulletin Of Marine Science

5. Norman, M. D. and Jones, G. P. (1984) "Determinants of Territory Size in the Pomacentrid Reef Fish, Parma victoriae". Oecologia

6. Reebs, Stephan (2001) "Fish Behavior in the Aquarium and in the Wild". Cornell University Press

7. Simpson, George G. (1960) "The Meaning of Evolution". Yale University Press

LATERAL LINES

MAKING WAVES WITH THE ECOTECH MARINE VORTECH

By Adam Blundell M.S.

While water motion will forever be debated, we can all agree that having options on water flow is always great. Thankfully we now the ability to produce water flow in all sorts of varieties.

Published June 2008, Advanced Aquarist's Online Magazine

© Pomacanthus Publications, LLC

Keywords: Adam Blundell M.S., Lateral Lines, Pumps, Water Circulation
Link to original article: http://www.advancedaquarist.com/2008/6/lines

The VorTech kicks ass and here's why: you can make waves, you can control the waves, and you can customize your flow. Is that enough reason for you? If not here we go....

THE BASICS OF WAVES

Well this is a whole can of worms to open here. In this article I want to cover some terminology and basics of waves. Future articles (Adams & Blundell) will go into depth covering the mathematics and dynamics of waves.

Wavelength is the name for a measured distance. It is the distance from one spot on a wave until the next point where the spot occurs. Did that make sense? In other words it would be the distance from the top of wave to the top of the next.

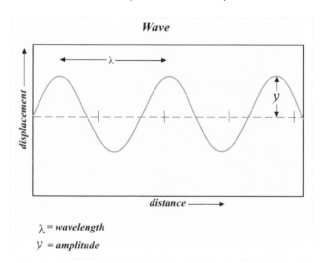

Picture courtesy of Wikipedia

AMPLITUDE

Amplitude is also a measurement of distance. The amplitude is a measure of how high (or low) a wave moves from the baseline. This measurement is magnitude of disturbance from that baseline. Note- many people are confused on this because the amplitude is measured from the baseline, and not from the peak of a wave to the trough of a wave. If you are measuring from the top of the wave to the bottom you are actually measuring 2x the amplitude.

FREQUENCY

Frequency is a measurement used in time. Frequency measures how many waves are produced during a certain amount of time. You could measure frequency in number of waves per 3.721 seconds, or number of waves per 11.184 minutes, or number of waves per full moons. To make things easy scientists prefer to measure frequency in number of waves per

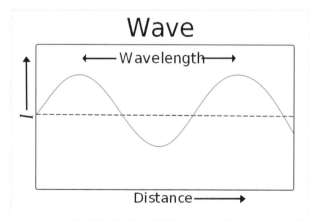

Picture courtesy of Wikipedia

second or per minute. It is a measure of how often something occurs.

WAVES IN AQUARIA

Waves have been absent from most home aquariums. A dump bucket or surge device can be used to create a transverse or traveling wave. But in most aquariums this isn't rhythmic and doesn't carry for long (because the aquariums aren't long to begin with). Some new items (like the VorTech featured here, and other water motion devices hitting the market) have the ability to produce wave flow in the aquarium.

Here are some examples of wave devices put into action (these tests were performed in an area 60 inches long, 24 inches front to back, and 16 inches tall. This is 100 gallons of water):

VorTech Undertow:

Video 1:
http://www.advancedaquarist.com/2008/6/
lines_movies/vortech_undertow.wmv

Video 2:
http://www.advancedaquarist.com/2008/6/
lines_movies/vortech_undertow2.wmv

These videos show the ability of the VorTech pump to draw sediment off the bottom of the aquarium and to lift it into the water column. This type of flow can greatly increase feeding capture of corals as the food stays in suspension and does not settle onto the reefscape.

Making Waves:

Video 3:
http://www.advancedaquarist.com/2008/6/
lines_movies/vortech_making_wave.wmv

As the VorTech runs it continues to "build up speed" as the inertial forces build and the wave is generated.

Wave Amplitude:

Video 4:
http://www.advancedaquarist.com/2008/6/

Picture courtesy of Wikipedia

lines_movies/vortech_amplitude.wmv

This video gives you an idea of the amplitude that can be created in a standard 100 gallon system.

Broad Water Flow:

Video 5:
http://www.advancedaquarist.com/2008/6/
lines_movies/vortech_broad_flow.wmv

This video shows the broad pattern of water flow from the VorTech. This is especially beneficial in reef aquaria. Notice how the beads stay in suspension and continuously move.

Water Flow 5 Feet From VorTech:

Video 6:
http://www.advancedaquarist.com/2008/6/
lines_movies/vortech_5feet_away.wmv

Shown here is the aquarium on the OPPOSITE side of the running VorTech. What you see here is that the beads are moving around in the water flow created by the pump... from 5 FEET AWAY. In other words one VorTech pump is creating all the flow in this 100 gallon display, and you are seeing the far end of the tank.

The VorTech Display: http://www.youtube.com/watch?v=rLPmea2II-A

Shown here Tim Marks of EcoTech Marine puts the pumps into action in a vendor booth.

VorTech Producing Differing Wave Patterns: http://www.youtube.com/watch?v=L9L2FaZwfwo

Jake Adam's video of VorTech's producing a 3rd Harmonic standing wave... the favorite flow pattern of Adam Blundell. The video then shows a transverse or traveling wave. (forgive the music... it is a Jake thing)

ITEMS TO CONSIDER

Do we want waves? I guess it depends on whom you ask. Fellow author and water flow guru Jake Adams is a huge fan of laminar flow. I however, am not sold on laminar flow being all that Jake says it is. To me, an oscillating standing wave is the ticket.

COMING TO A CONCLUSION

Flow patterns in aquaria are diverse. At least they can be. Some people like Laminar Flow (Jake) while others like Oscillation (Adam), and the vast majority of aquaria feature Chaotic flow. Why would someone chose one type of flow over another?.... well that question is to be addressed shortly....

CONCLUSION

While water motion will forever be debated, we can all agree that having options on water flow is always great. Thankfully we now the ability to produce water flow in all sorts of varieties. These options will undoubtedly allow hobbyists to produce the water flow they desire.... whatever it is that they desire.

AUTHOR INFORMATION

Adam Blundell M.S. works in Marine Ecology, and in Pathology for the University of Utah. He is also Director of The Aquatic & Terrestrial Research Team, a group which utilizes research projects to bring together hobbyists and scientists. His vision is to see this type of collaboration lead to further advancements in aquarium husbandry. While not in the lab Adam provides services for of one of the Nation's largest hobbyist clubs, the Wasatch Marine Aquarium Society (www.utahreefs.com). Adam has earned a BS in Marine Biology and an MS in the Natural Resource and Health fields. Adam can be contacted at adamblundell@hotmail.com.

PRODUCT REVIEW

CAPTIVE PURITY'S REVERSE OSMOSIS AND DEIONIZATION WATER TREATMENT DEVICE

By Dana Riddle

This Captive Purity RO/DI unit generally performs very well, especially when considered the low quality of the feed water. As such, it is worthy of your consideration when making a purchase.

Published June 2008, Advanced Aquarist's Online Magazine

Keywords: Conductivity, Dana Riddle, Product Review, RO/DI, Salinity, Temperature, Water Quality, Water Testing, pH
Link to original article: http://www.advancedaquarist.com/2008/6/review

Reverse osmosis (RO) and deionization (DI) water treatment processes have found wide spread acceptance among aquarium hobbyists, and especially among reef aquarists, for many reasons. A properly functioning RO/DI unit can deliver water meeting rigid criteria for 'pure' water, does so at a modest price, and requires no operational skills.

As saltwater aquarium hobbyists, we need pure water for a number of reasons. Perhaps the two most important are for ensuring that freshly mixed artificial seawater is not contaminated with various chemicals commonly found in tap water. Secondly, we do not wish to add tap water's chemicals when we 'top off' an aquarium to make up for water loss due to evaporation. Just what is in tap water that we want to avoid?

Before answering this question, almost every public and private water supply company is regulated by the Environment Protection Agency (although some very small systems are not). Minimum standards have been set in order to ensure that your drinking water is safe. For instance, water utilities must check the amounts of copper and lead found in drinking water. Copper and lead are usually not found in ground or surface waters, but instead are generally a result of degradation of copper pipes and old solder joints containing lead. If concentrations of lead and copper exceed a given amount in a certain percentage of homes, then the utility must develop and implement a plan to reduce these metals' concentration. This is usually accomplished by chemically treating the water to minimize pipe corrosion, and can be done with a number of compounds, including those containing phosphorus, zinc or tin. After the treatment process has had time to work, the pipes are coated with, say, phosphorus, corrosion is minimized and copper and lead concentrations meet safety standards. Phosphorus is benign and is not a regulated substance in tap water - but it is a critical element for algal growth. Some areas will have naturally occurring compounds such as iron, sulfur, etc., or, as the case here in Hawaii, nitrate and fluoride. This list could go on and on, but I hope the point is clear - we can have safe drinking water, but it is not really acceptable as aquarium water when we want to control algal growths and minimize accumulations of certain elements due to evaporation and contaminated make-up water which results in 'cycles of concentration'.

Captive Purity has been around for a number of years (reference one of their advertisements in a 2000 issue of

Figure 1. Not a glamour ad photograph - this Captive Purity Reverse Osmosis Device has treated thousands of gallons of water.

FAMA), yet their name recognition is not equal (at least to me) to that of some other pet industry suppliers. When considering a replacement of my ancient RO unit, I considered the purchase of several brands. Price was a consideration and Captive Purity's units were substantially less expensive than their competitors. But quality was an unknown. I decided to purchase a Captive Purity RO and DI unit and put it to the test. This would be a tough test too, as the tap water is chlorinated and has a high total dissolved solids (TDS, nearing the EPAs secondary standard of 500 mg/l) content, relatively high chloride (due to saltwater intrusion), silica, and nitrate.

There are many parameters to test when determining water quality. I decided to check for these:

- Conductivity
- Resistivity
- Salinity
- Total Dissolved Solids
- Phosphorus
- Ammonia
- Nitrate
- pH
- Silica

Here are the results for each item:

CONDUCTIVITY

Conductivity, or Electrical Conductance, is the ability of water to conduct an electrical current, and is reported in units called micro-Siemens per centimeter (µS·cm) at a given temperature (25°C). If the water is really trashed with conductive compounds, conductivity could be reported in milli-Siemens per cm, or mS·cm). It may come as a surprise to many that *ultra-pure* water will, for all intents and purposes, *not* conduct electricity (However, water contaminated with any number of compounds will conduct electrical current - we know that - we're conditioned to the old movie plot where the radio falls into the bath. If the girl in the tub had only used ultra-pure water instead of taking the bubble bath...).

Conductivity is measured with a special sensor, and it is inversely proportional to water purity - the *higher* the conductance, the *less* pure the water is. See Figure 2.

Absolutely pure water has conductivity of 0.055 µSiemens·cm. The DI unit initially produced water of 0.24 µSiemens·cm. This meets the requirement of 'pure water.'

RESISTIVITY

Resistivity is the reciprocal to conductivity, and is sometimes considered to be a method superior to conductivity when testing pure water. The *higher* the resistivity, the *higher* the quality of water.

The resistivity of absolutely pure water is 18.2 MΩ·cm (meg-ohm per centimeter). Resistivity values as high as 7.3 MΩ·cm have been noted in the discharge of Captive Purity's deionization unit, but is usually lower (~5.2 MΩ·cm). This value meets the definition of 'pure water'.

As a footnote, the feed water resistivity was 1,219 Ω·cm, and 27.1kΩ·cm for the discharge from the RO membrane (note the prefix to Ω - k, or M, or lack thereof - this makes a huge difference! As would be expected, the feed water has low resistivity, while removal of conductive substances by the RO device increases the resistivity, but only to the kilo-ohm range. Deionization really cleans up the water and boosts the resistivity into meg-ohms).

SALINITY

Salinity is usually considered to be a measurement of the mass of dissolved salts in a given mass of solution (water). Simply evaporating the water away and weighing the residual salts is not particularly accurate. Complete chemical analyses are expensive, time-consuming and offer little advantage over the method used in this report: Conversion of conductivity to salinity, using the Practical Salinity Scale 1978. Fortunately, the meter used (Hach HQ40d multi-meter) is programmed with this conversion and a simple push of a button reports salinity in parts per thousand (ppt).

In this case, salinity is due to seawater intrusion into the freshwater aquifer. Freshwater, since it is less dense, floats

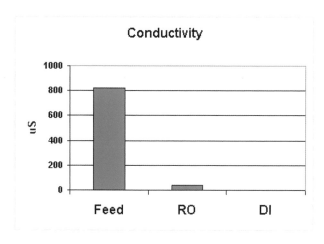

Figure 2. Conductivity of water in various stages of treatment. The DI water measured 0.24 µSiemens·cm - pure water indeed!

on seawater beneath this island. This floating freshwater is called the basal lens. When freshwater is rapidly withdrawn (in this case, by pumps supplying drinking water to the island), seawater is locally pulled upwards, and the aquifer is contaminated with saltwater. Obviously, this is not a good situation. Persons limiting their sodium intake are affected, and, when there is not treatment of top-off water in an aquarium, the sodium chloride content increases.

This RO/DI unit was very good in removing salinity. The RO membrane removed 95% of salinity, and the DI cartridge removed some of the remaining salts, with an overall removal rate >99%. See Figure 3.

TOTAL DISSOLVED SOLIDS, OR TDS

TDS is a measure of inorganic salts dissolved in water, and is expressed in units of milligrams per liter (mg/l, which is about the same thing as parts per million). The higher the TDS in mg/l, the higher the concentration of inorganic salts. The EPA has established a secondary, non-enforceable standard of 500 mg/l TDS. The feed water to the RO/DI unit was 401 mg/l (80% of the EPAs maximum concentration). See Figure 4.

The discharge permeate from the RO membrane was only 17 mg/l (a 95.7% removal) while the DI effluent contained only 0.041 mg/l (for an overall removal of 99.989% removal of TDS).

NITRATE

Nitrate in many drinking water supplies is relatively high on the Big Island of Hawaii. This is due to leaching of nitrate from relatively young volcanic rock by rainwater; however, the groundwater pumped in this particular district is not among those with concentrations approaching EPAs Primary Standard (enforceable) of 10 mg/l NO_3-N.

Nitrate removal was not as great as those seen with other parameters. The RO unit removed the nitrate with the DI unit

removing little, if any. Average nitrate removal was 56% (see Figure 5).

PHOSPHORUS

Phosphorous is sometimes added to a water supply in order to prevent corrosion of water pipes. This is not the case in this instance. Results (not shown in chart form) were at 0.02 mg/l phosphorus (as P), which is below the detection limit of 0.14 mg/l. Therefore, results for all three streams are reported as <0.14 mg/l P.

PH

pH, as we know, is a measure of hydrogen and hydroxyl ions on a scale of 0-14 standard units. A pH value of less than 7 is considered 'acidic' and those measurements above 7 are said to be 'basic'. A measurement of exactly 7 is called 'neutral'. pH is usually checked with an electronic meter using a probe specifically designed to report pH. However, see comments in the 'Methods' section below.

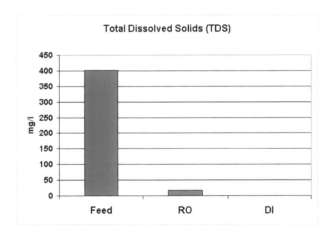

Figure 4. Total Dissolved Solids of water from various stages of treatment.

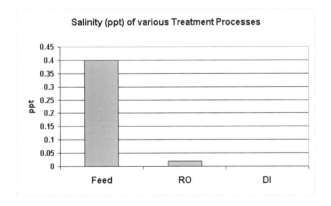

Figure 3. Salinity - inorganic salts - from each treatment stage.

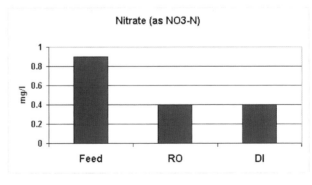

Figure 5. Nitrate removal by the various stages of water treatment.

pH values will generally drop as water becomes more pure - this is usually due to removal of alkalinity and substances buffering against the effects of carbon dioxide as it dissolves in the water (carbon dioxide and water mixed makes carbonic acid). It takes very little CO_2 to drop the pH in pure, un-buffered water. See Figure 6.

SILICA

There is some controversy over the negative impacts of silica in aquaria. Relatively small amounts apparently cause no harm, but, at higher concentrations, could help promote diatom growths. I have included silica in the testing results since some pet industry suppliers tout their products' abilities to remove silica. Silica (as SiO_2) was monitored on all water streams. The silica concentration of the deionized water read zero, but is reported as <1 mg/l. See Figure 7.

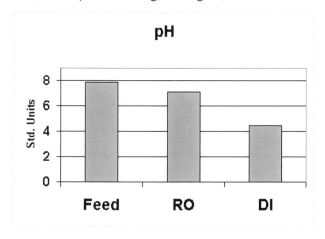

Figure 6. pH of fed water, and discharges from the reverse osmosis and deionization units.

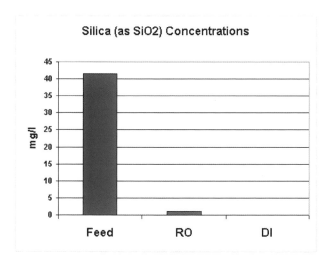

Figure 7. Silica - whether good, bad, or indifferent - is effectively removed by the Captive Purity RO/DI water treatment device.

AMMONIA

Ammonia concentrations in the feed, RO and DI waters were analyzed using the salicylate method. Ammonia concentrations were below the detection limit of the instrument, and are reported as <0.01 mg/l NH_3 as N (results not shown in chart form).

TEMPERATURE

For the record, temperature was monitored on all samples. This is especially importance for conductivity (EC) samples (although the meter used has an automatic temperature compensation feature, EC is reported at a temperature of 25°C - or 77°C). Temperature also affects the performance of the reverse osmosis membrane. Temperatures ranged from 24.1°C to 25.4C° (~75.4 to ~77.7°F).

PRODUCTION AND REJECTION RATES

This Captive Purity RO/DI device is rated to produce 75 gallons per day, and came close (~67 gallons/24 hours) after some tweaking. Since production and rejection are competing processes for a given amount of feed water, we should pay close attention to physical variables. Among variables, temperature and water pressure are two important factors to consider when attempting maximizing the efficiency of your RO unit.

A drawback to the reverse osmosis treatment is its water consumption (though it is more efficient in this respect than some water distillation units). The water containing the removed elements is called the 'reject' or 'concentrate' water, and its volume is always greater than the volume of the 'pure' water, or permeate (if the permeate flow suddenly increases, this is an indication that the membrane has failed catastrophically, or that a seal, such as an o-ring, has failed).

In my particular case, the RO/DI unit produced pure water at a rate of ~170 milliliters for every 768 mls of feed water, which means, of course, ~598 milliliters were rejected. Your situation may, and most likely will be, different and the amount of product water will be higher. (To give you an idea of how poor the drinking water quality is here, I can taste the salt - the tap water has a flat briny flavor).

OVERALL RESULT AND DISCUSSION

This Captive Purity RO/DI unit generally performs very well, especially when considered the low quality of the feed water. As such, it is worthy of your consideration when making a purchase.

The strengths of this device are:

1. Price,

2. Availability (it is distributed through a national network),

3. Replacement parts such as carbon, DI cartridges and membranes are also readily available. Replacement fittings are available at any well-stocked hardware store,

4. Though not a physical strength, Captive Purity's advertisements are grounded in fact, and not subject to a great deal of salesman's hyperbole. They understand that the quality of water produced is influenced by the quality of the feed water, and express removal rates as percentages in their ads.

5. Hardware (with the exception of a few screws) is non-metallic and not subject to corrosion.

The weaknesses are:

1. No directions are included,

2. There is no website with instructions or FAQ at the time of this writing

3. The deionization resins are not rechargeable.

Next time, we'll look at what it took to get the most out of this water treatment device (and these recommendations are applicable to any RO unit).

And for hardcore hobbyists:

METHODS

A colorimeter (Hach Model 890) was used for testing of nitrate, phosphorus (ortho-phosphate), silica, and ammonia. The procedures involved were cadmium reduction, amino acid, silicomolybdate, and salicylate methods, respectively. See here for an evaluation of this colorimeter: http://www.advancedaquarist.com/2005/6/review/

A meter capable of multiple electronic measurements (Hach H4oq) determined salinity, conductivity, resistivity, total dissolved solids and pH (pH of the feed and reverse osmosis permeate). See here for a product review of this instrument: http://www.advancedaquarist.com/2006/10/review/

Electronic measurement of pH in 'pure' water is not recommended unless the pH sensor is specifically designed for pure and/or ultra-pure water - mine is not. So, in the case of the deionized water, pH was determined with a litmus paper strip. See here for a review of various 'test strips': http://www.advancedaquarist.com/2007/4/review/

Comments, suggestions? Reach me at RiddleLabs@aol.com.

A NOTE FROM THE EDITORS

This original book was created from select content from the website of Advanced Aquarist's Online Magazine, http://www.advancedaquarist.com/, a monthly internet magazine for the marine aquarist dedicated to promoting exchange between the scientific community and amateur aquarists, for the benefit of both disciplines and the environment.

If you have enjoyed reading this volume and would like to order additional copies, they can be purchased from our website at **http://www.advancedaquarist.com/print-editions** or at our online store at CreateSpace (**https://www.createspace.com/3354927**) or from Amazon.com (search for Advanced Aquarist).

We also think that you will enjoy reading the latest articles online as they are published. The latest articles can be found online for free at http://www.advancedaquarist.com/.

If you are interested in writing for Advanced Aquarist's Online Magazine, please email our Editor, Terry Siegel at terry@advancedaquarist.com. We offer very competitive pay rates for articles.

For information on advertising with Advanced Aquarist's Online Magazine, please contact advertising@advancedaquarist.com. We have a variety of packages that should be suitable for your business needs.

We welcome your feedback. If you have ideas for new subjects, articles, or for Advanced Aquarist's Online Magazine in general, please let us know at feedback@advancedaquarist.com.

If you are interested in keeping abreast of issue releases, please subscribe to our email list at reefs-newsletter-subscribe@reefs.org.

Thank you for your continued support!